SLIDELL
"CAMELLIA CITY"

SLIDELL'S FIRST RAILROAD STATION CA. 1885.
THE CONSTRUCTION SITE HAD BEEN CALLED SLIDELL
STATION BEGINNING IN THE EARLY DAYS OF 1882.

DAN A. ELLIS

The Author – Dan Ellis

765 Brill Street, Pass Christian, MS 39571

(228) 224-1695

email: danellis@danellis.net

danellis@cableone.net

Web Site – www.DanEllis.net

First Release: September 1999

Second Edition: October 2015

ISBN-13: 978-1514266021

ISBN-10: 1514266024

Comment from Becky Taylor, Archive Librarian
St Tammany Parish Library
January 18, 2007

Dear Dan:

I want to tell you that we continue to use your Slidell Book at least weekly. Someone regularly needs information on Slidell and your book is the most informal and easy to use book written to date.

INTRODUCTION
The Book – by Dan Ellis

This Second Edition of Slidell (2015) has been structured by using much of the preceding data collected for the First Edition of Slidell (1999). Although fifteen plus years is not a generous extent of time when an accounting for the history of a community, much has happened during the intervening years that required this update and expansion of information.

In preparing for the first edition during the years of 1998 and 1999, it was first necessary to read all available books relating to Slidell's history. At that time, published books were not large in quantity, but nevertheless rendered a treasure of information. Research for the earliest historic incidents was garnered from resource documents and personal interviews. Much of the information was also sifted from newspaper clippings from area resources. Gratefully, many of the photographs came from those who faithfully answered the call to browse through their attics and closets. Very helpful were the staff members of the St. Tammany Public Library System. In particular, Librarian Becky Taylor was most helpful in guiding me through the "hanging files."

Welcome and meaningful access to the Slidell Museum archival files in 1998 and 1999 was warmly offered by G.O.S.H. personnel. Interviews with a number of City and Parish residents were most informative.

My personal gratitude is extended to Judge Frederick Stephen Ellis, Judge Peter Garcia, Annie Rogers, Becky Taylor, Charles Fritchie, Irma Cry, Judy Voelker, Suzanne Parsons, Mildred "BeBe" Pearce, and Jack Galatas for document and photo support and to Beth Martin with the *Times Picayune* for her responsive press announcements. Of significant support was Dudley Smith for his gathering of data and furnishing contact persons. — And to Mrs. Suzee Lampton Williams for her "Fritchie Files," and to Mrs. Maris Pravata Leitz for her "Pravata Files" and to Mrs. Kay Phillippi for her "Evans Files."

It is with sadness that many of these wonderful contributing persons were not around to assist for this revised edition.

The Cover – "The Slidell Depot"

Some people maintain an ongoing nostalgia for the essence of the old railroad days when rail cars and coaches were pulled by the "Iron Horse" engines that puffed heavy smoke and spouted cinders into the faces of passengers as they leaned out their windows for fresh air. However, anyone having boarded a troop train may beg to differ about any love for riding the tracks.

It goes without saying that the City of Slidell was cut and molded around the construction of the same roadway route that courses along Highway 11. The labor of many men cleared the land and cut the timbers that were processed at the Creosote Plant that caused the early camp town to become incorporated in 1888. Through World War I and World War II, the life's blood of Slidell was centered in Olde Towne and around the Depot Train Station. This book is about those men, their predecessors, and those who have come afterwards. Truly, Slidell has a rich heritage and the Railroad Station is the symbolic soul of that existence.

Slidell's First Railroad Station, ca. 1885

Chapter Index

Bibliography of Readings

Slidell, the City of the Future, 1980
City of Slidell, Annual Report, 1996
City of Slidell, Annual Report, 1997
City of Slidell, Annual Report, 1998
Inside Slidell, Slidell Sentry-News, 1998
History of Slidell, Jeraldine S. White, 1957
History of Louisiana, Charles Gayarre, 1854
The Times-Picayune, St. Tammany Editions
Along the Line of the NOGN Railroad, 1978
Piney Woods, John Hawkins Napier III, 1985
Louisiana's Historic Towns, Jess DeHart, 1983
Pamphlet, Guardians of Slidell History, undated
All for the Want of a Name, Geri U. Staines, 1988
Lake Pontchartrain, Walter Adolphe Roberts, 1946
History of the Ozone Camellia Club by John Geise
British West Florida, 1763-1783, Cecil Johnson, 1943
Historical Collections of Louisiana, B.F. French, 1851
Mississippi Harvest 1840-1915, Nollie Hickman, 1962
St. Tammany 1885 - 1945, Kemp and Colvin, Jr., 1981
Dubuisson Family History, by Cheryl S. Castelin, 1997
Pete Pravata Autobiography, Compilation and Notes, 1979
Historic Slidell, UNO Courseworks, Charles Fritchie, 1998
History and Progress of the Slidell High School, 1909 - 1935
Chata-Ima and St. Tammany Choctaws, Blaise C. D'Antoni, 1986
Leon Fremaux's New Orleans Characters, by Patrick J. Geary, 1987
St. Tammany Parish, *L'Autre Cote Du Lac,* Frederick S. Ellis, 1981
Slidell Magazine, Greater Slidell Area Chamber of Commerce, 1998
Slidell 1888-1938, Centennial Supplement, Daily Sentry News, 1988
Slidell Centennial, 1888-1988, Times Picayune Special Edition, 1988
Lighthouses, Lightships, and the Gulf of Mexico, David L. Cipra, 1997
Hunting for Bears, St. Tammany Marriages 1808-1900, by D.L. Murray
Business Connection, St. Tammany Chamber of Commerce, 2014-2015

Many and sundry Internet gleanings during this update and rewrite

A preface to Slidell

I am most pleased and grateful for Bill Blackwell whose photographs are displayed throughout. I extend my gratitude to Bill's mother, JoAnn, who participated with very beneficial editing and advice in this Second Edition. As always, when writing a book, I meet so many wonderful folks who impart their passion for living and their passion for Slidell.

Utmost, I miss those persons who have passed on – but were most worthy contributors to this book in its First Edition format — Dudley Smith, Jack Galatas, Annie Rogers, and other most genuine people who loved to talk "Slidell."

As a departure from the standard "Preface" tendered by book writers, when I asked a friend to write something on Slidell, at the time I did not forecast that I would place his remarks on these pages. —My thanks to Donald Moore, who related. . . .

"I spent half my life in Slidell, spending some of the best years of my life as a teenager cruising the strip, hanging out at the Movies and roller skating rink, and enjoying many recreational and outdoor activities the area had to offer. Slidell had the best schools with the best school rivalries, and was a place a kid could run free without worried parents anxiously calling neighbors trying to track us down.

"**M**y family always lived on the outskirts of Slidell, or the "greater Slidell area." We lived in the suburbs of the suburbs. It was quiet. It was beautiful. There were trees and open spaces. We never even locked the doors on the house for the first 25 years of my life.

"**I** had many friends whose families moved to the area as a result of the boom in the aerospace and oil industries. Slidell experienced rapid growth during those times but always retained its small town feel. I went to school with people from all over the country along with many people whose families were longtime residents of the area. Our south Louisiana upbringing made all newcomers to the area welcome and Slidell went from a sleepy town nestled on Lake Pontchartrain and Lake Borgne to one of the most desirable places to live for those working in and around New Orleans.

"**I** made lifelong friends growing up in Slidell. Like me, some have moved away for jobs and other pursuits. Many have stayed because it is such a great place to raise a family. Slidellians can experience all that south Louisiana and the New Orleans area has to offer while enjoying a quality of life that one can only find in small towns. Slidell takes pride in everything that it does, from its own weekly Mardi Gras celebrations during the carnival season, to its many festivals, sports and recreational activities. The town is rich in history and while it has grown tremendously over the years and becomes a bustling epicenter of North shore activity, it has maintained its identity and celebrated its past.

"**I** miss Slidell and think often of the many great years I had while growing up there. It is a great hometown . . .

Welcome to Slidell —

I have been blessed to represent the City of Slidell as Mayor and Chief of Police, and it is an honor to serve you and our great City.

Over the years, I have traveled around the country representing this great city.

And over the course of traveling, I always meet people who ask me where I'm from.

Here's what I tell them.

I live in a city with a strong sense of community.

People live together and work together. And we are a great city.

We live in a city that has some of the best schools in the state of Louisiana.

We have a very low crime rate, thanks to our great, nationally accredited police department.

We live in a city that when businesses close for the night, they don't pull down chain link gates across their doors or have bars across their windows.

We live in a city that has a great quality.

Slidell provides all the amenities of a great metropolitan area, with the shopping, entertainment and benefits that a big city provides.

We live in a city where cultural activities thrive.

On any given weekend, there is an abundance of things to do, from free concerts in Heritage Park, art exhibits in area galleries to festivals in Olde Towne.

There is always something to do in Slidell.

We live in a city that has some of the best food in the world. You want it. We have it.

We live in a city that has 31 beautiful parks and playgrounds, and it's usual to see children playing or ladies out walking and jogging late at night or early in the morning.

We live in a city that's only 40 minutes away from an international airport, where anyone can fly anywhere around the world.

And if aviation is your hobby, Slidell has a full service airport to suit your needs.

We live in a city that's only 40 minutes away from professional sports teams. Who Dat!

We live in a city that's 40 minutes away from the beautiful beaches of the Mississippi Gulf Coast where you can find numerous casinos and the great food and entertainment they provide.

We live in a city that has five fresh water rivers and plenty of bayous in our parish.

We have access to one of the largest salt water lakes in the United States, and that lake flows into the Gulf of Mexico, which has some of the best fishing in the country. Louisiana is a sportsman's paradise, and Slidell is no exception.

What more could you ask for?

I am proud to call Slidell my home. It truly is the best kept secret in the south.

Your Mayor,

Freddy Drennan

Slidell *"Camellia City"*

Welcome to Slidell! Welcome to this near-tropic abode of sun filled days surrounded by bayous, rivers, and lakes. Welcome to this country abounding in beautiful tall pines, moss-layered water oaks and fragrant magnolias. Welcome to the land of hospitality!

The parish of St. Tammany and the city of Slidell are steeped in a historic revelation of heritage and culture, which unfolds through centuries filled with truth and fact. In addition there are also the legends and myths of the early Indians, French, and Spanish that capture our imagination. Just as the native Indians were intermingled with the early settlers, so were the ensuing generations that followed.

The tributaries to Lake Pontchartrain, Lake Borgne, and the Mississippi Sound have proved to be a bountiful breeding ground for shrimp, oysters, crabs and edible fish of every description. Each community along St. Tammany's lake shores supports its own safe-harbor or small craft marina with awaiting adventures in water sports, while unrevealed and hidden within the tall pines north of the shore are manicured golf courses, parks, trails, and majestic gardens.

For these and many more reasons, folks have been selecting Slidell water havens as their choice for retirement. The inducements are many . . . Just ask anyone!

A City on the Move

East St. Tammany Parish consists of the sprawling municipality of Slidell in congruence with the cities of Lacombe to its west and Pearl River on its northeast. Encroaching these outlying cities are subdivisions which abound in rapid development, each offering homesites for varied interests. More and more commuters are finding their way in seeking low crime areas and superior school environments for family living, which includes recreation and entertainment outlets commensurate with their distinctive tastes.

Slidell offers the best of selective choices. By undirected evolution, it has become a prime city — enmeshed with small communities and lofty pristine estates which meld within a network of many natural waterways.

Slidell's location as a crossroad of State and Interstate Highways provides quick and easy access to New Orleans, Baton Rouge, Hattiesburg, and the Mississippi Gulf Coast.

Slidell has a social structure which produces a strong spirit of community and family friendly atmosphere.

Slidell has outstanding youth centered programs encompassing youth sports leagues in baseball, football, basketball, and soccer.

Slidell has outstanding restaurants and an increasing Real Estate market with affordable priced new construction as well as an inventory of previously owned homes.

Slidell has numerous Hotels, Motels, and Bed & Breakfast Inns which truly provides a Crossroads made more significant by its growth in hotel motel rooms approaching 1200 rooms by year's end 1999.

Slidell has various subdivisions for any discriminating home seeker -Oak Harbor, Masters Point, The Inlets, The Fairways, Mariner's Cove and exclusive home developments at Eagle Point, off Spartan Drive behind Salmen High School, and at Stoneridge, located off St. Joe Road.

According to the 2010 US Census, 27,068 people, 10,050 households, and 7,145 families live in the city

Exploration and Development

The Explorers

The first explorers were the Spanish and the Portuguese, who in the 1500s, mapped the shores of the Gulf of Mexico. The Spaniard DeSoto is credited as being the first European to encounter the flowing Mississippi River having traversed the gulf coast region in 1542. The early French influence in the New World began with the founding of Quebec, Canada in 1608. Father Marquette and Joliet initiated explorations of the Mississippi valley followed by De La Salle's expeditions. Robert Cavalier de La Salle, a native of Rouen, France, bought provisions using his personal resources in order to explore the Mississippi valley. His first voyage from Montreal in 1669 was unsuccessful and was followed up in 1680. Finally arriving at the mouth of the river on April 9, 1682, La Salle erected a cross blazoned with the French Coat of Arms and proclaimed formal possession of the Mississippi River and all its tributaries, and of all the lands, in the name of Louis XIV, King of France. He named the lands Louisiana. The French had a penchant for immediately christening everything they discovered. LaSalle's final voyage by way of the Gulf of Mexico was unsuccessful as he attempted to find the Mississippi's mouth.

The baton was passed to Pierre Le Moyne, Sieur d'Iberville, of French Canada. According to *Iberville's Journals,* he was instructed by King Louis XIV, to "go to the Gulf of Mexico, locate the mouth (of the Mississippi River) . . . select a good site that can be defended with a few men, and block entry to the river by other nations."

Aware of English commitments to establish a trading post upon the banks of the mouth of the Mississippi River, Iberville made the first move. He commissioned and outfitted the *Badine,* the *Marin* and several slower vessels called *Travasiers,* or transports. With careful discretion and determination, he selected his men. With a prime staff including his brother, Bienville, he picked Spanish-speaking Frenchmen, Spanish deserters from Mexico, and other French Canadian *voyageurs.* He ordered trade items for the Indians and stored guns and ammunition. He was prepared to fight the English if for any reason he didn't arrive at the gulf before them.

The small fleet of ships left from Brest, France in October of 1698 and arrived at the Spanish controlled island of Santo Domingo in January of 1699. Spending just enough time to take on new provisions and hiring fresh local hands, they started searching the coast lines westward delving into each water inlet in search of the mouth of the Mississippi. The journey was made more difficult because he had to rely on faulty charts and journals as described by the former explorations of La Salle in addition to using incorrrect Portuguese maps. Painstakingly, during his exploring expeditions he designed new journals and charts with the help of native Indians. Encountering Spanish ships in the Pensacola harbor they continued westward, arriving at the Bay of Mobile.

During each careful scrutiny along the way, Iberville raised crosses and cut the bark of trees to establish their presence. Further west they encountered Horn Island which was so named because a soldier had lost his powder horn during a landing.

D'Iberville's first landing party.

They then encountered Ship Island off the coast of present-day Gulfport, Mississippi, on February 10, 1699, wherefrom they made foraging landings on the mainland to make contact with the Indians.

On communicating with the natives, they were told of the Mississippi River further west. So they set sail once more to investigate Cat Island on March 1st and from there they continued to the Mississippi.

On Monday, March 2, 1699, as a storm was pounding the schooner, the French, in attempting to seek haven coincidentally discovered the mouth of the Mississippi River. The following day they celebrated Mardi Gras with a catholic mass and raised a cross as a symbol of their manifestation. Here, they planted one of a series of the *Fleur-des-Lys*. They traveled upriver in order to verify that the vast body of water was actually the Great Mississippi. After passing Baton Rouge, they retraced their voyage to return to the Gulf by way of the Rigolets. Iberville, in realizing the need to establish a fort for protection of France's claim to the Mississippi River, began seeking a safe harbor with adequate deep waters to anchor their ships.

On return to Biloxi Bay on Wednesday, April 8, 1699, they selected a settlement site, cleared the land, and built a fort for protection of the garrison which would remain. This location is present day Ocean Springs, Mississippi.

During the building of the fort, the Indians assembled and five chiefs celebrated for three days; dancing, chanting and sounding drums and rattles. One Indian placed his back to Iberville to mount his shoulders as another carried his feet to a planted stake in a sign of peace. The French made alliances with the Indians and taught them how to use tools such as picks and shovels and how to make and replace handles for axes. In turn, the French learned Indian cultivation methods and how to make dugout canoes.

The Settlers

Iberville chose *"old Biloxi"* (current Ocean Springs, MS) as the first Capital of Louisiana in 1699, followed by Mobile, Alabama. and later a return to the Coast at *"new Biloxi"* (current City of Biloxi, MS), before finally moving the French seat of government to New Orleans.

During the intervening time, Mobile was founded in January 1702, and for a brief period became the center for Indian trade and French diplomacy. In 1704, the *Pelican* arrived with the first of New World brides. Ship's carpenter and historian, Penicaut described the passengers, "there were twenty-three marriageable girls who were reared in piety and who were drawn from sources above suspicion and who know how to work." These were the forerunners of the Casquette girls. They were the predecessors, too, of a group of "wayward ladies" from a house of correction in

Paris who were willing to come to Louisiana in exchange for freedom. Needless to say, the colonists who desired a European wife were not particular about their prior demeanor.

Andre Penicaut, while traveling with d'iberville, kept a journal that reported, *"We continued along the (Mississippi) river making a circuit around back to Lake Pontchartrain by way of Pass Manchac (which means back entrance). From there, northward around the Lake we carne upon the Tangipahoa River (which means white corn). After circling Lake Pontchartrain, we passed through the Rigolets (which means Channel) to return to the Bay of St. Louis. Once more we took to the hunt, taking back to the Fort (Maurepas) with us, many cows and deer and other wild game, which filled our long boats."*

The French governing officials primary goal was to seek wealth from the Mississippi region. However, Europe fell into economic hardships due to wars and famine, which resulted in the early French settling along the coast simply to display their flag and to protect their political dominion from English or Spanish takeover. Early inhabitants perceived the sea primarily as a supply route rather than as a source of food. Therefore the early colonists settled mostly in sea-oriented, unkempt villages and depended on trade with the Indians and supplies from France for survival. As time passed, the early settlers found themselves left to fend for themselves. There was no food or supplies or even trinkets to keep the Indians happy. Eventually, the colonists learned to fish and to probe the local oyster beds.

During the early 1700s, the French spread out along the Coast and invaded the inland bayous, the bays and the rivers. These new settlers consisted of French and Canadian soldiers; craftsmen, such as carpenters and millers; the *Voyageurs* were sturdy, experienced, Canadian scouts and guides who rowed the canoes and pirogues; *Coureurs du Bois* were Canadian woodsmen and fur trappers; and later arrived the *habitans* who were settlers seeking to establish homesteads on land grants owned by rich friends of Royalty.

The French Canadians were not like the other colonists. From the first days of the settlement, they took the comely Choctaw women as concubines and the young girls of the Natchez and Chickasaw as slaves. They adamantly insisted that they had to have women to do their washing, and their cooking in order to make *sagamite,* and to maintain their cabins. No military order and no religious edict could keep them from the Indian girls. As time passed, small dusky half-breed children were found playing about their cabins. They would grow up to be approved by the blood-tolerant Frenchmen and Canadian French. As years passed, this custom became concealed as newcomers criticized the practice.

As time passed, several regions along the Coast were being taken up by such pioneering settlers like Jean Baptiste Nicaise, Chevalier Dedeaux, and Pierre Moran in addition to existing settlers such as the Sauciers, the Ladners, the Cuevas's, the Favres, the LaFontaines, the Dubuissons, and many more.

Why did these pioneering people stay? What caused them to fan out over the entire Louisiana/Mississippi Coast? These seekers evidently found the peace of *joie de vivres* and Gulf breezes and the greatness of a paradise unfolding. They remained in spite of adversity.

Large grants of land on the Mississippi River, its tributaries, and along the Gulf Coast were made by the French, English, and Spanish governments on the condition of colonization. Joining the new influx of people were the Acadians who had been expelled by the British from Nova Scotia in 1763. They became known as Creoles.

After 1763, under British dominion of the Gulf Coast region, and the withdrawal of French troops, the priests also left the territory. Once the British exacted pledges of allegiance from the remaining settlers, the English enforced an isolation which resulted in the inhabitants frequently being in harms way.

Since the Indians were no longer being traded supplies to keep them peaceful, they began to raid the farm sites causing the remaining French *habitans* to flee their settlements.

During the period of 1771 to 1773, Captain Bernard Romans, a map maker, wrote about the West Florida region of the Gulf Coast. "The scarce *habitans* living in the wooded areas learned to produce lumber, pitch, tar, and charcoal from the pine forests, as well as herding pigs and cattle."

With political restructuring in Europe, the New World lands were becoming influenced by the ensuing war games resulting in coastal area ownership being shifted from one European national control to another. The British took possession away from the French in 1773. They took some of Florida and some of Louisiana and created the fifteenth colony which they called West Florida. When the original 13 colonies rebelled in 1776, the two Florida colonies remained loyal to King George III of England.

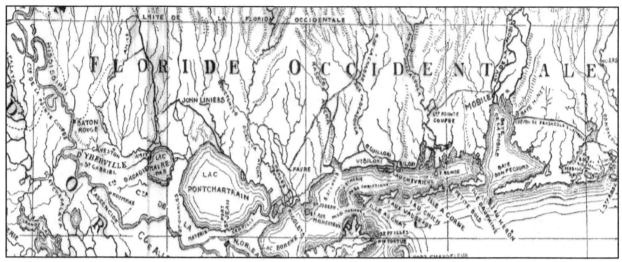

This is part of a Map of 1806 showing West Florida, as drawn by New Orleans cartographer, Lafon. Spanish West Florida was located south of the 31st parallel and situated between the Mississippi River to Pensacola, Florida with Baton Rouge and St. Francisville in Louisiana, established as its western boundary.

In 1779 the Spanish appropriated the two Floridas hoisting their colors adorned by Lions and Castles. The Spaniards held Louisiana until the year 1800, when it was ceded back to France. Napoleon couldn't hold it against the English so he decided to sell the vast Mississippi Valley territory to the United States on April 30, 1803.

The West Florida Territory, which included the Gulf Coast from Baton Rouge to Pensacola, had become settled by eight to ten thousand, many of whom were Anglo-Americans who primarily inhabited the areas of Natchez and Baton Rouge. The end of Spanish reign took place when the settlers lost patience with the frequent switching of allegiance to different national flags. The rebelling Americans in Baton Rouge established their independence by raising the *Lone Star Flag*.

The Indians

As d'Iberville and Bienville had encountered new Indian tribes, they would quickly make allies of them. Alliances were cemented at 3-day Feasts which were celebrated by the *Dance of the Calumet*. Afterwards, gifts were distributed consisting of knives, hatchets, axes, picks, mirrors, rings, beads, and trinkets. In exchange, the Indians would offer food and teach the French their ways of cultivation and making pirogues. They also cooperated by giving detailed descriptions of local terrain and Indian villages for the map makers.

The Indians remained shy of the white man following their encounter with the Spaniard, DeSoto. During DeSoto's 1540s trek along the coast from Florida to the Mississippi River, he had killed all Indians he came in contact with. However the French finally made amends with the Indians and by 1730, the Choctaws and the French accepted each other as equals. Intermarriages even produced some Choctaw-Creole leadership as characterized by the famous Chief Greenwood LeFlore.

The part of Louisiana that lies north of Lake Pontchartrain and east of the Mississippi River is even today called the Florida Parishes. The Choctaw tribes lived mainly in this section of the state. Much of the area is either flat land or hills covered with pine forests. For the Indians, pine forests were not good hunting grounds nor were they cultivated for farming. Most of the Choctaw villages were located either on the Mississippi River, along the Pearl River, or on the shores of Lake Pontchartrain. The pine hills were visited usually when the Indians sought stones to make their arrowheads. The Indians would make camp for just a few days at places where they could find gravel. Once they had all the stones they needed, they returned to their homes on the rivers or the lake.

The early Spanish and French explorers encountered various tribes along the Gulf coast such as the *Duma, Acolapissa, Bylocchy, and the Pascoboula*. Near the mouth of the Mississippi River they encountered the Tangipahoa, Mougoulaschas, and the Bayagoulas; and further upriver they smoked the peace pipe and celebrated the dance of the *Calumet* with the *Nipissas* and the *Quinipissas*.

The Indians called the great Mississippi River the *Malbanchya*. The early Spanish called it the *Rio de Palisades* or *Rio de Espiritu Santo*. The early French called it the St. Louis River, or by the Indian name *Myssysypy* as recorded in Iberville's Journals.

Most Indian villages were cleverly hidden deep in the interior above the limits of tidewater and hurricanes, while coastal sites were typical to seasonal encampments of fair weather. As part of their diet, Indians made Sagamite from corn, which was prepared like a porridge mixed with meat for variety. Lizards and snakes were added when the hunt was poor.

"The Choctaw dispersed in small, presumably family-based, groups in the Spring after the crops were planted. They subsisted on fruit and aquatic foods until the early summer when they returned to the home community for the annual *Green Corn Ceremony*. Following this, they dispersed again until harvest time. After the crops were harvested in the fall, the men were away on the Fall hunt and the remaining villagers gathered nuts and other resources for winter and early spring consumption.", as described by R. Barry Lewis in his *Fires on the Bayous*.

Choctaws were, by far, the strongest Indian tribe in southeast Louisiana and southern Mississippi. Because the tribe was too large to be ruled by one man, the Choctaws divided their people into three groups each ruled by a chief known as a *Mingo*. Chief Tacala Yarbo ruled the Devil Swamp's tribal group.

Through the years, yellow fever epidemics, warfare and colonial encroachment, greatly affected the Indian population.

With the Indian Removal Act of 1830, the tribes east of the Mississippi River were forced to exchange their home lands for new lands in the West. The Choctaws and Chickasaws of Mississippi and Louisiana were included, as well as the Creeks from Florida. This enforced migration was later called the *Trail of Tears*. Many of the mix blooded Indians dropped their native names in favor of their European

family name and discreetly remained concealed in the wooded areas.

One famous Frenchmen who intermingled with the Indians was Jean Baptiste Favre, Jr. He originated from Rouen, France where he married Madeleine, his first wife, on July 2, 1714. He then married Marie Anne Arlut in 1720. He left four children at his death, one of whom was Jean Claude Favre who was the official Government Interpreter for Louisiane.

During his extensive travels, it has been reported that he sired many children, including five legitimate children by his wife Marguerite, the daughter of a Swiss soldier. One of these was Simon Favre who also became an official government interpreter and traveled the whole of southern Louisiana and the Gulf Coast. His descendants reported that Simon had many illegitimate children – white, red, and black – scattered from New Orleans to Mobile. Simon Favre settled along both sides of the Pearl River in 1806, following the explorations of his predecessor, Jean Claude Favre, who had cultivated some of the area in 1767. Simon was sufficiently educated and participated in the negotiations and signing of many Indian Treaties. He also served as one of the four magistrates appointed by Territorial Governor W.C.C. Claiborne in 1811, and planted the American Flag there. He played a prominent part in currying the Choctaw Nation to the American cause, however, he died before the Battle of New Orleans took place.

Today, Indians are few in number in the former West Florida territorial region and much of their heritage has been forgotten. However, we might justly remind ourselves that many of the names of towns, counties, rivers and bayous, proclaim the omnificense of their progeny.

For the amateur archaeologist, or Indian lore seeker, there are still traces of native Indian inhabitants along the coast. Archaeological components are unfortunately based entirely by results of limited excavations, thereby providing limited data. However, some Indian shell piles called *middens* still have potential historical significance.

Thus, the early Indians who created these mounds, had done so long before DeSoto ever made his *Pasada,* or bloody trek, from Florida to the Mississippi River in 1541.

The Pirates

Another flag had fluttered both ashore as well as throughout the waters along the Gulf Coast. It was the flag of the Pirates. These included; Captain Pitcher, and the infamous Lafitte brothers who scurried throughout all of the water inlets from Grand Isle in Louisiana to the Mississippi barrier islands.

Several of Lafitte's kin remained ashore to settle along the villages of the coast.

Then, too, there was the ignoble Pierre Rameau, the King Pirate of the Honey Island Swamp (the French called it the (*Marais de l'île-de-Miel*),.

Pierre Rameau was not French, but Scottish born. He arrived at the Pearl River area about 1800. Choosing piracy as the quickest means for getting rich, he soon assembled a big band of lawless men and established his headquarters and hidden treasures in the Honey Island Swamps across the river from Gainesville, Mississippi.

When General Jackson marched from the Creek Wars in Florida, Rameau used his ships to transport the heavy artillery to New Orleans. Like Lafitte, he volunteered to fight with the Americans, but the British offer of money and his belief that the superior British Army would be victorious, resulted in his switching allegiance just before the Battle of New Orleans. Justly enough, he was killed during the Battle. This left his treasure hordes to be laid rampant to many seekers.

The "Pirate King of Honey Island" and his band of *"Chats Huants,"* or Screech Owls, were thought to have buried Mexican coins dating from 1827. These were discovered in an iron chest in 1907 by two hunters in Honey Island Swamp.

Jean and Pierre Lafitte were the most famous of all the pirates who scavenged the coastal areas from Galveston, Texas to Mobile, Alabama. Because of their participation in the Battle of New Orleans by helping to thwart the British, they were exonerated.

Piracy was practiced for hundreds of years. Many of the privateers ignored allegiance to anyone country's flag. They flew their own and abided to their own laws. However, during times of war between countries, it was always considered fair game for citizens to plunder or to protect those who were actively engaged in such profitable ventures.

Many stories have been told of Jean Lafitte's infamous journeys. After his pardon in New Orleans, he was reported to have disappeared in the West Indies. However, there were many reportings of his having established residence at different places throughout Mississippi and Louisiana.

A story goes that "one of Jean Lafitte's pirates slipped away from the moorings at one of the coast inlets and absconded with some of the booty in order to bury the cache. In carrying the hefty chest, he also took along his huge vicious dog which was left at the treasure site to perform guard duty.

The buccaneer, however, was killed while plundering for more treasures. The dog continued his vigilance until dying of old age.

It is still told by many folks that the ghost of the dog lives on. It has been reported to be seen beneath an old oak tree on dark nights as it prowls and growls all night long at the banks of the river.

The Flags

The first banner to wave was actually planted in 1682 by LaSalle. It was the French standard known for the House of Bourbon represented by the *Golden Fleur de Lis* in a field of white. D'Iberville planted the flag for a second time in 1699.

When the British arrested control of the territory in 1773 they took some of Florida and some of Louisiana, thereby creating the fifteenth colony which the English called West Florida and raised their flag known as the *British Red Ensign.* When the original 13 colonies rebelled in 1776, the two Florida colonies remained loyal to King George III of England.

In 1779 the Spanish appropriated the two Floridas hoisting their colors decorated with *Lions and Castles.* However, when Napoleon took control of France, he induced the Spanish to release Louisiana back to France, which they did.

In 1803, President Jefferson sent James Monroe to France to purchase New Orleans and West Florida. Napoleon countered the request by generously including Louisiana into the sale package. With the Louisiana Territory acquisition from France in 1803, the southern-most portion was designated the Territory of Orleans, conforming with much of present-day Louisiana. Claiborne was then transferred from the governorship of the Mississippi Territory to assume territorial governorship of the newly organized lower Louisiana territory.

Spanish West Florida spread from Baton Rouge and Natchez to Pensacola on the east, the Gulf of Mexico on the South and the 31st parallel on the North. (The northern boundary at that time was the 31st parallel which is approximately 40 miles north of the gulfshore.)

In 1810, a group of enraged settlers, staged a revolution in the vicinity of St. Francisville and Baton Rouge upon learning that they were excluded from being part of the new Territory of Orleans. The leaders of that revolution declared West Florida to be an independent Republic naming Fulwar Skipwith as its president. They then raised the Lone Star Flag and appealed for United States statehood. Even though President Madison had

proclaimed West Florida as a part of the "Louisiana Purchase," Spain had disregarded this maneuver. Shortly thereafter, the American Stars and Stripes replaced the Lone Star flag.

On December 10, 1810, Governor William C.C. Claiborne gave instructions to Col. Leonard Covington to proceed to the north shore of Lake Pontchartrain to raise the American Flag. Gov. Claiborne also instructed Dr. William Flood to enlist each settlement along the Mississippi Gulf Coast. On January 9, 1811, Flood docked his sloop, *the Alligator,* at Simon Favre's east bank farm on the Pearl River. There, Flood raised the American flag, and appointed Favre justice of the peace for Biloxi Parish, which consisted of the area from Pearl River to Biloxi Bay.

When Louisiana became a state on April 8, 1812, its boundaries were extended to absorb the four parishes west of the Pearl River, leaving the remaining West Florida lands from the Pearl to the Perdido River to be included in the Mississippi Territory. That remaining West Florida coastal region was then known as the County of Mobile.

Louisiana and the Mississippi Territory were further populated and settled following General Andrew Jackson's defeat of the Creek Nation in the Battle of Horse Shoe Bend on March 27, 1813. Further expansion took place after January 8, 1815, when he defeated the British in the Battle of New Orleans with his legion of Kentuckians, Mississippians, Louisianians, Free Negroes, and Pirates.

They flew the *American Flag with fifteen stars and fifteen stripes.*

St. Tammany Parish

Description

The natural beauty of St. Tammany has delighted and charmed residents and visitors alike for almost three centuries. Artists, poets, naturalists, and photographers have sought to capture the scenic splendors and quiet secluded retreats that manifests as one of Louisiana's loveliest regions. Encircled by Lake Pontchartrain and the Pearl River, the land is intermeshed with sandy-bottomed creeks, rivers, and bayous. Much of St. Tammany's beauty is associated with its grassy forest cover. In the southeast is the Honey Island Swamp area where cypress and tupelo gum trees rise in profusion. Upon the high ground abutting the lake and along the river banks, Live Oaks majestically rise, gracefully extending limbs adorned with strands of Spanish moss continually swaying in the breezes.

The southern and eastern sections of St. Tammany Parish are flat, and rise slowly to the rolling hills of the north-central and northwestern regions. The parish is drained by two major and four minor stream systems. Almost the entire western half is drained by the Tchefuncta-Bogue Falaya system, which also includes the Abita and the Little Bogue Falaya rivers, Pontchitolawa Creek, and other smaller tributary creeks and branches.

The northcentral, northeast, and extreme eastern sections are drained by the Bogue Chitto-Pearl River system, while the southcentral part of the parish drains into Lake Pontchartrain through Bayou Castein, Cane Bayou, Bayou Lacombe, and Bayous Liberty and Bonfouca. In the lower reaches, all the streams are quiet, winding and relatively deep, and furnish some of the loveliest scenery and most desirable homesites in Louisiana.

Judge Ellis remarked in his book that, "St. Tammany Parish offered a varied terrain, well-watered and well drained, heavily-timbered with long-leaf pine, and sustained a healthy climate and beautiful environment. Extensive deposits of sand, gravel, and clay for bricks are still available. For much of its early history, the area had been kept isolated by its surrounding lakes, rivers, and swamps."

The wooded areas shelter quail, turkeys, deer, rabbits, foxes, squirrels, and a multitude of rare birds. The Tchefuncta, Bogue Falaya, and Pearl rivers as well as the Lacombe, Liberty, and Bonfouca bayous provide ample opportunities for superb fishing. The wealth of this transcendent backdrop captivates visitors and vacationers all year round.

L'autre Cote DuLac
Across the Lake

The first Europeans to affect life in St. Tammany were the French, initially by their explorations of the Lake Pontchartrain Basin, but more importantly, by their building of the City of New Orleans in 1718. Bayou St. Jean (St. John), which empties into the lake from the south, provided water access to the rear of the Crescent City and served as a major port between New Orleans and Mobile during much of the eighteenth century. As the French settled along Bayou St. John, some

> **Frederick S. Ellis,** author
> *St. Tammany Parish,*
> *L 'autre Cote DuLac*

venturesome souls moved across the lake to settle along Bayou Bonfouca, Bayou Liberty, and Bayou Lacombe. Their reasons for coming to the northshore were varied: some as traders, businessmen, farmers, tradesmen, and fugitives. The common link was the land, the water, and the natural resources.

Wilderness life in early St. Tammany centered around the bayous and streams. Travel was mostly by piroque, canoe or schooner. Roads were few and far between. Many were no more than beaten Indian paths, while some of the larger land owners maintained make-shift roads through their own property.

D'Iberville was the first European to describe the area as he had written in his

Journal on March 28, 1699.

> "We traveled along the shore of this lake about ten leagues to the east, a quarter southwest, the wind in the northwest. The water of the lake is too brackish to drink and camped on a treeless, grassy point, pretty bad, having no water to drink and many mosquitoes, which are terrible little animals to people who are in need of rest. For the last four leagues, there are prairies along the lake, which are about one league wide, back to the forest. I cannot see the other side of the lake ... "

On the next day, d'Iberville proceeded along the shore east by southeast, and at about four leagues from the previous day's campsite, he exited Lake Pontchartrain by way of the channel he named the "Rigolets."

According to Judge F. Stephen Ellis's calculations, he reported that d'Iberville would have passed the night at Goose Point which "lies about 30 miles from Pass Manchac and about 12 miles from the Rigolets, and is the only prominent point in the area."

There were primarily two main road connections. One was the mail road which crossed into Louisiana from Mississippi over the Pearl River ending at Simon Favre's farm. From there the mail was taken by water route through the Rigolets and across the lake to Bayou St. John.

Another road was the Military Road which left from Ford's house on the Pearl River above the 31st parallel, and then proceeded to Madisonville. A smaller road ran east-west, through Mandeville across Bayou Castine, then northward through Francois Cousin's property to the west bank of Bayou Lacombe. After crossing Martin's ferry, another path led from the east bank of

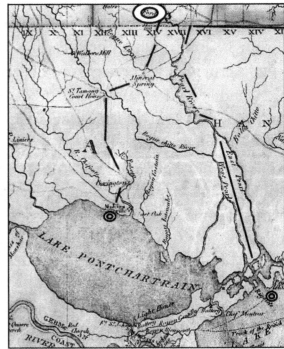

1820 Map – Top donut at Ford's, BottomRight donut at Rigolets, Mid-map donut at Madisonville.

Bayou Lacombe to Bayou Liberty, then on to Bayou Bonfouca. In 1867, it took three hours to travel by carriage along this route from Mandeville to Bonfouca..

Ford's Place

Due to seasonal Indian uprisings, John Ford's place served as a temporary fort and refuge with stockades built surrounding the area for protection. General Jackson proceeded to New Orleans following the defeat of the Creeks in Florida, crossing the Pearl River at Ford's Ferry and traveled 2½ miles to John Ford's Fort, in all – 31 miles and halted for the night. From there, Jackson's men traveled west

Ford's Place, located on Old Columbia-Covington Road in Marion County, MS. Built in 1810, it is listed on the National Register of Historic Places. Image courtesy of Historic American Buildings Survey.

of the Pearl down to the mouth of Tchefuncta on Lake Pontchartrain at Madisonville, where a navy yard was located with a mustering point for the Louisiana militia.

In review of Judge Ellis's well-documented history, *"St. Tammany Parish, L'autre Cote DuLac,"* he described that the first recorded white resident of the northshore was reflected in a lawsuit filed on August 22, 1725, between and Indian trader, Pierre Brou, "resident at the Colapissas," and a man named Bertrand Jaffre, called *"La Liberte,"* who had a pitch and tar works in the Bonfouca region at Bayou Liberty. While there, Jaffre hired Indians to aid in his plant operations. He was the namesake for Bayou Liberty. Brou retired to New Orleans in 1745, where he filed his Will.

Another early French settler was Rene Chairman, or "Du Chesne," as reflected in a census of 1727. Also, listed were names, such as: Lacombe, Lacroix, and Jean Vis and son. A report in 1735, listed La Liberte, Lacombe, and Jacques Chauvin as living on "the other side of the lake." Also, Antoine Brunel operated a tar works employing Francois Gaspalliere, Joseph Gatoir, and a man named Perron. Antoine Brunel, Antoine Aufrere and a Michael Brosset jointly owned the *St. Anne,* which was the first recorded vessel from the northshore.

Judge Ellis surmised that Brunel died, based on records showing Michael Brosset having married the Widow Brunel on October 12, 1737. Other business associations were between Claude Vignon, called "Lacombe" and Louis Joseph Bizoton, in a tar works business until 1738, when Lacombe then entered into a partnership with Juan Baptiste de Cavannes. In 1739, Jacques Chenier also joined that business venture.

Lacombe was also active in raising cattle on Grand Coquille Island. In Lacombe's Will, he acknowledged giving freedom to his female slave, Mariane and her two children, Joseph and Pierre, in addition to providing them with cattle and money. Lacombe is known as the namesake for Bayou Lacombe, where his tar works was evidently located. Reported also, was a Michel Pacquet, who lived in that vicinity for whom Bayou Pacquet is named.

The French called the tar works industry a *Gaudronnerie,* which included charcoal as a by-product

Antoine Aufrere is assumed to have kept his residence at New Orleans, but participated in several tar works partnerships at the northshore, including an association with Louis Tixerand in 1738.

Another plantation owner was Francois Hery, called "Duplanty." He was one of the few men who made the obligatory trip to Mobile in the 1760s, to pledge his allegiance to the British Crown and confirm his land grant. He owned a tar works that was located at the Bayou Lacombe-Bayou Liberty area, which he called *Tanchipaho.*

There was a Joseph Chauvin Delery operating a sawmill before 1736. His widow appeared before the Superior Council at New Orleans on March 12, 1736, to plea for her land by showing the gate-locks, which were the only remaining articles from the mill that burned down.

Jacques Milliet and his wife, Jeanne Poitier Milliet were living in the area of the north shore when he died in 1763. His Will indicated a cabin, furniture, hogs, cattle, and three Negro adult slaves with two children.

In 1763, from British West Florida, 25 citizens journeyed to Pensacola, the capital, to pledge oath of allegiance to British rule and their new flag. Among them were: Carriere, Dupont, Farve, Gollot, Krebs, Meaut, Nicaise, and Ladner.

The weak exposure of British occupation forces proved a boon and a bane. French settlers were alienated from the English, both in language and religion, therefore many were able to freely adopt the trade of smuggling. They were induced to fend for themselves since there was no protection from the Indians or government support during catastrophic occurrences such as the devastating hurricane of 1772.

In 1766, Montfort Browne, Lt. Gov. of British West Florida, took a tour of inspection through the area which led westward from the Bay of St. Louis, past the Pearl River, through the Rigolets, into Lake Pontchartrain to "Tanchipaho," which was an old French settlement. In his report, he described that most of the land was used for grazing cattle.

Early activity between New Orleans and the St. Tammany was also reported by another Englishman, Captain Harry Gordon in 1766, as he reported seeing three schooners plying the lake carrying tar.

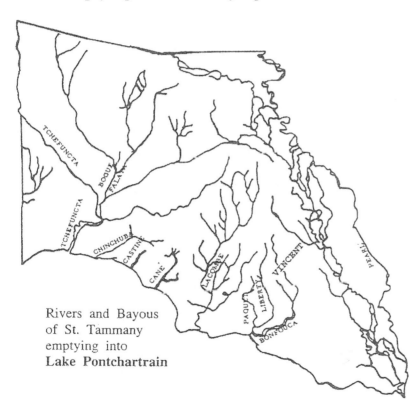

Rivers and Bayous
of St. Tammany
emptying into
Lake Pontchartrain

Also, Englishman Jacob Blackwell observed Indian traders on pack horses at a town on Lake Pontchartrain called "Tangipahou," which was settled by Frenchmen and Choctaws. He observed that there was smuggling activity between New Orleans and St. Tammany. The town he described was most likely in the Bonfouca, Liberty, Lacombe area, as presumed by Judge Ellis.

When Englishmen began moving to the area, the earliest British grant was given on July 28, 1766, to John Jones on a creek named *Chefuncte* followed by another land grant of 500 acres to Richard Dixey on Bayou *Chief Mentieno* (Chef Menteur). On September 29, 1767, Jerome Matulich was granted 1000 acres at the head of Lake Pontchartrain and

1778 map by Englishman George Gauld
Bonfouca was spelled Boucfouca

John Gradinego, with a family of 10, was granted the adjoining 1000 acres. Other grants along the east end of Lake Pontchartrain were awarded to John Marshall, Cornelius Bradford, John Moor, Edmund Milne, George Hawkins, and Peter Miller. In 1768, five-hundred acres of Bayou Lacombe property was given to Babe St. Martin.

Henri Millon (alias Matala) sold his dairy farm to Gabriel Peyroux in 1790.

Others who followed during that era were Letchworth, Spell, de la Barthe, and Goodby families.

A second wave of settlers came into St. Tammany's north shore area during the 1770s including Jean Claude Favre, who claimed two plantations on the Pearl River. One was located on the west bank of the Little Pearl where Favre took over a dairy farm with a building that was used as a tar kiln; another grant on the right bank of the Large Pearl became Favre's indigo dye factory.

Nicholas Ducre, (aka Bell Humeur) purchased 800 arpents of land on Bayou Bonfouca in September 1785.

Joseph Laurent also owned a large tract on the Bayou which was sold in 1793 to

From a 1774 English Map by Bernard Romans, he stated that "there was scandalous illicit trade carried on between the inhabitants of the Country between Tangipaho to the Bay of St. Louis and (with) the Spaniards at Orleans, the former of which many have taken the Oath of Allegiance to and hold estates under both Governments, (English and Spanish) while supplying the latter with Pitch, Tar, Charcoal, Live Oak, and Cattle by way of St. Johns Creek."

Vincent Rillieux, the namesake for Bayou Vincent. In 1825, widow Rillieux, Maria Tronquet, sold the Bayou Vincent plantation, including the slaves, and the schooner, *"Le Reductable de Bonfouca"* to her husband's manager, Barthelemy Martin.

Another Rillieux was Francois, who expanded his lands all the way to the Pearl River and purchased the small island known as *"Las Conchas"* from a Mr. Deruisseaux who had owned it since its purchase from the Biloxi Indians in May 1757. Other reports suggest that *"Las Conchas"* was purchased by his widow, Marie Chenet.

Most prodigious in the Bonfouca region were the Cousins, Carrieres, Rouquettes, and Pichons, who will be further described.

American Revolution

Following the opening shots of the American Revolution in 1776, new arrivals to the north shore were mainly from New York, including: Matthew Arnold, James Connett, Lewis Davis, William Webb, James Kirk, Paul Labyteaux, John Loofbarrow, and Thomas Loofbarrow who settled around Bayou Castein (Madisonville). Many others came afterwards and were classified as escaping Loyalists, who wished not to rebel against the British.

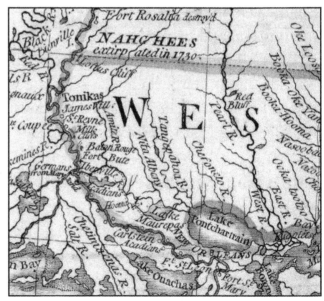

The American Revolution moved into Lake Pontchartrain in 1779 with a British armed sloop, the *West Florida.* Orders were to maintain vigilance and to deter American smuggling activities. With the aide of the Spanish at New Orleans, Captain William Pickles, Lieutenant Rousseau, and their crew aboard the *Morris's Tender,* captured the *West Florida.* The British ship was led to New Orleans which was under the command of the Spanish.

Captain Pickles, while landing on the north shore of Lake Pontchartrain on September 21, 1779, raised the American Flag for its first time and forced those British settlers living between Bayou LaCombe and the Tanchipahoa River to sign an oath of allegiance to the United States. However, it wasn't long before the area was placed back in command of the Spanish.

Vincent Rillieux, commanding a Spanish ship with only 14 Creoles, captured an English warship manned by 56 soldiers and 12 seamen near Pass Manchac.

During the 1780s and early 1800s, Charles Parent, Sr. served as the first commandant of the District of Chifoncte where his duty was to settle local disputes. Parent owned a large tract of land north of Madisonville where he raised about 1500 head of cattle. Following his death in 1804, Charles Parent, Jr. continued to operate the family plantation and brickyard until his death in 1868.

After Spain recovered West Florida from the British in 1783, a number of citizens became interested in buying land on the far side of Pontchartrain, therefore with the end of the American Revolution, greater numbers of settlers arrived. Included among these were Francois Dubuisson in 1788, John Baham in 1797, and Joseph Baham in 1800.

Pierre Philippe de Marigny de Mandeville was also one of these. His brother-in-law, by virtue of their marrying the d'Estrehan sisters, was the new Spanish Governor Bernardo de Galvez. Marigny bought up vast lands and became the largest land owner and richest resident of New Orleans and the north shore area. While engaged in fighting the British north of the lake, he became enamored with the lands there. At his large estate west of the future Madisonville, which he called Fontainebleau, he had as his guest, the young Duc d'Orleans, the future of France, King Louis Philippe.

Louisiana Purchase

With the Louisiana Territory acquisition from France in 1803, the southern-most portion was designated the Territory of Orleans, conforming with much of present-day Louisiana. However the land east of the Mississippi River and north of Lake Pontchartrain remained under control of the Spanish.

Spanish West Florida spread from Baton Rouge and Natchez to Pensacola, Florida; the Gulf of Mexico on the South, and the 31st

parallel on the North. (*The northern boundary at that time was the 31st parallel which is approximately 40 miles north of the Mexican Gulf shoreline.*)

Following the Louisiana Purchase, by adding such a vast domain to U.S. continental boundaries, *"Manifest Destiny"* became the geo-economic doctrine.

This doctrine was further pursued into the islands of the Caribbean, the Pacific, the South Pacific, and into Alaska.

The Spanish had encouraged English immigration to West Florida and "St. Ferdinand," their name for the St. Tammany district. Although some Carolinians moved in, Choctaw uprisings frightened away many prospective settlers. Regardless, some people emigrated from Mobile; among these was Juan Baptiste Baham, who with his sons received a land grant along the Tchefuncta including the site of the town of Madisonville. Other grants went to Cataline Badon, a widow, who received 1600 acres on the Tchefuncta, and Jacques Drieux, a New Orleans Creole, who obtained land on the Bogue Falaya in 1803.

Numerous settlers continued to move to St. Tammany regions during the period of temporary Spanish control from 1803 to 1810. Such immigration increases eventually weakened Spanish authority.

Republic of West Florida

On July 25, 1810, a convention was assembled for the District of "Tanchipaho and Chifoncte" and continued grievance meetings were held until September 23, 1810. The Spanish fort at Baton Rouge was captured without bloodshed, the garrison imprisoned, a capitol was set up at St. Francisville, and the Lone Star Flag was raised. These actions were followed by a Declaration of Independence and a new constitution, which was accepted by the inhabitants of St. Ferdinand (later, St. Tammany) as part of the Independent Republic of West Florida.

New Orleans was not part of West Florida

Shortly following their independence, on October 27, 1810, President James Madison issued a proclamation declaring that West Florida formed part of the Louisiana Purchase. On December 10, 1810, Governor William C.C. Claiborne sent Col. Leonard Covington to lower the Lone Star Flag and replace it with the 15-star American Flag. In the following month, on January 9, 1811, Dr. William Flood aboard the *Alligator,* was also sent by Governor Claiborne to the Gulf Coast to raise the American Flag.

At Pearl River, Simon Favre was appointed Justice of the Peace for that district as he pledged his allegiance and support to the American cause.

On December 22, 1810, Claiborne proclaimed that the County of Feliciana would be divided into the four parishes: Feliciana, East Baton Rouge, St. Helena, and St. Tammany (which was originally named for the famous Delaware Indian chief). These Florida Parishes, carved from old Spanish West Florida, were amended onto the Louisiana statehood bill shortly before Louisiana entered the Union of the United States. On April 8, 1812, Louisiana was admitted as the eighteenth state, however, the Florida parishes were not included until August 4, 1812. Of interest, the Florida parishes, including St. Tammany, had petitioned President Madison to attach them as part of the Mississippi Territory.

At that time the population of St. Tammany was reported at approximately 1700 free people and 300 slaves. The biggest taxpayer was reported as Francois Cousin who owned 42 slaves, 2 schooners and 1300 cattle.

By legislative act of March 25, 1813, Thomas Spell, Robert Badon, Benjamin Harvard, Joseph Hertraise, and Benjamin Bickham were appointed the first police jurors of St. Tammany Parish. They selected a centrally located spot near Enon on the Bogue Chitto River to erect the parish courthouse. However, in 1817, an election was called to fix the seat of justice at or near Covington. A new slate of commissioners was installed, consisting of David B. Morgan, Jesse R. Jones, John Wright, James Tate, and Daniel Edwards. Near Covington, a newly platted town of "Claiborne" was named, and a courthouse was built.

After a few years, a new courthouse was built at Covington, establishing it as the official county seat.

War of 1812

With renewed conflicts between British and Americans, the War of 1812 erupted. Eventually, the Gulf Coast and New Orleans were threatened by British invasion. At Madisonville just above the mouth of the Tchefuncte River, several small American gunboats were built to face 50 British men-of-war, however, they were soundly trounced even before the Battle of New Orleans took place.

In 1812, the Assembly at New Orleans directed that the Pearl River be cleared for navigation from New Columbia to the mouth. Included on the commission were Simon Favre, Jordan Morgan, William Hunt, John Burnett, John McGavie, and Joseph Ford. Everyone living within five miles of the river were required to work six days a year to clear the river of its natural rafts and other obstructions.

Madisonville had two shipyards, including a U.S. Navy facility. However, the Tchifonta, a 22-gun ship, was never finished despite desperate pleas from Jackson and Gov. William Claiborne, who wanted to use it to defend New Orleans from the British.

A typical schooner of war

Because the Tchefuncte and Lake Pontchartrain have shallow drafts and were not deep enough to handle the Navy vessels, they were outfitted with lifter barges that were strapped onto the hulls of the vessels in order to float them out to the Gulf.

Preparing for the Battle of New Orleans

General Andrew Jackson marched from Florida, along the 31st parallel Military Road, through St. Tammany to Madisonville where he took the mail packet boat across Lake Pontchartrain to assume command of the defenses at New Orleans. Joining them were a number of St. Tammany men who served under General David Banister Morgan of Madisonville. St. Tammany troops were mustered into the 13th Regiment under command of Col. Thomas C. Warner, with whom, the regiment saw battle duty at various locations during skirmishes and at the Battle of New Orleans.

One Militia Man's Story
(Contributed by William Blackwell, 3ʳᵈ great-grandson of Nathan Blackwell)

One young soldier that served under Colonel Thomas C. Warner was 19 year old Nathan Blackwell from northern Washington Parish (then part of St Tammany). Born in Warren County Tennessee, he had joined the ranks of the early colonists that came to Louisiana in search of homestead property and a better way of life. Nathan's land claim of 670 acres along the Pushepatapa Creek was where he chose to settle with his wife Mary and to raise a family.

When the general mobilization order for the Louisiana Militia was issued, Nathan enlisted at the Naval Yard in Madisonville on December 23, 1814. His military records indicate that he served at an outpost on picket guard for the duration of the war and was discharged on March 10, 1815. In his book, "St Tammany Parish-L'Autre Cote' Du Lac", Judge Frederick Ellis describes Nathan's military career as probably typical of a St Tammany volunteer in the War of 1812.

When the war was over, Nathan returned home where he and his wife lived out their lives and raised a family of 10 children. It was in 1855, at the age of 60, that Nathan signed a corrected affidavit attesting to his military career in order to obtain bounty land for which he was entitled. His carefully scripted signature on this document along with several years of census records indicate that he had received an early childhood education that was not typical of the early 19th century experience.

In March of 1870, at the age of 75, Nathan Blackwell passed away and was interred in the Blackwell Stateline Cemetery. Mary died some years later and was buried beside her husband.

Today their graves are properly marked with period headstones because of the good graces of their 3rd great grandson, Dr. J. Larry Crain, former President of Southeastern Louisiana University from 1980-1986. Dr. Crain held a formal monument dedication ceremony at the gravesite in 1979 which was attended by more than 100 descendants of Nathan and Mary Blackwell. Members of the local VFW were in attendance and prayers were offered by the clergy.

Dr. Crain's genealogical research and records of the 1979 ceremony are included in the J. Larry Crain Historical Collections housed in the Center for Southeast Louisiana Studies on the SLU campus in Hammond, Louisiana. Dr. Crain passed away in January 2014.

Ante-bellum Period: 1815 - 1861

After General Andrew Jackson's defeat of the Creek Nation in the Battle of Horse Shoe Bend on March 27, 1813, the antebellum years witnessed further growth in St. Tammany. The area became even more populated and settled after Jackson's defeat of the British in the Battle of New

In 1815, the steam driven New Camellia commenced crossing Lake Pontchartrain between New Orleans and Madisonville.

Orleans on January 8,1815. The parish attracted cattlemen, boat builders, brick makers, and lumbermen. They brought in more slaves to service in manufacturing lumber and bricks as well as the more familiar agricultural pursuits. Besides the small settlements at Chifoncte and the Barrio of "Buck Falia," two towns were founded in 1813 and 1814, and a third in 1834.

Population Reports

In the mid 1820s, the first U.S. Government Surveys were made on the Township Grid system, however due to many discrepancies, the Parish was re-surveyed in the late 1840s and early 1850s. There were two early roads, one running northeast to meet the Pearl River Road and another ran southeast towards the Rigolets.

Sampling of Earliest Marriages
1834 Anatole Cousin to Cormith (Camille) Pichon
1839 Nicholas Galatas to Baselide Laurent
1839 Sidoine Pichon to Adelle Carriere
1841 Pierre Gusman to Moliute Piernas
1841 Bartholemew Gusman to Louisiana Childress
1843 Zeno Pichon to Emily Loving
1845 Francois Rouquette to Marie Antoinette Favre
1845 Louise Cousin to Joseph Ordogne
1848 Artemise Dubuisson to Jean Coevas
(daughter of Silva in Dubuisson & Louise Nicaise)
(son of Juan J. Cuevas, Jr. & Eugene Ladner)
1848 Jacob Frederick to?
1850 Henry Vincent to Jane Little
1852 Francois Dubuisson to Aimee Marie Pena
1852 Eugene Parent to Marie Rodrigues
1853 JeanGusmantoMathiidaBaham
1856 Adolph Dubourg to Eglantine Dubuisson
1859 Emile Dubourg to Louisiana Fontaine
1885 Nelville Pichon to Maria Galatas
1886 John Salmen to Elise Sollberger

The 1820 Census reported a St. Tammany population of 1,821 of which 760 were men and women and 460 were children the remaining were Negroes, Free and Slave. Some of the large slaveholders were John Gusman, who inherited the Rillieux property on Bayou Bonfouca from Bartholomew Martin. Gusman owned 35 slaves, Terrence Carriere owned 69, Francois Carriere owned 39, Terrence Cousin owned 37, and Charles Parent owned 34.

The quantity of slaves indicates economic industries which may not have been agriculturally centered. According to Judge Ellis, there was an old document showing a brickyard on Bayou Bonfouca in 1826. By 1850, John Gusman and perhaps others were engaged in brick works businesses.

The 1850 Census reported 6,385 residents with a little more than 50% being white. There were 786 households reported.

From 1830 to 1850, more settlers arrived in St. Tammany to take lands along the roadways and on unclaimed lands adjoining old land grants.

Covington

Jacques Dreux arrived in St. Tammany in 1800 to develop a Spanish grant on the west bank of the Bougue Falaya River. His unsuccessful development of a small town that he named St. James was acquired by John Wharton Collins, who, on July 4, 1813, rededicated it as the town of Wharton. On March 11, 1816, the state legislature formally incorporated the town and renamed it Covington. Located on the Military Road and the Bogue Falaya River, Covington became an important port. From there, agricultural and timber products were shipped by barge, schooner, and steamboat across the lake to New Orleans.

Current View

Madisonville

At the time that Louisiana achieved statehood in 1812, marauding Indian tribes had begun stealing cattle and pillaging some of the homesteads, causing a number of families to abandon their homes to seek safety elsewhere. This resulted in troops being stationed at the cantonment and at the navy yard at Madisonville.

In late 1999, legislation transferred the light to Madisonville

In 1814, the Bahams, boat builders on the Tchefuncta, laid out the town of Madisonville. The natural beauty of the area with its fine water and pure air fostered the development of resorts abounding in hotels, boarding houses, and restaurants. Mandeville, Madisonville, and Abita Springs began attracting guests overland from upstate plantations and New Orleans. Excursions became quite popular and boats operated on regular schedules between Milneburg on the south shore and Madisonville on the north.

Mandeville

One of the most famous names associated with St. Tammany was that of the great Creole, Bernard de Marigny, who owned the renowned Fontainebleau Plantation (Fontainebleau Park) and who was prominent in the development of the town of Mandeville in 1834.

Pierre Philippe de Marigny, father of Bernard, had bought a summer retreat in the forest by the lake. During the Spanish regime in 1799, Governor Gayoso had granted Antonio Bonabel 4,020 square arpents on the northeastern part of Lake Pontchartrain at a place then known as *Punta Verde,* situated about one mile and a half southeast of Bayou Castine. This grant was added to Bernard de Marigny's property, expanding his family holdings to 3,545.68 acres.

This was one of the loveliest spots in the lands of the Choctaw. The beach was broad and clean. A short distance back from the shore grew magnificent Live oaks draped with Spanish moss. The area flourished with magnolia trees.

Bernard de Marigny delighted in improving his paradise during the 1820s, treating his sugar plantation as a show place. He bought additional land to the west and laid out streets as he had done in New Orleans at the Faubourg Marigny. He personally supervised the construction of public buildings, a church, and a market hall. Construction projects also included a hotel by the shore complete with wharves. There were also charming miniature bridges that crossed a nearby stream. He placed lots on sale, with restrictions designed to attract the sort of people he wanted. He established a ferry service across the lake which coincided with the opening of the Pontchartrain Railroad. He named the new site Mandeville, from one of his family titles and declared it a town in 1834. He even had a mayor and council elected.

He invited his friend John Davis, a gambler, to open a gaming casino which was one of Bernard's personal passions. Davis took charge of hiring chefs from Paris to provide for the best of restaurants. Mandeville developed an air of European sophistication.

He also engaged the *Blackhawk* steamboat to schedule regular lake crossings. Other land deals followed. In 1850, two more steamers the *Lenora* and the *Jenny Lind* began running regular excursions to the towns of West St. Tammany where tourism was being developed with the building of hotels.

Marigny managed to keep Fontainebleau until 1852 when it was sold to satisfy his creditors. It had several subsequent owners, among them the Nort family, having bought it in 1881. Eventually, one fifth of the plantation was organized into the Tchefuncta State Park and afterward renamed the Fontainebleau State Park. The remaining property was converted into a conservation area.

Trolley crossing the Bogue Falaya River in Covington (at left). The line ran from Mandeville, through Abita Springs and to Covington in the early 1900's. Orleanians had access to the north shore by taking day trips via excursion boats across Lake Pontchartrain.

Boat Building, Brickworks, and Sawmills

Activity reports at the Port of Bayou St. John in 1803 showed 314 boats had left the bayou bound for the north shore. Apparently, the most active land holder to transport his products, was Terrence Carriere, who owned property at Bayou Lacombe where he operated a large brickwork. Another registered vessel was captained by Pierre Robert, who owned land just north of the Rillieux property at Bonfouca. Eugene Dubuisson and Francois Cousin were others to make lake crossings.

Boat building between 1811 and 1820 resulted in 23 schooners, seven built at Tchefuncte, six at Madisonville, one at Covington, and seven at Bayou Bonfouca. The remaining were built at Lacombe and the Pearl River. In the years 1821 to 1829, there were thirteen schooners registered. Five were from Tchefuncte, two at Bayou Bonfouca and the rest from Lacombe, Bayou Pacquet, Bayou Castein and the Pearl River.

From 1830 to 1840, 27 boats were built including the first steamer, the *Pontchartrain.*

Eleven were built at Bonfouca, six at Tchefuncte, three at West Pearl River and the others at various places.

Before the Civil War there were fifteen brickyards and fourteen sawmills in operation, but in the late 1870s, the only remaining brickmakers in the Bonfouca region were Max Cousin and Hypolite Cousin.

Civil War

Although St. Tammany was opposed to secession, Louisiana ratified the Constitution of the Confederate States of America on March 21, 1861. The St. Tammany Militia was organized in June 1861. However, throughout the war a Unionist sentiment prevailed there. Of the several regiments raised for the Confederacy, one of these was known as the Washington Rifles, commanded by Hardy Richardson of Washington Parish.

Smuggling across the lake continued for the duration of the war, despite efforts by the Confederacy and the

Water Battles

In April 1864, Union Major Martin M. Pulver led four companies of the 20th Infantry, Corps d'Afrique (Black Federal soldiers) from Fort Pike at the Rigolets up the West Pearl River aboard the steamboat *Lizzie Davis* on a raid. He brought back stores, sixty-four slaves and recovered the steamboat *J.D. Swain.*

On September 9, 1864, Union Lt. Col. Alfred G. Hall led a detachment of the 74th U.S. Colored Troops from Fort Pike aboard the refitted *J.D. Swain* up the West Pearl River. The *J.D. Swain* was a side-wheel steam boat completed at Jeffersonville, Indiana and was lost in 1869.

Federals to end it. In 1863, the *U.S.S. Commodore*, a New Orleans built side wheel steamer, under command of Acting Master F. M. Green, was sent to Lake Pontchartrain to break up the blockade runners, but no records indicate capture of anyone. The small steamer remained there throughout the war.

Confederate troops did their share to help stop smuggling by burning two schooners in Bayou Lacombe and two other boats in Bayou Bonfouca. On a number of occasions, Federal troops were sent to St. Tammany to forage for food, cattle, and stock in addition, seeking timber and charcoal. St. Tammany was further left defenseless, as the Confederate troops also made their swoops for food and recruiting of man power. These raids were interspersed by the Jayhawkers who took whatever was left.

In Judge Ellis's history of St. Tammany, he described a letter from Brig. Gen. Taylor addressed to Messrs. F. Cousin, L. Cousin, Joseph Cousin, and John Cousin of Bayou Lacombe; and T. Cousin, Anatole Cousin, A. Cousin, and a Mr. Jones at Bayou Bonfouca:

"I have been informed that you are the owner of a number of boats which are engaged in running the blockade with passengers and property, and thus carrying on an illicit business. Such being contrary to law, I order that it be immediately stopped."

When New Orleans fell to Federal troops, those citizens refusing to sign loyalty oaths to the U.S. Government were allowed refuge on the north shore.

Post-bellum

Following the Civil War, the 1870 census revealed a population of 5,586 with eleven brickmakers and six sawmill operators still in business, however, boat building businesses had fallen off. Paul L. Gusman was reported as a schooner captain indicating a resumption of trade with New Orleans.

Following the Reconstruction Period, the census reported between 1870 and 1880 showed an increase in population from 5,586 to 6,887. The 1880 Parish census reported 6,911; in 1910, it was 18,917; and in 1920 the count was 20,645.

Prior to 1882, Slidell sawmills had already been established by Messrs.

Hamlet, Bliss, and Elliot, years before the Salmen Brothers arrived to establish theirs.

Another early industry was located on Honey Island in 1893, where F.M. White had a sawmill, a spoke factory, and a logging railroad which ran across the center of the island.

Laissez les bon temps rouler *(let the good times roll),* was the feeling of the times as the people shared the new economic good without concern that timber resources would eventually become depleted.

In 1908, when John A. Todd moved his mill from Bayou

A good Squirrel Hunt always provided great sporting entertainment for men folk such as exhibited in this 1893 string of peltries hunted by Gene Joyner, Will Watts and Bud Cuneo in the Honey Island Swamp.

Lacombe to Bonfouca, the *St. Tammany Farmer* reported that he had bought the last stand of yellow pine in the area. Previously, in April 1906, the *Farmer* stated, "The timber lands are rapidly being denuded by the saw mills, and it will not be long before the piney woods and the ozone belt will be a thing of the past . . . "

In 1913, Poitevent and Favre Lumber Company moved its mill from the Pearl River region to Mandeville. It was located just east of the causeway toll plaza, where Mariner's Village is now located.

At Lacombe another well-known mill was owned by John H. Davis which became better known as the Davis-Wood Lumber Company.

Ultimately, through reforestation, parish timber lands have undergone second, third, and fourth generation growths, but seldom can be found, the slow-growing long-leaf yellow pines.

Battle over the Bivalves

For years, oyster-men from Louisiana and Mississippi had been battling over their oyster beds and fishing processes. This resulted in the need to satisfy the differences in harvesting the bivalves.

Many people are familiar with a "fish story" about this boundary settlement between Louisiana and Mississippi. The prevailing story as retold many times by many persons of intellect, as well as commercial and sports fishermen, was that the argument was decided over a keg. Some say an empty nail keg and others claim a beer keg was simply floated down the Pearl River. The fishermen followed the keg as it was carried by the current, thus the boundary became established.

Indubitably, it was all a fish story.

The truth of the matter can be found in a lengthy legal case settled by the U.S. Supreme Court on March 5, 1906, known as the Louisiana v. Mississippi suit.

The dispute began due to the difference between state laws concerning oysters. Mississippi permitted the dredging of oysters on its natural oyster reefs, whereas, Louisiana prohibited such dredging. At that time, neither state marked their boundaries by the use of buoys or other line dividers, except as maintained by the United States Government in deep water channels.

To prevent the intrusion of Mississippi oyster-men with dredging vessels, a call was made to mark the water boundaries by Louisianans.

Further, to prevent fishers and sheriffs from taking up arms, each state agreed to create separate commissions to solve the boundary disputes and to mark the stipulated water bodies. However, since neither commission could agree with the other, they decided that a friendly suit was their only recourse.

After several years of preparation, and three days of legal arguments before the U.S. Supreme Court, the final ruling was ultimately settled in Louisiana's favor. "A true boundary was established as the deep water channel sailing-line upon emerging from the most eastern mouth of Pearl River into Lake Borgne, then extending through the northeast corner of Lake Borgne, north of Half Moon or Grand Island, thence east and south through the Mississippi Sound, through South Pass between Cat Island and Isle aux Pitre, into the Gulf of Mexico." This was reenforced by the delineation shown on an 1898 geodetic map, which was made a part of the decree.

Judge Frederick S. Ellis

Judge Frederick S. Ellis served in the 22nd Judicial District Court, the First Circuit Court of Appeal, Chief Judge of the First Circuit, and served Ad Hoc in a number of Civil and District courts as well as the Louisiana Supreme Court after his retirement in 1982.

Judge Ellis is a Tulane graduate in Geology and in Law. He served in many legal and professional associations, and numerous business, cultural, and social organizations.

He served during World War II as a U.S. Navy ensign, which military engagements involved foreign invasions and occupation forces.

Author of *"L'Autre Cote du Lac"*

On February 4, 2015

Hon. Frederick Stephen Ellis received the President's Award tendered by the parish's Commission on Cultural Affairs. As an attorney, retired judge, and World War II veteran, Ellis has worn many hats, but his work as a St. Tammany historian has earned him a spot among honored St. Tammany artists. One might say Ellis literally "wrote the book" on St. Tammany, publishing "St. Tammany Parish: L'Autre Côte du Lac" (the other side of the lake) in 1981.

His book explores the parish in the early 1800s through around 1920.

The Piney Woods

In the southern portions of southeastern United States were located the most valuable timbers for naval architecture. Stretching through North and South Carolina, Georgia, Alabama, Mississippi, and Louisiana were vast forests of the long yellow pine, of matchless height and straightness; it was considered one of the most useful and valuable of the forest trees, not only because of its excellent timber quality, but also for its byproduct of tar, pitch, and turpentine which it yielded in great abundance.

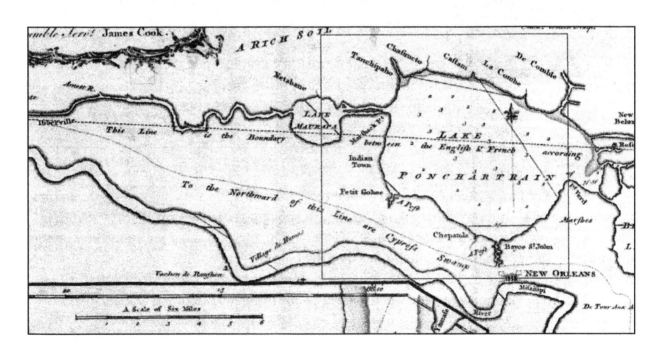

First France, and later England and Western Europe, had placed great demands on the exported timber. Cuba, Mexico, and Texas, in proximity to the area, also provided early markets for lumber. But, the earliest market for lumber products arose at nearby New Orleans where the population, trade, and industry grew rapidly in the years 1830-1850.

Although sawmills and loggers had been operating for almost 200 years and tar burners for nearly 300 years, they barely scratched the surface of the timber resources. Timber had only been cut near the banks of the rivers because there were but few roads. The Poitevent and Favre Lumber Company which originated on the Mississippi side of the Pearl River, began to buy up vast sections of public lands for its timber. By 1910, as other companies began to purchase acreage, virtually all public lands were in the hands of investors or lumber companies.

In the pre-railroad era, creeks, bayous, and rivers were of incalculable importance to the economy of the pine country. The Bonfouca and Liberty bayous and Pearl outlets drained the area into Lake Pontchartrain and Lake Borgne.

Lake Borgne at the mouth of the Pearl River provided quiet waters and a relatively safe passageway to Lake Pontchartrain and New Orleans. Large ocean-going vessels could usually take on a full cargo in still waters behind the barrier islands located two to twenty miles bordering the Mississippi Sound.

The first steam mills were introduced in the mid-1830s. Mills were located a short distance up the Pearl River from Lake Borgne where mill towns were constructed on the banks of the Pearl. Far into the back country, the logs were cut and hauled to the Pearl and its tributaries, and then floated downstream where the logs, both cypress and pine were manufactured into lumber, staves, and shingles and being shipped by schooners and brigs to the outside markets.

Because logs had to be brought to the mills by water from interior forests, and lumber was shipped to outside markets by boat, almost all of the early mills in the coast country were erected at river mouths or on the banks of bayous which extended a few miles into the interior. Before the advent of the railroad, commercial lumbering would have been impossible without cheap water transportation.

With the building of the first railroads, such as the Great Northern, commercial lumbering on a small scale arose in the interior of the long-leaf pine belt. Railroads began to penetrate the pine country in the years following the Civil War. Steam mills were erected along the paths of the roads, and their products were transported by the railroads to regions beyond the long-leaf pine belt.

Beginning in the 1830s, lumbering developed slowly at first, then rapidly in the years 1845-1850. There was a considerable commerce in pine plank, charcoal, and cordwood. The cordwood went to the mouth of the Mississippi River to be used as fuel for boats employed in towing steamers on the river between New Orleans and the Gulf.

In the latter part of 1846 and early 1847 a number of sawmill men and manufacturers of sawmill equipment arrived in the fast growing Bayou Bernard (Gulfport, MS) area. Among the immigrants were two Swiss families, Henry Leinhard and his relatives, Fritz, Albert, and Jacob Salmen, who in time, accumulated large fortunes from brickworks and lumbering in the subtropical coast country.

After the war, lumbering was one of the first of the southern industries to revive. In 1865, lumber brought good prices at the New Orleans market. Smoke began to pour from sawmill boilers as the whine of circular, gang, and sash saws was heard along the banks of rivers and bayous.

Gang saws consisted of a series of adjustable blades set in a frame, that were able to reduce a log into boards in one operation. Circular saws were used to remove the slabs from the logs, while gang saws were employed to complete the sawing operations while cutting uniformly with less waste.

The first crude dry kilns, erected during the 1870s and 1880s, contributed much to the subsequent development of the yellow pine industry. Before the kiln was invented, lumber was cured by air-drying in the open. In the South, where rainfall was heavy, weeks often passed before the cut lumber became sufficiently dried. The advantage of kiln-drying over air-drying was two-fold. The weight of kiln-dried lumber was decreased thereby reducing the cost of shipping, and the wood was less subject to bluing, which was a discoloration caused by fungi.

As forests along the Pearl River passed into private ownership, the Poitevent & Favre Lumber Company had to relocate their mill operations closer to their timber properties in Louisiana. In 1884, its company-owned East Louisiana Railroad began

Lumber Mills

Henry Weston arrived from Maine for New Orleans about 1845 at age 22. He worked as a laborer in the mills of the Pearl River and in the early 1850s he bragged that he made money like smoke.

Following a short depression when only four out of forty mills were running on Lake Pontchartrain's north shore – business picked up during the 1850s and was booming by 1860.

bringing logs out to the West Pearl River at Florenville, from where they were floated downriver to the mills through Jug Bayou. With the completion of the NO&NE Railroad, a new era was ushered in. New mills were built along the railroad.

Between 1870 and the early 1920s, the introduction of railroads created a greatly rejuvenated economy in the Piney woods. But, by mid-1920, all the timber was gone — displaying an unbroken vista of stumps as far as the eye could see.

H. Weston Lumber Co. at Logtown on Pearl River

Lake Pontchartrain
Ports and Lighthouses

Historically, Lake Pontchartrain was once a wide spot in a bayou which originally formed the easternmost pass of the Mississippi River. Traces of the original bayou can be found north of Lake Maurepas. Today, it is the largest inland lake second to the Great Lakes. Its north shore is composed of high and sandy terrain, while its south shore consists of marshy river deposits.

The *Rigolets* (pronounced RlG-o-leez) is a crooked bayou providing the main outlet from Lake Pontchartrain to the Mississippi Sound. During the development of colonial New Orleans, it was the Rigolets shortcut that provided an outlet to the Gulf – which advanced the growing town as a port of significance. Sailing ships arriving at the Gulf were greatly hindered by the Mississippi River's swift, turbulent currents and 100-mile distance upriver to reach New Orleans. The Rigolets also caused several other smaller ports to develop along Lake Pontchartrain's south shore.

The first port on the lake was *Port St. Jean,* which was connected by the *Canal de Carondelet* when built in 1794. The digging of the five-mile canal linked the natural bayou with the heart of New Orleans. By 1797, schooners sailed into the new waterway to moor in its central basin. Eventually, most boat traffic from the Gulf and the Lake passed through Port St. John. There, the U.S. Government placed its first lighthouse on territorial soil on August 5, 1811. From the Spanish Fort located nearby, Lieutenant Sands was hired to be its first Lightkeeper in addition to his primary military duties. Pierre Brousseau became its first civilian keeper. With the attraction of the fort and light, the Lake Pontchartrain waters attracted many citizens to its shores for recreational swimming and fishing.

Following the Battle of New Orleans, in March 1815, Governor Claiborne strongly encouraged the building of schooners over steamboat development. Although, steamboats could proceed quickly down the river with the flow of currents, the same current prohibited upriver maneuvering by steamboats. However, the following year in 1816, Captain Shreve (Shreveport) succeeded with a more powerful improved steam boat.

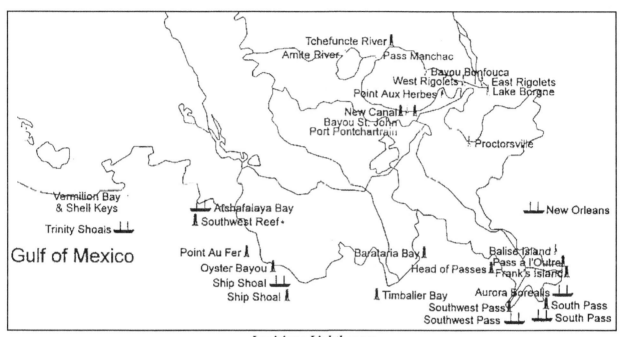

Louisiana Lighthouses

The first steam boat crossing on Lake Pontchartrain occurred in February 1819 with the maiden voyage of the *"Maid of Orleans,"* piloted by Captain Morrison. However, steamboating on Lake Pontchartrain grew slowly.

Over time and with further development, Port St. John was less used with the opening of the new Port Pontchartrain at Milneburg where, in the late 1820s, Alexander Milne had built the first steam railroad west of the Allegheny Mountains. With the dredging of the Lake's first artificial harbor, a lighthouse was established there in 1832, diverting more boat traffic to it. By the 1850s, Port Pontchartrain had even drawn traffic away from ports as far as Mobile.

A few miles west of Bayou St. John, a new canal, later called the "New Basin Canal", was excavated from the Lake extending to New Orleans near the site of the future Union Railroad Station. The cypress Light-tower at the Lake was completed in February 1839, near where the present Coast Guard Station and Lighthouse keep vigilance.

On the north shore at Madisonville, at the Tchefuncte River, a 30-foot Light-tower of hard-burnt lake brick, probably from the brickworks of Bayou Bonfouca, was built in November 1837. The first Lightkeeper was Benjamin Thurston. Following the hurricane destruction of the Cat Island lighthouse in 1860, its lantern was shipped to the Tchefuncte River Lighthouse for use there.

The East Rigolets lighthouse was built on Rabbit Island in 1834, and the West Rigolets tower was placed at Petite Coquilles near Fort Pike, in 1855.

Other lake lighthouses included one at West Pearl River in 1838, and another at Pass Manchac, and one at Proctorsville at the south end of Lake Borgne, in 1850.

Bayou Bonfouca Lighthouse

The Bonfouca lighthouse construction contract was bid for $2,975 by New Orleans contractors Joseph Howell and Moses Coats. The tower was 30-feet above sea level, topped by a small lantern with four lamps. It was three feet in diameter and six feet high providing a 12-mile visibility range during clear weather. The light was commissioned in early March 1848. The lighthouse consisted of two rooms with a nine foot chamber between the rooms.

The chamber was the base of the tower. The house sat on a five foot wall with the tower extending twelve feet above the roof. The original optics was four small lamps in a lantern that measured six feet by three feet. It was small in stature because the light did not need to be seen more than five miles distance.

It's first keeper was John Wadsworth followed by Vincenzo Scorza who served until being captured by the Confederates in 1862.

The burning of the Lighthouse during the war resulted in restricting further growth of the small village. Instead of replacing the Light back at its location near the mouth of Bayou Bonfouca, after the Civil War, a replacement lighthouse was built at *Point Aux Herbs* a short distance across the lake on the southshore.

Point Aux Herbs Lighthouse

Located on the southeastern side of Lake Pontchartrain the Point Aux Herbes light station was described as being a black lantern on a square white dwelling. It rested on five white piers having a total height of 38 feet. It was completed on August 1, 1875.

The Point Aux Herbes Light was built to replace the Bayou Bonfouca Light that had been destroyed during the Civil War. The light was deactivated after World War II and was burned down by vandals in 1950's.

It wasn't until the coming of the Railroad in 1883, that the Bonfouca settlement along the bayou once more followed a path of progress.

Bonfouca
A North Shore Paradise

The name Bonfouca is a derivative of the Indian and French languages, a likely source being *Bouk Fouca,* which some historians have translated to mean "fork in the river" and others, as "house on the river." Another possibility is *Bogue Fooca,* meaning "Forked Bayou." English cartagrapher, George Gauld, in a 1778 map spelled it as Boucfouca. Regardless, old time locals pronounce it Bohn-foo-CAH.

Bonfouca is much more than the Bayou which takes its name. Originally it included the entire region between Slidell on the east to Lacombe on the west. The other large region west of Bonfouca was early on called "Chifoncte."

Many historians report that Bonfouca was already founded by 1725, just a few years after New Orleans, thus submitting it as the oldest settlement on the north shore of the Lake. When the United States was making claims to the Spanish West Florida regions and American settlers were pressing for independence, a small Spanish military garrison had been posted at the settlement, remaining there until 1807. The settlement was located about six miles above the lake and was known for cattle exports and hard-burnt lake brick which was apparently used in several Louisiana lighthouses as well as many New Orleans buildings. The boatyard industry at the bayou catered primarily to the lake trade. At the time the lighthouse at Bayou St. John was authorized, eighteen lake schooners had been conducting trade from the northshore by carrying bricks to New Orleans. There was a post office established at Bonfouca in 1875, and another at Fort Pike, which was manned by a Mr. O'Rourke in 1853.

Early Settlements

Land grants in the area north of Lake Pontchartrain were issued during the 1700s and early 1800s by France, then England, then Spain, and finally by the American government.

La Liberte (Bertrand Jaffre) and his son Ricard owned a shallop rig named *La Liberte,* which in 1739, was sold to Antoine Aufrere who had a tar works on the west bank of the Tchefuncte River. La Liberte died in 1740, having indicated by his Will that he lived at Bonfouca, where his tar works was located – situated at the first rise of high land on the west bank of Bayou Liberty. La Liberte's Will also listed a 30' high by 30' wide kiln; one large house and three smaller cabins which housed 18 slaves; and a number of oxen, a 40- foot boat, and several pirogues.

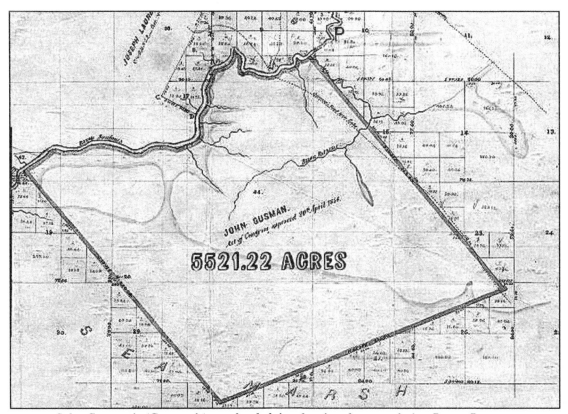

John Gusman's (Guzman's) vast land claim showing the meandering Bayou Potassat crossing Gusman Road at the northeastern edge of his property. Bayou Bonfouca is shown as its northwestern boundary. The southern tip almost reached Lake Pontchartrain. The claim, section 44, was officially confirmed by an Act of Congress on April 23, 1856.

Francois Rillieux arrived at Louisiana in 1720 and settled on Bayou Bonfouca as early as 1737. After Francois's death in 1760, his widow, Marie Marguerite Chenet, bought all the lands between Bayou Bonfouca and the Pearl River from the Biloxi Indians, a tribe which was then in residence at Indian Village. However, the claim was not recognized by the U.S. Government because the widow had never made registration with the Spanish, nor with the English governments. Francois Rillieux's son Vincent, for whom Bayou Vincent was named, lived at that settlement for many years. He also maintained a New Orleans, Royal Street residence, which is the present location of Brennan's Restaurant. Among his descendants were the Musson and Freret families of New Orleans. A large part of the original Rillieux tract was sold to Bartholomew Martin in 1825, and this property was later inherited by John Guzman.

There were other early settlements along Bayou Bonfouca, which were occupied by holders of early French land grants.

These were followed by homesteaders during the short period of the West Florida Republic and followed later by forerunners of the "American Migration" pursuant to the Louisiana Purchase and the Battle of New Orleans.

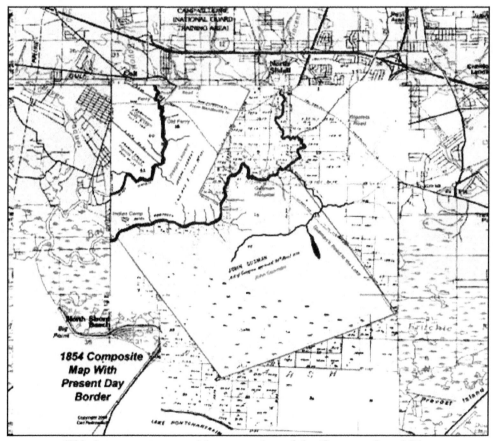

This is a recent map with an overlay of the Guzman Land Plat

One of the early land grants in 1803, was to Francois de Buisson (Dubuisson) who built his home in 1805. This Bayou Liberty property was later acquired by Terence Cousin in 1840, where he erected the current main house that stands at that site. Amongst majestic oaks and stately pines, the 19th Century plantation estate is surrounded by natural loveliness and was suitably named *"Tranquility"* by later owners.

By 1840, one of the early industries along Bayou Bonfouca and West Pearl River was shipbuilding. Judge Ellis reported one old document showing a brickyard on Bayou Bonfouca in 1826.

Tranquility

Judge Ellis reported that, "Some of the early French settlers at bayous Liberty, Bonfouca, and Paquet, were Francois Cousin, who died in 1819; Francois Pichon, (Sr.,) died in 1820; and M. (Francois) Dubuisson, died in 1821. These dates are recorded in Covington courthouse records along with their testamentary Wills."

The arrival of the Cousins

(Cousin is pronounced Kooz-EHH)

The Cousin family arrived from France sometime during the 1700s. Terence Cousin was an uncle of the famed poet-priest, L'Abbe Adrien Rouquette, aptly known by the Choctaw Indians as *"Chahtaima."*

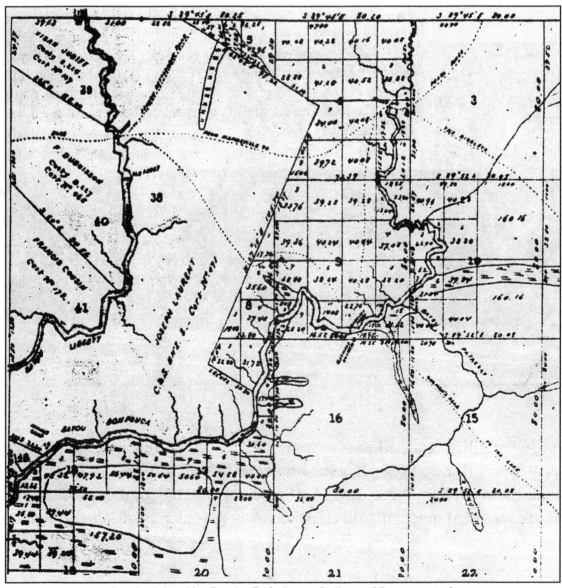

Lands claimed by Cousin, Dubuisson, Judise and Laurent, et al.

Francois Cousin, Sr. married Catherine Peche, who was first married to Jacques Carriere with whom she had two sons, Francois and Terrence Carriere. Francois Cousin Sr. and Catherine produced their three children; Francois, Jr., Celeste, and Louise Cousin. Before moving to Bayou Liberty and Bayou Paquet, they operated a brickworks in New Orleans at Bayou St. John.

Upon Catherine's death, Francois, Sr. went on to marry Cesaire Ducre, producing five more children: Terrence, Adolphe, Anatole, Eliza, and Myrtle Adele.

St. Genevieve Church at Bonfouca Settlement about 1890.

Upon the death of Francois, Sr. on October 31, 1819, he left a large tract running east-west from Bayou Lacombe to Cane Bayou (*Ravinne aux Cannes*) – and, another large tract above Lacombe and one on Bayou Bonfouca. With such a large family estate, Francois Cousin, Jr. was in extended litigations for many years.

Some claims were settled in 1855 and a final settlement took place in 1876.

In 1820, Francois Sr.'s estate resulted in his family heirs entering into a business agreement to manage the businesses and properties. One of Francois, Sr.'s daughters, Myrtle Adele, married Louis Donne and upon her death, in keeping

Current St. Genevieve Chapel - at Bayou Liberty.

family interests together, Donne married one of Francois Sr.'s granddaughters, Antoinette-Adele, who was Pere Adrien Rouquette's sister. Donne then became a business partner with the Cousin and Carriere brothers on Bayou Bonfouca, producing hard-burned lake brick at their brickyard. Widow Louise Rouquette bought out her sister's interest in Lacombe where she raised her children.

The Bonfouca Mission of 1915 shows the Quietness and Serenity of the area even as it remains today.

Dominique Rouquette, Sr.

Dominique Rouquette Sr., a wine importer and large landholder, married Louise Cousin and brought her to New Orleans. Following his death, the widow Louise Cousin Rouquette brought her young family to Bayou Lacombe in 1820, settling near the plantation of her brother, Francois Cousin, Jr. and her half-brother, Terrence Carriere. While there, in 1825, Louise died leaving her orphans in the care of her brothers and half-brothers.

The surviving Rouquette children were:
• Antoinette-Adele, who married Louis Donne of New Orleans and Bayou Liberty, (Henry Clay stayed at their northshore home while he was visiting New Orleans.)
• Francois-Dominique, Jr., a poet as was his brother Adrien. He married Marie Laurie Verret producing three children. In grief, following his wife's early demise, he thereafter wrapped himself in a mourning blanket. Along Bayou

Bonfouca is a small spring called *La Source de Dominique* where he was inspired to write two history books, one on the Choctaws and the other on the Chickasaws.

• Adrien-Ernmanuel as a young boy was a poor student who often played hooky. However, he later received his degree from the College of Rennes, France. Instead of pursuing a vocation, he became the famous priest to the Indians, *Chata-Ima*.

• Francois-Terrence, married Marie Aimee Favre and had three children; Adrien, Marie, and Louise.

• Felix built his house in the cypress swamp on the west bank of the winding Bayou Lacombe. In 1836, he married his cousin, Delphine Cousin, daughter of Francois Cousin, Jr.

It was on this land that Adrien (*Chata-Ima*) built his private haven he called the *"Nook"*.

Abbe Adrien Rouquette
Chata-Ima

The young Rouquettes were born of wealthy Creole parents, who had a house on Royal Street in New Orleans and a country place on Bayou Lacombe to the northeast of Fontainebleau, Marigny's plantation. In 1810 the poet Francois Dominique Rouquette was born there. His brother Adrien Emmanuel spent his lifetime there. When they were still young boys, the family deserted the downtown mansion for a semi-rural home on Bayou St. John near the lakefront. There were still a few Indians living in the swamps near by, and Adrien was much attracted by them. They taught him nature lore which he never forgot.

*Father Adrien Rouquette as a young **man**.*

At the age of eight he attended the College d'Orleans, the leading French school in the city. He and his brother were later sent abroad to France for further education where they frequented literary circles and commenced to write verse.

Adrien's elder brother, Dominique Rouquette was the better and more original poet of the two. While he lived in Paris, in 1839, he published a volume entitled *Les Meschacebeennes* (The Mississippians) in addition to other works.

However, Adrien, or *Chata-Ima* as the Choctaw Indians had renamed him, holds a significant place in the history of the lake and its northshore. He possessed many individual virtues and a well-disciplined strength of character. Adrien spent much of his time at the Bayou Lacombe residence making friends with the Choctaw Indians who lived in scattered villages.

There was a tale that he loved and wished to marry a Choctaw girl named Oushola *(Bird·Singer),* the daughter of a chief. Her father gave his consent, but on Adrien's return from the city, where he had gone to consult with his own family, he was lastingly grief-stricken to find that Oushola had, during his absence, died of pneumonia.

In 1837, on his return to New Orleans from France, Adrien purposely failed his bar exam because he didn't want to practice law. In 1842, he joined the priesthood after ordination in 1845, and became secretary to the Bishop, remaining in that position until 1859. He spent his life in the northshore wilderness with his adopted Choctaw families and his nearby family and friends. He took a minimum of baggage to the piney woodlands where so much of his boyhood had been spent.

With his own hands he built a small wooden chapel near Bayou Lacombe, and little by little he won over the Indians respect for his ministry. Later he established several other chapels in groves beneath the live oak trees. Occasionally he would preach from a low bough of the tree that sheltered his chapel at

Even as a young man, Adrien Rouquette was well known on both sides of the lake. In New Orleans, for his poetry and writings of the Choctaw Indians, and in St. Tammany from Mandeville to Bonfouca, Adrien was a friend to all – invited to settlers' homes and Indian villages. He was Chata-Ima, *"He who is like a Choctaw."*

Chinchuba. Much of the time he went about dressed as an Indian and was widely known as *Chata-Ima,* meaning "like a Choctaw."

It was September 9, 1859, when Adrien moved to St. Tammany to begin his full-time Choctaw Ministry at the headwaters of Bayou Lacombe. Had it not been for his writings and of those he mailed to his friend John Dimitry, the intimate lifestyle of the Choctaw Indians would have remained insignificant. He wrote:

The five cabin-chapels built by Pere Rouquette included: *Our Lady of Solitude* on Ravinne aux Cannes (Cane Bayou) overlooking Lake Pontchartrain; *Le Coin* or "The Nook" on Bayou Lacombe; *Buchuwa Village chapel* at the headwaters of Bayou Lacombe; *Chuca-Chaba* or the Night Cabin on Bayou Castine near the Lake; and *Kildara* or the Cabin in the Oak on Chinchuba Creek.

"I lived as an Indian, without regretting civilization; and it never occurred to me to civilize them, to have schools for them and to teach them to read; it was sufficient for them to read in the great book of God, open before them — Nature."

"I have not organized their traditional industry, disciplined their occupations, for to do so, would be to destroy the Indians. You must take him as he is. I would not civilize him if I could, but I cannot. I tried, but tried in vain and ought not to have tried at all."

It wasn't long before the clouds of the Civil War would affect his mission. After New Orleans surrendered on May I, 1862, a federal blockade was imposed on Lake Pontchartrain, and Adrien had difficulty securing goods from

A Palmetto house, or Latanier, as built by Choctaw Indians in St. Tammany once flourished along the bayous and rivers of the northshore as typified in this photograph taken in the 1870s.

the city.

The St. Tammany Parish was also over-ridden with looters and jayhawkers. Adrien Rouquette wrote the following dramatic account.

"Before the War . . . the Choctaw had the finest fields and cultivated corn, sweet potatoes, melons, pumpkins and other vegetables and were happy and rich."

However, during and following the War, he stated, "Their houses and fields were destroyed by jayhawkers and deserters . . . Since that time the tribe has been scattered, and many who could not come to the city, nor find any place to raise or obtain food upon which to subsist, perished horribly."

On many occasions, Adrien defied the blockade by crossing the lake in his pirogue to

In typical Choctaw fashion, Emile John of Lacombe showed his native array in this 1909 photo.

secure food and medicine for his ministry, often times having to beg because he had no money. On one occasion, after an appeal to Admiral Farragut, he was supplied with food, clothing and quinine and given a Federal gunboat escort up the Bayou Lacombe.

By the mid-1870s, Adrien Rouquette's ministry

Adrien Rouquette's wilderness retreat was his headquarters where be meditated and wrote his poems and histories. He called it his "Nook," Le Coin, which be was forced to abandon as the trees were being felled by the ax of timber men.

at Bayou Lacombe came to an end. His brother, Felix, had died in 1873 and within a few years, Felix's widow, Delphine Cousin Rouquette, was selling off parts of her property to timber interests. Soon after, Adrien lost the solitude of his *"hideaway nook"*.

By mid-summer 1876 his beloved woods had already been desecrated by the ax when he wrote:

"My trees! My romantic trees! The grand old trees of my secluded *Nook!* They had resisted the repeated shocks of all the warning elements, and still they stood up, towering with tranquil stateliness, in their green and unfading mantle."
"They were destined to overshadow my quiet and recollected old age, and at last to throw their mournful gloom over my solitary grave."
"But, alas! You barbarous men, ... ye have dared achieve the sacrilegious deed of irreparable devastation, covering my dear *Nook* with a desolating heap of moldering trunks and leafless boughs."

The loss of his brother, Felix, the loss of the presence of his Choctaw, and the destruction of the trees — forced Pere Adrien to abandon his once secluded, wooded forest along the banks of his childhood bayou. He departed in bad health and old age from his *Le Coin de l'Eglise,* "The Nook of the Church".

In 1886, Pere Rouquette's health failed. He was removed to Hotel Dieu Hospital in New Orleans where he endured a lingering illness. The following year he died

Father Adrien Rouquette as an older man .

and was buried in the old St. Louis Cemetery No.1. At his funeral, a delegation of Choctaw mourners in tribal dress followed the cortege to the tomb.

Adrien Rouquette, the poet-priest of the Lake Pontchartrain piney woods, continues to be loved by the members of his faith, in particular the old families of Bonfouca and Lacombe.

Light at East Rigolets

Light at West Rigolets

All Aboard!
The Railroads

Before the Civil War, the first railroad lines in the South were primarily built as competition to northern rail transportation owners and were thought of as passenger or light freight conveyors to support the movement of port trade that was ordinarily too slow for upriver passage.

Following the Civil War, the first railroad construction was the L&N railroad, 139 miles from New Orleans to Mobile. The railroad engineers first drove pilings that in 1869, were not adequately creosote-treated. Within nine months, a train plunged into Bay St. Louis due to blighted pilings. All the pilings needed replacement because they were eaten through by marine boring worms called *"Teredos."*

The 139-mile line of tracks required engineering feats crossing six major water-ways. The four water-bodies of Pascagoula, Occan Springs-Biloxi, Pass Christian-Bay St. Louis, and the Rigolets required pivoting bridges for vessel access to inland waters. Of these four bridges, the crossing on Bay of St. Louis was the first to exhibit a problem. Even though the ties and timbers were well treated with the best preservatives of that time, in a matter of months, the marine mollusks, *Teredos Navalis* were boring deep holes into the pilings.

An adult teredo, the size of a school pencil, had a voracious appetite for sub-surface timber and created almost complete deterioration as they multiplied. The wooden bridge crossing the Bay of St. Louis became so frail as to prevent railroad traffic, because even those pilings, having been replaced, were soon infiltrated by the marauding shipworm.

In quest of a solution, J.W. Putnam was sent to England to examine a waterproofing and preserving process discovered by a Dr. Bethel. His technique was to pressurize timber logs causing the inherent sap to coagulate, resulting in the wooden fibers becoming thoroughly waterproofed. This concept was brought to the Mississippi Gulf Coast at Gautier. There, in 1874, Putnam established the first creosote plant in the United States. The process began with soaking and boiling the timbers in oil, then, under pressure, the oil was forced into the heated wood. Today, creosote pilings endure for decades, foiling the Teredos destructive nature and stymieing the marine mollusk problem.

As a result of this improved creosoting treatment method, a creosote plant was built near the north shore at what was to become the town of Slidell. The result was a more durable lumber product that impeded Teredos and even extended the life of the pilings, poles, and ties from natural decay.

Illinois Central

On August 23, 1854, the New Orleans, Jackson and Great Northern (later the Illinois Central) was open for business. Its construction was due to the rivalry between New Orleans and Mobile. The Illinois Central route went from New Orleans, west around Lake Pontchartrain, through Bogue Chitto, through Jackson, on to Chicago.

Mobile had built their own railroad about the same time in competition for northern trade. At that time, the vast long-leaf pine forests which laid to the interior were largely unknown to lumbermen who continued to cut timber only at the bayous and rivers near the Gulf coastline. However, it was the need for lumber for construction of the increasing numbers of railroad freight cars that resulted in the Illinois Central railway carrying timber to northern cities.

In the late 1870s, freight agent T.K. Edwards sent the first carload of yellow pine lumber north of the Ohio River without an advance buyer. The cut lumber was offered at whatever price it would bring. From that small beginning in 1869; and by 1885, lumber had become the largest single class of freight carried by the Illinois Central Railroad.

The expansion of the yellow pine industry was greatly aided by the dwindling supplies of northern white pine. By 1883, there was a sawmill at every train stop along the railroad. By 1902, the Illinois Central had reached its peak in servicing the lumber mill industry.

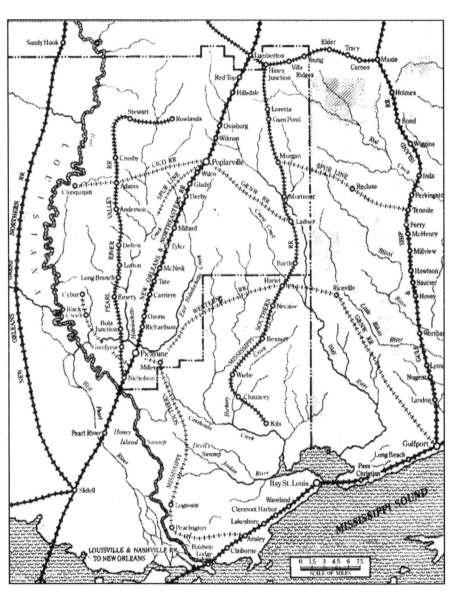

The map at right shows the major railroad lines that were built through Louisiana and western Mississippi during the period of the Railroad Era. Slidell is shown with three lines linking through the heart of the City and the L&N coastal railroad passing nearby across the Rigolets.

On October 29, 1870, at 5 p.m., two trains, one from Mobile and the other from New Orleans, met near Chef Menteur Pass, 27 miles east of New Orleans. Two representatives of the railroad drove in a gold spike and a silver spike joining the final rails that united the Gulf City with the Crescent City. The next day the first excursion train traversed the 139-mile run between the two cities. Regular passenger and freight service officially began on November 21, 1870.

While riding the L&N line in May 1895, Charles Dyer described the following in his book entitled *"Along the Coast."*

"The Chef Menteur is a place which should not be missed when one is making a trip along the Gulf, as it is honored in the heart of every fisherman in the south. Chef Menteur is the name of the bayou which connects Lake Borgne with Lake Pontchartrain and here the fish abound at almost all seasons of the year. As a consequence, fishing clubs of all descriptions are located on the banks."

"It was in the dining room of one of these clubs, that we were served with a fish breakfast, truly fit for the gods."

"After passing a few hours very pleasantly at the Club we took the (L&N) train once more for the East, catching a fleeting glance of Lake Catherine as the train stopped a

A Sportsmen's Club dining room at the Chef

moment to drop a small percentage of its human freight. We arrived at the Rigolets in a few moments thereafter."

(N.O. & N.E. RR) The Northeastern

As early as 1868, George Ingram organized the Mandeville and Sulphur Springs Railroad Company. Upon Ingram's death in 1870, the Charter was purchased by Captain William H. Hardy who changed the name to New Orleans and Northeastern Railroad Company. It was completed in the mid- 1880s running from New Orleans in a northeasterly direction through the forests of east Louisiana and Mississippi to Meridian, Mississippi.

In 1880, the *St. Tammany Farmer* reported: "Able engineers have pronounced it practicable to build a line directly across Lake Pontchartrain, about 22 miles". In another news release, in May 1881, the *St. Tammany Farmer* reported the preliminary survey complete, and that the road would cross Lake Pontchartrain to Mandeville on a trestle. However, a major change in plans was made, and the decision was to build the New Orleans Northeastern Railroad through the eastern part of the parish. It was scheduled for completion by December 31, 1882.

It wasn't until the evening of October 15, 1883, that the first train arrived at New Orleans from Meridian, Mississippi. Aboard, were, Chief Engineer G. Bouscaren, General Superintendent R. Carroll, Division Engineer S. Whinnery, and General Freight Agent H. Colbran. It was the building of this railroad that provided the impending destiny for Slidell.

Building the Railroad

When the railroad surveyors were looking for high ground due north of New Orleans; they found the Bonfouca area met their requirements. The local settlers were agreeable to provide the right-of-way in exchange for economic progress.

During the early months of 1881, small parties of surveyors for the New Orleans and North Eastern Railroad began to break through the neighboring forests, swamps and marshes. Theirs was the difficult task of giving New Orleans a rail outlet to the North and East. Their job was made easier by the combination of comparatively high ground and a junction with an established link of water transportation in the immediate area.

On October 29, 1881, the contract was let to build the NO&NE RR bridge over Lake Pontchartrain. The project included 21 miles of trestlework and its approaches of sixteen miles which required that pilings, cross-ties, and bridge timbers be creosoted. This required the construction of a creosote works near to water access and proximate to future rail-line roadways that would be carved through the teeming forests.

Contracts were let all along the proposed route between New Orleans and Meridian creating a continuing requirement for creosote processed products. Contracts were also let for the bridge across the Pearl River and other bayous and streams.

One of the early inland settlements was at *Robert's Landing* on the banks of the Bayou Bonfouca. Reportedly the ferry crossing was located just behind the present railroad station. Early commerce took place there with the import and export of lumber, cattle and wildgame in exchange for needed supplies. With the entrance of increasing numbers of railroad employees, *Robert's Landing* became the headquarters site for the work crews which built the needed creosote plant for the bridge. Work commenced at Robert's Landing on December 3, 1881. On January 7, 1882, at Meridian, Captain William H. Hardy was the principle speaker for ground breaking ceremonies in announcing the opening of road constructions.

At ***Robert's Landing,*** engineers, foremen, and work crews made camp for the next three years. The encamped workmen bought their food, clothing, and large quantities of whiskey, thereby generating business enterprises near the campsite which later became the rudiments for the town of Slidell. Work teams were brought in from many areas to build the creosote plant.

Slidell Station was named during the first months of 1882, and a building was constructed near the future depot site called the *"Robert Brick House"*. This building was soon converted into employee lodgings by a Mr. Beer of Tallulah, who also built a general store adjoining it. Close by, a lumber mill was constructed by the company of Hamlet, Bliss, and Elliot, new arrivals from Alabama. It was not long before other construction sites began developing into hotels and boarding houses.

Newspapers reported that "at the creosote works, there is quite a town being built, called Slidell, and a great deal of land in the vicinity has been bought by speculators. Several houses and stores have been put up lately, and town lots are selling at good prices."

Farmers were able to sell all the cows and hogs they could raise and all the produce they could grow to feed the construction crews. Any able-bodied man who wanted a job could get one.

After surveyors staked the right-of-way, contractors let sub-contracts for every few hundred feet of construction. All the grading was done by hand with men using axes, shovels, and wheelbarrows. Where water access was not available, oxen carts pulled hand-hewn timbers to road sites and bridges.

The creosote plant treated pilings and cross-ties for construction of the railroad bridge across Lake Pontchartrain. Cypress logs as long as 90 feet were pressure-treated at the creosote plant and driven into the lake bottom to build the rail line trestle. (The railroad bridge was rebuilt in the 1990s. None of the original structure remains.)

The Creosote Plant began as part of the railroad project in 1882. Careless handling caused major toxic pollution in the Bonfouca-Vincent watershed.

By August 1882, a telegraph line had been installed connecting Slidell Station to New Orleans and Meridian. The creosote works was completed and in operation. Bridge construction cross the lake was nearly half finished while the tracks were being completed to the lakeshore from Slidell Station. From the North, a clearing was in progress across Honey Island Swamp and the rails had already been completed to within 40 miles of Slidell Station.

The construction which followed, brought the rail line from Meridian, Mississippi to Slidell. On October 15, 1883, the first train from Meridian completed the awaited trip to New Orleans. On November 18, 1883, the first passenger train, the Queen and Crescent ran between New Orleans and Cincinnati.

With the completion of the NO&NE Railroad in 1884, a new era was ushered in, as lumber mills and towns sprang up along the railroad line.

The year 1884 was an important one for Slidell, not only had the railroad been completed, but the first telephone and telegraph line was extended to the town.

Some of the significant railroad personalities were Baron Emile von Erlanger and engineers Leon Fremaux and Bouscaren.

Many early investors in Southern railroads were British. The New Orleans and Northeastern Railroad (NO&NE) was under British financial control in 1883, the year it began operation. However the financial picture changed for them after the start of World War I in Europe. The British had become hard-pressed for American dollars needed in their fight against Imperial Germany, therefore, on December 29,1916, Southern Railway was able to acquire the NO&NE.

Construction of the NO&NE Railroad was, at first, a narrow-gauge line until 1886, when it was converted to a standard-gauge line.

This 1905 photo shows Engine #429 which was later involved in a train wreck near Slidell.

In 1889, a "double-header" with two engines pulling nineteen coaches packed full of male passengers headed north from New Orleans. Aboard were heavyweight prize fighters John L. Sullivan and Jake Kilrain with their handlers, hangers-on, and members of the sporting fraternity looking for a place to hold the world's boxing championship, after New Orleans and Mississippi authorities refused to allow the event. They reached Richburg, south of Hattiesburg, where in an open field covered with sawdust, Sullivan defeated Kilrain after seventy-five rounds. In those days a round continued until there was a knockdown.

In the early years of the 1900s, interstate or intrastate roads were nonexistent. Transportation was limited to rivers and railway lines. The two major railroads through Slidell were the Northeastern (N.O.N.E.) and the Great Northern (N.O.G.N.). Once the tracks were laid, towns grew along the way to Meridian and to Jackson.

East Louisiana Railroad

The East Louisiana Railroad was constructed by W.J. Poitevent and his brother-in-law Joseph Favre in 1884 to accommodate their lumbering interests. The railroad ran from Pearl River and reached Abita Springs in June 1887 and Covington on May 16, 1888. It served as a feeder to the vast lumber properties in St. Tammany, but also carried freight and passengers. A spur was also sent from the main route to Mandeville in May 1892.

Logs were rolled from the flatbed timber cars into the West Pearl River at Florenville, north of Slidell, and from there drifted down to the company boom located one mile from Pearlington. They were then towed to the mills through Jug Bayou and through the half-mile long canal that connected to the East Pearl River.

(N.O.G.N. RR) The Great Northern

The New Orleans & Great Northern was built and financed chiefly by F.H. and C.W. Goodyear and other lumbermen. Early plans of the company called for construction of a railroad from New Orleans to Bogalusa and thence up the west side of the Pearl River to Jackson, Mississippi. In 1904, the East Louisiana Railroad was purchased from Poitevent & Favre and was added as the southern leg to its main line.

The railway was completed in 1909. In the following year, 77% of the road's total tonnage consisted of timber products.

At Pearlington, MS, Asa H. Hursey, Jr., built Poitevent and Favre's new mill, nicknamed "Big Jim," in 1890; it was then the largest one in the world employing 600 men. In 1913, the Poitevents closed their Pearlington operation and moved to Mandeville on the north shore of Lake Pontchartrain.

The Salmen Railroad

The Salmen Brothers of Slidell also took a turn at building a rail-line which ran from Slidell to Mandeville. The road was to be completed during the winter of 1904-05, however, it only operated to Bayou Lacombe by 1905.

Nevertheless, this railroad greatly satisfied their lumber operations within seventy five miles of Slidell. The track connected with the NOGN RR, thereby allowing country wide access with their four engines and 250 railcars

1919 photo, at the site where railroad cross-ties were manufactured and loaded.

Captain William Hardy
The Railroad Magnate

Captain William H. Hardy was born in Alabama on February 12, 1837. As a young man he taught grade school during the day and studied for the bar exam during evenings and week-ends. He began his legal career in 1858 and volunteered in the Confederacy during the Civil War. Following the war, he returned to his law practice.

While at Paulding, Mississippi, in 1868, Hardy planned a railroad to run from Meridian to New Orleans. He stated that the project was conceived on the proposition that timber was becoming increasingly valuable and that a demand would soon arise for the products of the long-leaf forests. In 1870, he incorporated the New Orleans & Northeastern Railway Company. However, before meaningful construction began, the nation underwent a financial crisis in 1873.

This was the same year of his marriage to Hattie Lott for whom he later named the city of Hattiesburg.

With better economic conditions in 1880, Captain Hardy regrouped the railroad stockholders and completed his first railroad three years later. He had always contended that the lines of commerce must run North and South. When finished, he had mastered the engineering feat of completing the "longest bridge in the world," spanning twenty-one miles across Lake Pontchartrain. The approaches required trestles made of creosote pilings which entailed an additional sixteen miles of expanse crossing through the marsh and swamps.

Captain William Hardy — This statue is located in Gulfport, MS – facing the harbor at 25th Avenue.

On to Gulfport – another Venture

In 1886, Hardy was elected President of the reorganized Gulf & Ship Island Railroad Company. He had convinced the Mississippi State Legislature to change the company charter to meet his requests in establishing the railroad terminus at a point on the Gulf shore of his pleasing. He had already established and named one planned city, Hattiesburg, and he was determined to build and name his own city on the Gulf, which he named Gulfport, MS. Little did he realize that not only would the city of Slidell become established along his first rail-line, but in addition, many other towns and cities would follow.

However, due to financial reversals, the completion of the Gulf & Ship Island Railroad, the deep water port harbor, and the channel to Ship Island were left to Captain Joseph Jones to put in place.

The Slidell Depots

The first Slidell train depot was located on the west side of the rail line. According to Jim Selzer with G.O.S.H., the first Slidell Station was located at Milepost 167.2, near Pennsylvania Avenue and was constructed about 1883 at what was then a camp town. It was not long before eagerness and determination became the catalyst for the creation of a new town that was incorporated in 1888.

Slidell's First Railroad Station, ca. 1885

*The first Depot was built circa 1883
on the west side of the tracks.*

Within a few years Slidell's second train depot was constructed, this time on the east side of the rail line and further south near the corner of Front and Fremaux streets. Although photographs of the time depict the depot with a handsome Prairie style exterior, the condition of the building deteriorated rapidly. By 1910, the town council began demanding that the Northeastern

The Second Depot as seen circa 1910

Railroad Company remedy the deplorable conditions that existed.

The current train station was built in 1913. The New Orleans and Northeastern as well as the New Orleans Great Northern Railroads utilized the station for many years . Their successor, Norfolk Southern Railway, donated the depot to the city of Slidell in 1996, and through the years the city has made extensive renovations to the building. As of 2015, the depot is home to the Times Grill with other spaces available for lease. There is also a limited service Amtrak station on the west side of the building that is served by one daily passenger train, "The Crescent."

The 3rd station was completed in 1913

Second Depot circa 1910

Third and Current Depot was constructed in 1913.

Amtrak's "Crescent" departing Depot – photo by Bill Blackwell.

-73-

SLIDELL
Its Genesis

The Original Owners

Land ownership of large acreage tracts in the hands of a few persons had an immediate impact on the development of the railroad settlement. Ownership was primarily held by the Guzman and Robert families. The other large domain of Joseph Laurent was located on the west side of Bayou Bonfouca which led to later development.

A typical Palmetto Swamp Scene
Although this photo was taken in the early 1900s, pristine bayou scenes such as this still exist in and around Slidell today.

Township Map of 1852

A map of the Slidell area that encompassed Township 9 south, Range 14 east (T9SR14E), shows the land grants and early roads. West of Bayou Liberty were the lands of Francois Cousin, Francois Dubuisson, and Hiram Judiss (Judice). Laying between Bayou Liberty and Bayou Bonfouca were the extensive lands of Joseph Laurent. — And, to the south and east, the Guzman and Robert lands.

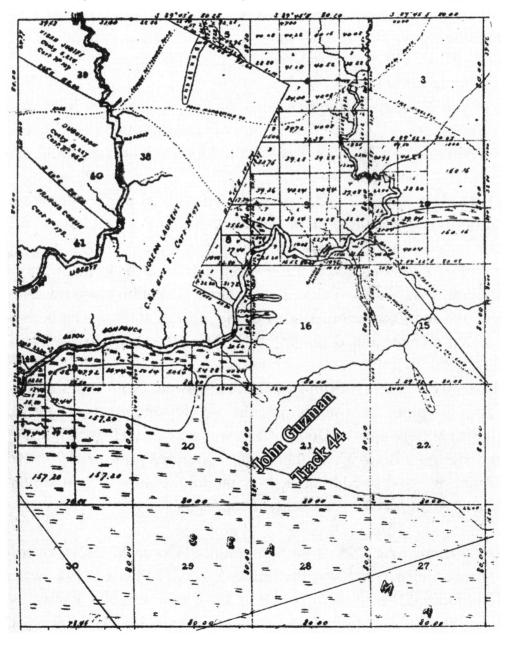

Several roads are visible on the map. At the top of the plat, a west-to-east main road from Mandeville is shown as a dotted-line. As the road crossed Bayou Liberty, a departing trail proceeds in a southeasterly direction to cross *Guzman's Ferry Landing* at Bayou Bonfouca; and continued on as *Guzman's Road* in a southeasterly direction, much resembling today's Old Spanish Trail and Rigolets Road. It then continued toward Lake Pontchartrain.

> **John Gusman's (Guzman's Tract)**
> The vast land claim shows the meandering Bayou Potassat crossing Gusman Road at the northeastern edge of his property. Bayou Bonfouca is shown as its northwestern boundary. The southern tip almost reached Lake Pontchartrain. His claim, Section 44, was officially confirmed by an Act of Congress dated April 23,1856.

Where the Mandeville road reached *Bayou Vincent* (north of West Hall Avenue), it further forked into two roads, one went northerly to *Pearl River* and the other continued southeasterly and was called the *Rigolets Road* (appearing much like today's "Hwy. 190" running east-west).

The vast *John Gusman Tract 44* is shown with its northwestern boundary, Bayou Bonfouca; and its northeastern boundary Bayou Potassat. East, West, and Southern demarcations are shown as straight lines.

The *Robert Claim* of nearly 1300 acres was located north of the Guzman property and east of Bayou Bonfouca. The Guzman plantation home was established near Bayou Lane and Cousin Street, west of the railroad tracks. The heirs sold the initial lands that architectural engineer Leon Fremaux (Frey-Mo) had laid out as streets and squares.

In 1880, there was a sawmill on Bayou Vincent, with a store at Robert's Landing. Bayou Vincent runs north, past the old creosote plant. There were also settlers at Indian Village and the Doubloon Bayou area, as well as families at Gause Landing and Herwig's Bluff where there was a shipyard prior to 1870. Nearby is Apple Pie Ridge, which derived its name from the soldiers traveling on Military Road who would stop to eat Mrs Taylor's delicious apple pies.

John Guzman, Sr. (1795 - 1858) (pronounced Goose-MAHN), inherited land from Barthelemy Martin which was the former Vincent Rillieux (RE-Low) property on Bayou Bonfouca. The northern stream of the bayou waters is known as Bayou Vincent (Veen-SON). The original land grant was approximately 5000 acres, which today includes south Slidell and Eden Isles. Guzman and his family lived on a large farm that was located near the former Slidell Vo-Tech School behind the Catholic Cemetery (Our Lady of Lourdes). He also owned a brickyard, hospital, ferry, and a store in the vicinity of the present bridge. His operations must have been substantial because records indicate that he owned 35 slaves.

Amongst his children was John E. Guzman, who was born about 1828 at the Bayou settlement. He married Mary Ann Cary on December 28, 1857 in New Orleans at the St. Louis Cathedral. They settled on his father's estate and had 10 children of whom seven survived to adulthood. When the railroad was proposed, Guzman was operating the family saw mill, but permitted a four and a half mile right-of-way for railroad track beds.

On July 7, 1884, John E. received the first telephone message to Slidell which was sent over the newly constructed telephone line from Mandeville to Slidell. The call was from General George Moorman whose company had just created the new line.

John E. Guzman died on December 12, 1914 and was laid to rest in the family crypt near the site of his birth. He and his wife have been remembered by the street names, Carey (Cary) and Guzman. Both of these streets intersect near Bayou Potassat by Brock Elementary School and Greenwood Cemetery.

A Guzman Family Photo at Robert's Landing on Bayou Vincent

Pierre Thomas Robert (1780 - 1867) (pronounced Row-BEAR) was born in Bordeaux, France. After marrying Emiline Joyner, they settled on the Pearl River at the *"Ridge"* where they raised two sons. Judge Ellis placed him in the Bonfouca area as early as 1803 and stated he had operated two boat docks on his property, one for schooners and one for lighter boats. He also operated a maritime supply retail store and a small sawmill as well as a brick plant, a tar mill, and he raised cattle and horses.

John Evans, with his wife Mary Ann Graham arrived from South Carolina to settle at the Pearl River area in 1812. He bought several hundred acres of land from the original Spanish land owner that was bordered by the West Pearl River and Doubloon Bayou. Just after his release from military action in the Battle of New Orleans he died and was buried in the cemetery on his land known as the *Rousseau-Evans Cemetery* which is just east of Slidell.

A daughter of John Evans was Mary Ann who married Antoine Rousseau Lacombe in 1823, for which the *Rouseau-Evans* cemetery was named. Access to the private family cemetery in Quail Ridge is from Military Road, continuing east on *Old River Road* until reaching Golden Pheasant Road. It is located on the left, which is the north side of Old River Road.

Another of John's ten children, was Joseph who married Elizabeth Margaret Crawford, a daughter of another immigrant family from South Carolina. Joseph served as St. Tammany Sheriff from 1848 to 1853.

First Steps to Development

The core of the original town had its roots just a few miles north of Lake Pontchartrain, first as a ferry landing known as *Robert's Landing,* and later as a railroad camp and flag-stop called *Slidell Station* along the New Orleans and Northeastern Railroad.

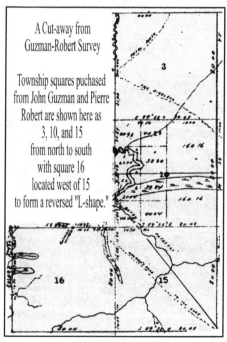

A Cut-away from Guzman-Robert Survey

Township squares puchased from John Guzman and Pierre Robert are shown here as 3, 10, and 15 from north to south with square 16 located west of 15 to form a reversed "L-shape."

The "Town Charter" of November 13, 1888, described the town as spanning 3 miles north to south and 2 miles east to west at its bottom leg. It encompassed township squares 3, 10, and 15 from north to south with square 16 located west of 15 to form a reversed *"L-shape."*

As stated by local historian Charles Fritchie:

"The east bank of Bayou Bonfouca where Slidell grew was owned by the family of John Guzman from Lake Pontchartrain approximately to *Bayou Potassat,* and by the family of Pierre Thomas Robert from Guzman's land to beyond the railroad depot, approximately to the head of navigation. John Guzman, who operated a small brick factory and a ferry near (the present) Bayou Liberty road, ceded right of way to the railroad through his land and (later) sold other

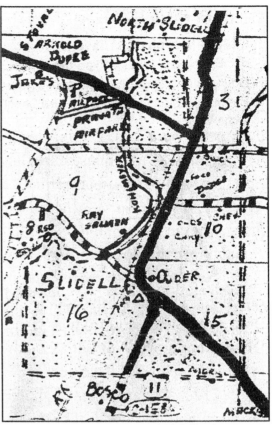

The 1888 incorporation of Slidell using Pete Pravata's map.

property to Fritz Salmen, who developed Slidell's first significant industry, a mechanized brickyard.

Junot Robert owned his family's bayou property, including the site of the earlier *Robert Ship Landing* and merchandise exchange which nucleated the railroad construction camp and first depot. He ceded right of way through these original few blocks of Slidell and sold other land to the first developers and arriving families."

"It is not known by whom the early town plan was authorized, but Junot Robert was owner of much, if not all, of this early area and many early purchases had been made directly from him."

"Branching from late twentieth century Slidell, Bayou Liberty Road reaches toward Ridge, Gause Boulevard stretches near the Honey Island site of George H. Gause's early store, and Robert Boulevard toward E.P. Robert's Pearl River farming property."

Birth of Slidell

As early as 1883, a 70-acre campsite was surveyed and laid out for workmen quarters and a creosote plant. As work progressed, more land area was acquired and developed. After the tracks were laid, a train depot was built and the station named "Slidell" as requested by Baron Emile Erlanger, one of the financial backers of the *New Orleans and Northeastern Railroad.* By his marriage to Mathilde Slidell, Emile Erlanger became John Slidell's son-in-law.

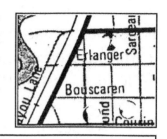

Slidell's first physical layout consisted of Fremaux Avenue to the North, Bouscaren to the South, Bonfouca (now Bayou Lane) on the East and Third Street at the West.

According to Historian Charles Fritchie, "The new town developed first along Bonfouca Street and Fremaux to Bouscaren Street, and from First to Third Street. The town was enlarged when Oscar Dittmar became mayor with the addition of Cousin to Guzman streets running from Front to Carey and First Street."

Fritchie reported that, "The first buildings were of wood and later of brick, (such as) the Bank of Slidell building on Cousin near Front Street and the Polk and McDaniel buildings on the two southern corners of Cousin and Carey streets. The Perilloux family also built an early brick building near the railroad depot, possibly either the Neuhauser Building, which now is a banquet hall, or the early Slidell Hotel Building, later *Laughing Pines Micro Brewery Restaurant"* — and now the renovated Chamber of Commerce Building.

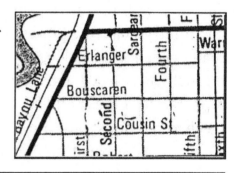

Slidell's first expansion included Fremaux at the North, Cousin on the South, Bonfouca (*Bayou Lane*) on the East, and Fifth Street on the West.

Entering a period of rapid growth, on November 13, 1888, the town was incorporated while it was still but a fledgling flag station. The town corporate limits shortly thereafter increased to approximately 2,320 acres including a northeastern portion of the John Gusman tract. Roughly, the expanded street boundaries were Fremaux Avenue to Fifth Street, then Cousin Street to Carey and to Front Street, then back to Fremaux Avenue.

Leon Fremaux (1821-1898)

After the final military defeat in Europe by Napoleon Bonaparte, one of his loyal military aides, Francois Etienne Fremaux (1788-1841) emigrated to New Orleans with his wife. Upon settling at New Orleans, Francois opened a book store while his wife continued her practice in midwifery.

Their older son, Napoleon Joseph Fremaux, was sent to the *College Louis Le Grand* in Paris, France, where he graduated in 1839, and returned to New Orleans to practice engineering. He was appointed State Engineer in 1855, the same year during which he was naturalized and changed his name to Leon. (*Shortened from Napoleon.*)

During the Civil War, he was appointed Captain of Engineers with the Confederate Army; and during the Reconstruction Era, Leon was involved with the Anti-Republican and Anti-Black movement called the White League which led

> One of Fremaux's descendants, **grandson, Judge Peter Garcia**, 22nd Judicial Court at Covington, also remembers his aunt, Seline Garcia, who kept a diary of the Fremaux family's pilgrimage while evading Federal troops during the Civil War.

the "Battle of Canal Street" on September 14,1874, where the Liberty Monument was placed. With the return of the Democratic rule in Louisiana, Leon was once more a favored surveyor, engineer, and architect; and later became a Lt. Colonel with the Louisiana National Guard in 1880. He was also an accomplished artist, drawing sketches and water color paintings of the various characters and scenes he encountered during his lifetime. In 1876, he published a selection of his water-paints produced during his surveying expeditions.

By virtue of his experiences, he was one of the engineers who assisted in the railroad constructions and reportedly performed the surveying and laying out of the early town of Slidell at which time, in 1882, he was 61 years of age.

John Slidell
1793 -1891

John Slidell was born in New York City in 1793 and graduated from Columbia College (Columbia University) in 1810. Completing his law studies, he was

> John Slidell, namesake for **City of Slidell.**
> He had never set foot in the town. The train stop was named *Slidell Station* by his son-in-law, Emile Erlanger, a financier of the Northeastern Railroad.

admitted to the bar in New York City and after moving to New Orleans, he practiced there from 1819 until his election to Congress. While at New Orleans he was assisted by his father's friend, the former mayor of New York City, a very prominent lawyer and New Orleans land entrepreneur, Edward Livingston.

Slidell was described as being of large stature and having "such silky, snow-white hair, that through it, the top of his head blushed like the shell of a boiled lobster." He was considered a strong willed, person who maintained tact and discretion. He emerged to become the dominant Democratic leader from Louisiana.

He was a member of the Louisiana House of Representatives, a U.S. District Attorney from 1829 to 1833, and was elected to the U.S. Congress from 1843 to 1845, followed by election to the U.S. Senate, 1853 to 1861. He was foremost in the movement to nominate Buchanan for President. When Buchanan was elected, Slidell became not only a strong political leader in Louisiana, but also a director of national politics and policies. He was the power behind the throne during the first three years of Buchanan's administration.

Slidell was perhaps the most successful political leader of his day. He wielded great influence during the 1850s.

When Louisiana seceded from the Union, he resigned from Congress and was later chosen Confederate Commissioner to France and assigned to present the

Confederate cause to England and France in seeking their aid. Sailing from Havana on the British Steamer *Trent,* he was arrested at sea by Captain Charles Wilkes of the U.S. Sloop *San Jacinto.* and imprisoned in Boston. However, he was soon released to proceed to France due to the illegal seizure aboard a British ship, which was a violation by the United States upon Great Britain's Fleet.

However, once in England, he was denied permission to return to the United States. Slidell died in exile at Cowes, Isle of Wight, England on July 26, 1871, and was interred in a private cemetery near Paris, France.

Regarding the heritage of John Slidell, in her booklet, Geri U. Staines, stated that, "the State of Louisiana which had catapulted him into anti-bellum social prominence through his relationship with Creole aristocracy, the war which devastated the South and stymied an era of prosperity, culture, and grace — all were left behind. He was never a part of the little town across the lake physically but, in all probability, his life story would have faded into oblivion, but for this small town which assumed his name back in 1888."

First Town Officials

During Slidell's first year of operation in 1888, the site on which the city now stands was still occupied with racoons, rabbits, and deer, which were almost undisturbed in their virgin forests. Small settlements had already been established upon the banks of Pearl River, Bayou Liberty, Bayou Bonfouca, and Bayou Vincent. These had been inhabited by families holding early French and Spanish land grants which were later substituted as homestead rights from the U.S. Government.

Early industry consisted of trade for timber and cattle which furnished the little money that was needed; abetted by fish and game that contributed an ample supply of fresh food.

Once the railroad established its temporary headquarters and built a creosote plant, it was inevitable that growth was imminent. Just behind the present railroad station, a small sawmill was beginning to thrive. Opposite the mill site, boats came more and more frequently to *Robert's Landing* and general store. From the boat landing, trails wound off through the pines to the widely scattered homes of neighboring settlers.

The first mayor was Seth H. Decker. His Board of Aldermen included H. Mandin, Oscar L. Dittmar, A.C. Prevost, Fritz Salmen, and Charles McMahon. One other town official, a marshal, was appointed by the town council made up of the mayor and five aldermen. The first marshal, Edgar P. Robert, was appointed on December 19,1888.

In the first council meeting, a committee was selected to look into the construction of a jailhouse, which in the next year, resulted in a small jail and mayor's office. It was moved in 1907, and a more permanent structure erected on its site. The two-story brick building was comprised of five jail cells with a marshal's office on the first floor and the mayor's office and a meeting room on the second floor. The final cost

Edgar P. Robert was appointed first Town Marshal in 1888, a descendent of Pierre Thomas Robert.

of the building was $3,685.40 as compared to $275 for the preceding building. In 1927, a 5,700 sq. ft. addition was made on the south side of the building in order to house the town's fire engine.

The town election of August 18, 1894, resulted in a tie vote for mayor. Of the two, C.V. McMahon and O.L. Dittmar, McMahon was sworn in. In December 1899, the mayor's race again resulted in a tie vote. This time, between J.M. Curry and O.L. Dittmar with Dittmar being sworn in.

Fritz Salmen
The Builder

One of the early arrivals to Slidell was Fritz Salmen, who arrived in 1884, with a Negro named Jack Peters and a strong determination. Salmen had spent a number of years in Handsboro, Mississippi, today an historic region of Gulfport.

During the years spent at Handsboro, the Salmen brothers learned much about technical advances in the highly industrialized town along the banks of Bayou Bernard, where lumber mills, shipbuilding, brick-making, and tar and turpentine kilns were thriving.

After developing his skills there, Fritz brought to Slidell just enough equipment to construct a manually operated brickworks. A plow and a mule were the only tools he needed with which to experiment for brick clay. It wasn't long before Salmen established his brickworks using the high quality clay found in the area. His original brickyard was located just north of the train station on Front Street. With his acquired profits he purchased more land.

By the following year, 1887, the enterprise

> **Fritz Salmen's early background in Handsboro, Mississippi**
>
> Fritz Salmen's father, John, and his mother, Catherine Lienhard, were born and married in Switzerland. They either arrived with, or joined later, Fritz's uncle, Henry Lienhard, who arrived in Handsboro in 1856, where he engaged in the lumber business. Prior to the Civil War, Handsboro had developed as the primary trading center on the Mississippi Gulf Coast. With the onset of the Civil War, immigrants were not compelled to enlist in the Confederate Army, however, with scant labor force and the Federal blockade, Lienhard closed his lumber mill. He resorted to operating a grist mill that produced ground corn for local consumption. After the war, he again operated his lumber mill in addition to starting a brick plant using mill slabs for fuel. He also operated a ship yard where he built schooners for the local trade.
>
> In the course of growth, Lienhard acquired large tracts of timber lands and constructed team-ways through the forests in order to bring the logs to his enlarged mill which afforded employment to several hundred men.
>
> His nephew, Fritz, born on August 22, 1854, was 13 when his father died. Lienhard took his sister's sons, Jacob, Al, and Fritz into his employ. Fritz later married Rosa Liddle, daughter of another saw-mill owner, who operated as Liddle and Seaman in Handsboro. It was with this background of experience that afforded Fritz Salmen the capability and finances to reap a harvest in the pioneer railroad town of Slidell.

had developed so well, that Salmen sent for his brother, Jacob, to join him, and in 1890, a third brother, Albert, joined the group in uniting their forces and business acumen.

In 1890, the Salmen sawmill was added to their growing property acquisitions between the railroad tracks and Bayou Bonfouca. About the same time, Salmen Brick and Lumber Company added a small shipyard and shipbuilding operations on the west side of Bayou Bonfouca to transport their products to nearby ports.

The company extended their operations and established offices and warehouses in New Orleans, Slidell, Tickfaw, and at Onville. Their large retail yards in New Orleans handled a large variety of building materials, including Portland cement, lime, and plaster as well as lumber, brick, and ornamental materials. Commercial lines were also opened into Central and South America.

In 1895, the Salmen Brick Works filled an order for 1,000,000 bricks to be used in the construction of the new St. Charles Hotel in New Orleans. The brickworks also furnished 23 million bricks for the storm sewers and drainage system of New Orleans; and bricks were shipped across the lake as construction material for nearly all of the New Orleans buildings; including the Roosevelt, St. Charles, DeSoto, and Grundwald hotels – the Maison Blanche and D.H. Holmes buildings, the Metropolitan and Whitney banks, and the Masonic Temple and Loew's State Theater. In 1910, the company employed 800 persons and at its general store, twenty clerks industriously worked. The "Commissary" at Front Street

Fritz Salmen was the builder and founder of several Salmen enterprises and a member of the first Board of Aldermen. He also promoted community development in religious, educational, and social welfare causes. He was also elected to the state legislature in 1904.

and Cleveland Avenue was the largest merchandise store in St. Tammany Parish.

In addition to the shipyard across the bayou from the brickyard, the company had timbering operations within seventy-five miles of Slidell which were reached by its own standard gauge railroad with four engines and 250 rail-cars. The Salmen track connected with the N.O.G.N. railroad thereby gaining countrywide market access. As a full-support operation, there was a machine shop, a blacksmith shop, a two-ton capacity foundry, a carpentry shop, and a sheetmetal shop.

Its primary company officers consisted of Fritz Salmen, president; J.A. Salmen, vice-president; E.G. Schneider, treasurer; and L.T. Miles, general manager.

Early Growth

After the railroad was completed in 1883, the town began expanding around its brick yards and lumber industries. In 1889, another lumber mill was built — this time by the Gause family, which had erected a large family home. And, soon after, another brickworks was initiated by the Fassman family.

Population Growth
By the year 1890, the population census for Slidell was reported at 364 people.
In 1900, it was 1,129
In 1910, it was 2,188
By 1920, it was 2,958, making it the largest town in St. Tammany.

In continued competition, saloons and boarding houses sprung up along the railroad right-of-way and the town resembled those from old west movies. It was rough and wild and there was no established town government until 1888 when a mayor was elected and a town marshal was appointed.

In typical frontier fashion, other businesses began to spring up, too. On the site which is now the corner of First Street and Fremaux Avenue, the famous *Birdcage Saloon* was soon doing a booming business. Its success led to the establishment of thirteen saloons along Front Street which furnished night life and entertainment for the early settlers.

Other stores were opened to offer commodities which included general merchandise, furniture, clothing, food, tools, hardware, medicines, and services. These were centered around Carey and Cousin streets. The nature of businesses occupying each of the old streets, gave them a long lasting reputation in contributing to Slidell's heritage today.

The famous Bird Cage Saloon was located in the former Commercial Hotel, where it set the air of peculiar atmosphere that was to distinguish the northern half of the town from the southern end for years to come.

More hotels were built to meet the demands of the ever increasing newcomers, transients, and traveling businessmen. A.C. Prevost operated the *Pioneer House* in 1890; E.H. Linton, the *Bird Cage Hotel* in 1894; Captain Cornelius Cooper built the *Crescent Hotel;* and there was also, Mrs. Eunice *Carroll's Hotel* that burned down in 1895.

During the heyday of River Sawmills, Italian fruit peddlers from New Orleans would maneuver their barges upriver to sell their wares door to door. Also, there were "floating saloons" which operated on the Louisiana side of the river. Taxi boats were pressed into service to carry the flourishing bar-trade back and forth.

Mississippi voted itself *"Dry"* in 1908. This resulted in Slidell participating in the "jug trade" as supplied to the people dropping in from Mississippi. William King maintained a bar on a flat-boat moored on the Louisiana side of the Pearl River, just across from Pearlington.

Olde Towne Origination

Before the turn of the century, Slidell became more accepted as an industrial community. It was blessed with a large but not inexhaustible supply of timber in the surrounding area, superior clay deposits for bricks, and fortified by rail and water transportation. Then as now, its prosperity depended upon the building trades. Many of the structures in New Orleans were built from brick and tile made in Slidell — most of those buildings are still sturdy and standing today.

One of the new arrivals in 1898, was Dr. Joseph Feston Polk who set up his medical practice and a pharmacy. Dr. Polk initially made his house calls on horseback until the city and the road system grew enough to justify a horse and buggy. Following his return from World War I, as an Army medic, he treated himself to a new Model-T Ford.

> **Mrs. Kate Lawler Able** was one of the pioneering ladies of the early community whose father had arrived as a construction foreman from Ohio. Her father with five daughters and two sons stayed to homestead on 162 acres at Brown's Switch. The family home was located at the former site of the *Massimini Estate.*

He and his wife, together, were early community activists who were on the planning committees to build the original First Baptist Church, a grammar school, and later, promoted the highschool. The doctor's wife, Marganie Langston Polk, taught regular school in addition to Sunday school classes. Their son, Clyde Feston Polk, was born in 1901.

Dr. Polk, with his brother-in-law Joseph Langston, opened the *Crescent Drug Store* at the corner of Carey and Cousin streets. In 1911, Dr. Polk built the current brick building, where his son Clyde operated the pharmacy after graduating from pharmaceutical school in 1925 at Ole Miss.

Because of the emphasis placed on industry, almost the entire labor force was involved in manufacturing, therefore, farming and cultivation continued to receive but little interest.

In the mid-1880s, Fritz Salmen built his first Commissary of wood. This was replaced with the current brick building at the same corner location of Front and Cleveland streets.

In 1893, Perilloux and J.D. Kitchen built the *Slidell Brick and Tile Company* to compete with Salmen's operations. It was

there that the large uptown brick pit was dug near the current site of Northside Plaza. Their kilns were located just south of what was the former site of the *Slidell Grocery and Grain Company.*

Along with progress and growth, rivalry developed between the *"uptown"* and *"downtown"* residential areas. For years, political elections, the selection of public buildings, and other local issues brought disputes which fell just short of a feud. Ultimately, this local problem was alleviated by increased progress and growth. The demarcation line had been the narrowing *Bayou Potassat* (patassat) which was reportedly named for the small perch that filled its waters.

1927 Flood - corner Cousin and Carey.

An old saying about Slidell was that it was "two-towns-long and half-a-town-wide." Of course the reason for this was that the main street (known variously at different times as Bayou, Railroad, Harvey, and Front Street) followed the course of the railroad and bayou. Front Street has remained essentially the same, but the town has expanded so much that the saying is no longer true. Many of the streets that branch off from Front Street are named for the men who were instrumental in making Slidell a town – for example; the railroad people: Fremaux, Erlanger, and Bouscaren; and the long-term inhabitants: Cousin, Robert, and Guzman.

Early 1900s

A 1901 article from the *St. Tammany Farmer,* a weekly newspaper printed at Covington, reported that "Slidell had six churches, three schools, a sawmill, five saloons, six stores, two brickyards, three barber shops, four fruit stands, and several other local favorites too numerous to mention."

The "minutes" of the Town Council meetings for 1901, show that St. Tammany parish gave the town $600 to help in the fight against smallpox during that year.

By 1903, the Southern Creosoting Company was conducting a thriving business. On December 15, 1903, the Slidell branch of the Covington Bank and Trust Company was opened as the first banking institution in the town. In 1906, the local branch broke from its parent institution which resulted in the creation of the *Bank of Slidell,* later known as First Bank. In 1998, it was included in the purchase by First NBC Bank, later Bank One. The original historic landmark building was singled out and awarded to the city.

Homes, stores, and saloons grew like mushrooms. Stores were built by R.A. Bourgeois and R. Richie. Still more hotels were built to accommodate new workers employed at the various plants. In the central section, a bank, a grammar school, and the *White Kitchen* restaurant, replaced the thickly pine covered corner. A number of homes were built surrounding the old Pank's home, today's Polk's corner. The Langston corner was the former site of *Keyser's Saloon* and the Decker home. Across the railroad track, on the bayou was the *Linton Place.* In the lower part of town, on the great 5500 acre *Gusman Tract,* many homes were developed for employees working at the Salmen mill and the lumber kilns. The *A.J. Mire's Store* replaced *Sabrier's* well known pavilion and health resort which had supplied healthful waters from its springs. Many people had claimed their ills to be cured, and after a short while, had gained back their good health.

A post office was established at Front Street and Cleveland Avenue.

Mr. and Mrs. John Provost came to Slidell from Zurich, Switzerland. John Provost was the foreman at the first *Slidell Ice House,* which was located on the corner of what is now Seventh Street and Gause Boulevard. Following the death of her husband, with nine children she opened a boarding house on the site of the *Old Salmen Hotel.*

Mrs. Taylor's Boarding house at 1955 Second Street and Erlanger was bought by the Taylors on March 5, 1913. That house had been built by Leonard Oalmann, the son of German immigrants. The house was torn down in 1986.

U.G. Neuhauser

Neuhauser Bros. (D.G. and A.S.) was one of the largest and most completely stocked general stores in St. Tammany. The building was 75x150 feet in addition to warehouses. They handled general merchandise, groceries, clothing, dry goods, hardware, feed, fertilizers, farming implements, and furniture. In 1905, the company advertized, *"Everything to Eat and Wear."*

The Original 1905 store burned down.

The Neuhauser Bro's Store was one of Slidell's oldest businesses. The original store burned down and was replaced at the same site with a modern building.

U.G. Neuhauser was a director of the *Bank of Slidell* and the *Slidell Ice, Light & Mfg. Company* and a member of the School Board and he was also an agent for the N.O.N.E. railroad.

This store burned down in the late 1950s

T.J. Hand

T.J. Hand was owner of *Pickle & Hand Wholesale Wine and Liquor* in addition to being agents for many of the best high and medium grades of liquors serving Louisiana, Mississippi, and Alabama. Hand was also president of the *Slidell Ice and Manufacturing Company* which had a 150-foot warehouse fronting the

1890 Photo of the Old Reed House.

railroad with a well-equipped packing department in the rear. Hand was also one of the organizers along with Fritz Salmen and others, to form the *Bank of Slidell* and he served many years as a Town councilman.

Henry Cornibe owned the leading livery and undertaking establishment. His two-story building which also housed the stables was located opposite the train depot. In addition, he conducted a livestock business with cattle and horses. – And Blacksmithing.

1905 Photo of George Cornibe's Blacksmith Shop on First Street

Solomon Levy was proprietor of *Lalumia & Levy's Theater* and amusement house. He was also owner of *Levy's Meat Market* that had cold storage facilities and a carriage and cart business to transport his products as far away as 20 miles. He also was a cattle dealer and owned *Levy's Building* in addition to other commercial sites as well as a country store at Bayou LaCombe.

Edgar J. Perilloux and his father, owned *E.F. Perilloux and Co.* Together, they also had a liquor store and a large brick building near the Depot which in 1905 was sold to Harry Hoyle of Gulfport, MS. Edgar died at age 39 in September 1910.

Perilloux Saloon circa 1905

Simon Levy was owner of *Slidell Bakery,* wholesaling into Mississippi by rail and retailing with two delivery wagons from his confectionery store. He operated one of the first soda dispensers in the town.

Dr. J.C. Minturn, was a Dentist with his offices located in the Slidell Bank Building.

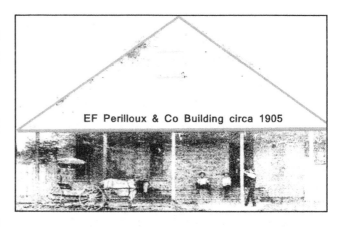

EF Perilloux & Co Building circa 1905

Edward L. Evans owned and operated the *City Saloon.*

Thomas Bros.

L.W. and J.F. operated a mercantile store handling groceries, crockery, tin ware, feed, hardware, and farming implements.

J.F. Thomas also operated a jewelry, watch, and clock repair store.

Mrs Evans Boarding House circa 1905

Charles M. Liddle was the brother-in-law of Fritz Salmen. A native of Handsboro, MS., who served for ten years as Harrison County Treasurer before moving to Slidell. He served for many years as a member of the St. Tammany Parish School Board and ran a successful insurance business in Slidell beginning in 1887. His son, J.T. Liddle served on the city council for many years.

Spring View Distributing, Co.

The company was a liquor distributor to Louisiana, Mississippi, and Alabama with store buildings and warehouses located along the railroad from where they shipped whiskeys, wines, beers, and fancy liqueurs.

J M Currie Saloon

Slidell Liquor Co.

The company was a wholesale and retail dealer of liquors, wines and medicines limiting their customer trade exclusively to jug or bottle products from their 100-foot warehouse.

Slidell Grocery & Grain Co., was a wholesale and jobbing house dealing in flour, grain, groceries, and feed stuffs. The company also handled carloads of cement, lime, and heavy hardware. They occupied two squares of property facing the railroad which included warehouses and office buildings.

Slidell Ice and Manufacturing Co. was chartered on February 28, 1903, with Francis J. Cunningham president, E.J. Perilloux, Treasurer, and F.A. Bourgeois, Secretary.

1999 image of Ice House

In an Interview posted in July 1933, Dr. Polk related the following information about the Town.

Dr. Polk was born in Mississippi in 1875. After graduating from Mississippi College, he furthered his education at the University of Tennessee Medical College where he was awarded his medical degree in 1900.

He had moved to Slidell in 1898, when the census reported Slidell with 1,297 people. While at that time, Slidell did not have a bank, picture show, public school, attorney or dentist or even a resident minister of the Gospel. There was no ice and power plant, no undertakers, no automobiles, and no radios.

Slidell, though small, did boast of one of the best saw mills, planing mills and brick yard to be found anywhere. The plant was owned and operated by the Salmen Brothers, Jake, Fritz and Albert. Under the name of Salmen Bros. & Co., they operated one of the largest stores in the parish – the Slidell Drug Co., which was the only drug store in Slidell then.

The following citizens were at that time most active in public life of the town: George Gause, E.P. Robert, U.G. Neuhauser, F.A. Bourgeois, Oscar L. Ditmar, C.A. Everett, W.E. Eddins, E.F. Perilloux, L.E. Harris, Ben Houghton, Sr., John Frederick, C.M. Liddle, W.O. Wilder, John Paterson, L.F. Miles, E.P. Hiley, B.P. Dunham, and H.L. Moore.

Miss Lilly Carr was Post Mistress of the post office in Slidell. Henry J. Cornibe owned and operated the only livery stable of which the town ever boasted and remained in business until his death in 1922. B. Houghton owned and operated the only bakery in the city.

In Slidell and vicinity there were four doctors: Dr. A.L. Dubourge, Dr. J.A. Harper, Dr. J.G. Smith and Dr. O.E. Parker, all of who are dead. Dr. Dubourge was resident physician of this section for nearly fifty years before his death in 1902. In 1901, the town was visited by a severe epidemic of small pox, which claimed many lives.

In 1902, during the yellow fever epidemic in New Orleans a quarantine station was established here.

In 1904, the Bank of Slidell was established, C.A. Everett was cashier, and later became its president, which position he held until his death.

In 1907, the Crescent Drug Store was established.

In 1908, Southern Railway (aka Queen and Crescent) and East La. R.R. trains collided claiming many lives. Jake Salmen, W.A. Martin and other Slidellians lost their lives.

Dr. Polk had seen many changes during his years while administering to the sick. During that period, the following took place:

In 1908, Slidell Ice and Light Co.,

In 1910, First picture show was operated by Pete Lalumni.

From 1913 to 1929, the post office was in the Polk Building.

In 1915, Cumberland Telephone Exchange moved into the Polk Building.

In 1918, the Flu epidemic took a heavy toll of human life.

In 1921, J.D. Grant died, at which time he was president of the Creosoting Co. He was the donor of the Community House and other properties to the town of Slidell.

For many years, James McKean was owner and operator of the only outfit for drilling wells and was instrumental in furnishing the town with much pure drinking water.

Dr. Polk and E.F. Hailey were the owners of the first two telephones installed in town. The doctor further recalled that in the early days, there were no automobiles or bicycles – travel was by foot or by horse. The major part of heavy hauling was done by oxen.

Remarking about community life in Slidell, former school teacher Laura Crawford related that in 1911, there was no electricity. "You could travel down Robert Road and see nothing in the world but piney wood flats. Robert Road was named after Jean Pierre Robert – and Gause Road was just a narrow dirt road," she added.

In touring Olde Towne Slidell, many local landmarks still abound.
The Country Cubbard gained an addition in 1939. *Mires' Hardware* opened in 1915. *The Mire Building* was built on the corner of Pennsylvania and Front streets housing the *Cake Castle* in 1988. *The Peach Tree* was opened by Gastrorondo, a French opera singer. *Slidell Cleaners* was built in 1939 by Joe Johnson. *Olde Towne Antiques* was formerly a saloon, –grocery store, and –meat market before remodeling. The present *Slidell Museum* was built in 1907 as the City Hall. *The Second Story Lounge* was originally a grocery store operated by the Carollo family. The original *Polk Building* at Carey and Cousin streets was the *Time Out Lounge* in 1988.

Other original family names associated with buildings in the area were Abney, Baker, Cornibe, Fontana, Gazano, Giordano, Neuhauser, Polk, and Pravata.

Circa 1905, Below Left — Cousin St at Front St;   *At Right — Bank of Slidell*

Bank and Masonic Temple Lodge #311

5 and 10 cent store

1914 Slidell High School Marching Band

Victory Celebration – End of WWI

Francois Dubuisson rode his horse to Town

Francois Dubuisson, was the son of Silvain Dubuisson and Louise Nicaise – born on January 27, 1828 and baptized on December 11, 1828 with Francois Pichon as Godfather and his aunt Genevieve Dubuisson as Godmother. He married Aimee Marie Pena, daughter of Adolphe Pena and Odile Pichon, on February 2, 1852.

His obituary in the *Daily Picayune*, November 29, 1914, reported that *Francois Dubuisson died this morning at the age of 89 years. Four daughters, seven sons and thirty-four grand-children survive him, all of them residents of this parish. He was a Confederate soldier in Co. A of the 9th Brigade and was in several engagements. He was also considered one of the best scouts in the Confederate service.*

Pichon's Journal
1848-1886

Francois Sidoine Pichon was born in 1818, the third child of Francois Pichon of Bordeaux, France and of Genevieve Isabel Dubuisson, daughter of Francois Bernardo Dubuisson and Anne Charite Krebs (Dubuisson) of Mobile. His older brother, Avenel, married Clementine Laurent; and his older sister, Camille, married Anatole Cousin, Sr. Another sister, Rose, married Joseph Galatas; and a brother, Silvano, married Louise Nicaise.

Francois and Adele Pichon

Excerpts from his Diary, relate to the living conditions before and after the Civil War.

The story is centered on Bonfouca Bayou before rails or roadways came to the area. Early transportation was by boat.

Francois's primary work involved a shipyard where he constructed new boats and repaired others. He subcontracted his slaves for outside labor as well as hiring others. As time passed, more of his repair work was on vessels of English speaking owners as revealed by the names he accounted for in his diary.

Most of Pichon's neighbors were French speaking settlers including the contacts he made at Pearl River and DeLisle to the East; Vacherie and New Orleans on the southside of the Lake; and Covington and Lacombe to the West. His close friends were Adolphe and Armand Cousin, Eugene Dubuisson, Raimond Carriere, Nicolas Galatas, Dubourg, Big Anatole, Eleonor and Paul Guzman, among others. He frequently spoke of one of his brothers, Avenel Pichon and was tender towards his wife, Adele, who was administered treatments for sleepwalking.

On December 26, 1839, Francois Pichon married Marie Adele Carriere. Both of these families already had many relatives living in the area. His diary, covers the period of 1848 to 1886, as it relates living conditions at "."

Francois's arduous workweeks were consumed in caulking and repairing local fishing craft, barges, ferries, and schooners. The earliest settlers were French descendants, many of whom represented the family names honored by street names throughout "Olde Towne."

Before the Civil War, slaves supplied labor at his shipyard and toiled in the forests cutting cord wood.

Following the War, the labor force was supplanted by his grown sons. As time passed, his family extended their agricultural sustenance along with their shipyard trade.

Francois was a respected honorable businessman, a practicing Catholic, and responsible citizen attending to taxes, jury duty, election processes, filing permits, clearing stumps from bayous, maintaining roadways, levees, cemeteries, church buildings, as well as accepting positions in community organizations.

Farming duties consisted of planting and harvesting potatoes, oats, peanuts, corn, vines, beans, melons, rice, okra, cabbage, onions, tomatoes hay, garlic, sugarcane, figs, pears, oranges, and pecans. In addition, they raised horses, cows, sheep, and pigs.

There was an abundance of deer and wild

Francois Pichon of Bonfouca, was a religious man, supporting the church by attending Mass at least as early as 1858 and he contributed time and labor to its maintenance. He referenced the arrivals of Father Grasse on December 11, 1875, Father Flanagan on October 26, 1878, and Father Barnardin on June 6, 1879. While crossing the bayou on July 12th, Father Barnardin's horse drowned. Father Avelier, a new Missionary, having arrived on September 6, 1881, continued on through at least 1885. During one of his earliest visits, he administered communion to the children. The Church and rectory were repaired March 24, 1883. Francois cleaned the cemetery frequently and prayed there.

Francois Pichon was a loving father, who provided for his children in boarding schools at New Orleans and Mobile, and visited them when they were ill. With nine children, three of them having died early, others married, and three of them, particularly Hypolite and Nelville, remained close at home to support the shipyard and farmlands. One of the consuming chores was in splitting posts and cutting stakes which were used in fencing his property as well as neighboring farms, and some of which was sold at New Or leans as game in the area. Also many trips were made to the Bay of St. Louis, DeLisle, Grand Lagoon, and other nearby locations to shoot ducks and geese, or to fish and shrimp the waterways. While at DeLisle, he probably stayed with his brother-in-law, Eugene Dubuisson.

Prior to the Civil War, many trips were made to New Orleans, Vacherie, Mobile, Pearlington, Covington, and Lacombe to purchase supplies and possibly to work on vessels at other shipyards. While there, he would spend a week, or spend overnight at a neighboring family usually by camping out on their property.

Notations described going to a Post Office in 1860, which was probably at Covington, or perhaps at Fort Pike where a postmaster was established in 1853. He described, briefly, mustering into the Confederate troops at Camp Ruggles with his oldest sons during preparations for the Civil War. In 1873, he reported another lumber mill owned by the Evarise family; and he would frequently go to his brother-in-law, Anatole Cousin's to get the *Gazette Newspaper.* Industriously, he also built his own sugar-cane mill.

He reported that Bayou Bonfouca froze over during the first week of January 1881 in addition to several other winters. The *"Society of Loyal Friends"* was organized on October 8, 1881, and Francois was elected its Treasurer; and on October 25, 1884, the *Bonfouca Hunting Club* was organized; while for other entertainment, dances were usually held at the Cousin's home or business.

In December 1884, Francois purchased food supplies from "Frederick's," which was probably a general store. He made his first mention of the Town of Slidell when his son, Romilia Pichon, went there on June 28, 1885, followed by paying his taxes there in late 1885.

Interspersed in his ledger book, Francois Pichon kept strict accounting for his business activity as well as maintaining the notes that composed his diary. This may be the only accounting of this nature for the Bonfouca Region.

The original document was translated from the French and commemorated in a publication by Jack Galatas and Dudley Smith. These gentlemen are credited for bringing forth an enlightenment for the folk life and culture of the early times of the Slidell/Lacombe region.

Primary Industries

Surrounded as it is by slash pine forests, Slidell's timber resources and allied products have always remained an important asset. During the early 1900s, H. Weston's Logtown mill on the Lower Pearl River produced six million board-feet annually.

The output of tar, turpentine, rosin, and charcoal gave profitable employment to hundreds of men and kept fifty to sixty schooners busy as witnessed by statistics of daily arrivals and departures of vessels to and from the Old and New Basins at New Orleans.

Until 1930, brick-making, lumber mills, shipbuilding, and service commerce made up the backbone of Slidell's economy.

Slidell, for many years, possessed a deep water harbor. Any vessel that could navigate Lake Pontchartrain could berth at its shipyards. Sheep wool and fleece also became major exports.

As for tourism, St. Tammany spas were touted as leading health resorts and were heavily frequented.

Shotgun Quarantines

Sawmills continued to operate in spite of Yellow Fever epidemics. The State Militia was called out to prevent anyone from leaving and to keep anyone from entering. This action was called a Shotgun Quarantine. Regardless, logs continued to be sent down-river in order to keep sawmills supplied.

On Agriculture

Grape vineyards were cultivated for their production of red and white wines in commercial quantities including grape vinegar.

The silk industry was advanced in the early 1880s, with mulberry trees planted for its silk product as well as raising silk worm eggs which were even sold to Italy in times of their seasonal calamity.

According to an 1885 story in the *St. Tammany Farmer,* "one ounce of silk worm eggs, fed on the leaves from one acre of mulberry trees (approximately 200 trees), would produced 120 ounces of eggs in six weeks, rendering a profit of $360 per acre."

High grade commercial tobacco was grown to a height of four feet by John H. Davis at Bayou Lacombe. He produced cigars from locally grown tobacco which were commonly called the *St. Tammany Special* selling for ten cents, and the *St. Tammany Maid* and the *Ozone* were sold for a nickel.

In the 1890s sugar cane and molasses were exported by schooner and rail carloads. Truck farming increased with such staples as corn, potatoes, vegetables, and fruits such as satsumas. Tung trees were farmed in great orchards for their oil by-product. Rice harvests began to produce such great quantities that St. Tammany became a leader in barrel production.

The Creosote Plant

In the 1890s, New Orleans businessmen bought the Railroad's creosote plant on Bayou Vincent and named it Southern Creosoting Company. There was a continued need for creosoted railroad ties, trestle pilings, and telephone and telegraph line-poles.

When Mr. R. L. Armstrong joined the management team of Southern Creosote, he built the "Manor House" overlooking the bayou. The manor had 12-foot ceilings with double doors opening to the gallery porch surrounding the two-story edifice. When Armstrong retired, J.H. Dunstan, the company engineer, occupied the home with his family until 1923. At that time Southern Creosote was sold to Gulf States Creosoting Company and the Dunham Family moved in and remained there until 1951.

In June 1972, the American Creosote plant burned down with its remains torn down in 1973, leaving behind toxic pollutants to remain in the Bayou Bonfouca until most recently.

During the plant's operation, numerous releases of creosote occurred through spills, runoff, and

Letter dated Oct 27,1888, from Methodist minister G.R. Ellis, describing Slidell, "I proceeded to the stupendous creosote works, belonging to the Northeastern Railroad Company, whose immense reservoirs, with millions of gallons capacity, and tremendous cylinders 100 feet in length and 6 feet in diameter, made of solid iron, were somewhat a sight of one not so costumed to such things every day."

discharges. The 1972 fire took place at the plant when several large storage tanks were ruptured, causing creosote to flow onto the site and into the bayou. In 1973 the remains of the plant was dismantled, leaving only a few shells of buildings and foundation slabs. Creosote contamination was so concentrated that it injured or killed aquatic animals and waterfowl, and posed a significant hazard to recreational users.

In March 2015, it was reported that: EPA and Louisiana Dept of Environmental Quality continue to review the operation and maintenance of the groundwater pump and treatment of creosote oil. Monthly operational reports are submitted to the EPA for review and comment.

The Louisiana Department of Environmental Quality maintains the site and performs routine monitoring of the ground water. Incineration of contaminated soils and sediments were completed on July 28, 1995. Ground water treatment began in June 1991 and continues to reduce the volume of contaminated ground water and prevent migration. Damage to some of the operating equipment resulted from hurricane Katrina in late August 2005.

LDEQ and FEMA assessed the extent of the damage and completed the necessary repairs. Sampling on and around the site took place in December 2005 to assess if any contaminants in the bayou were spread into neighboring areas. This sampling did not show any contamination problems on or around the site.

A third five year review was completed in July 2011 which determined that the overall remedy for the site is protective in the short term. The next five year review is scheduled for 2016.

Brick-making

At Bayou Lacombe there were three brickyards operated by different members of the early Cousin clan. During the same period there were brick manufacturers with kilns located throughout St. Tammany, which were producing bricks for export primarily to New Orleans.

With the coming of the railroads, the brick-works industry was revitalized. Prior to the coming of the railroad, brick-making factories and brickyards had to be located on navigable bayous and rivers.

Two of these were established in or near Slidell with the completion of the New Orleans & Northeastern rail line in 1883. The largest was the *Salmen Brick and Lumber Company* at Slidell which became the economic mainstay for the early development of the town.

Brick drying kilns at the Salmen Brick-works

The original Salmen brickyard was located just south of the train station.

The other was the St. Joe Brickyard, operated by Colonel Peter W. Schneider at St. Joe Station, a few miles above Slidell. The Schneider family has continued to maintain the business as the only major brickyard that is still producing in St. Tammany Parish.

> **Brick Making** was one of the early industries. With the many forts that were built to protect the water-ways, one of these brickyards produced the brick for Fort Pike at the Rigolets.

The noted "St. Tammany clay" eventually became used for pottery, terra cotta, and charcoal furnaces. The inexhaustible clay was shipped out in carload lots to other parts of the country. As the demand for these products abated, excavations of old clay pits and ruins of kilns are evidence of an industry from the past. Nevertheless, suitable clay beds still abound to serve the art-culture of southern pottery makers.

Salmen Brick and Lumber Co.

The lumber company manufactured yellow pine and cypress lumber, shingles, laths, and hewn and round piling. Their plant covered an area of forty acres. The first sawmill had a daily capacity of 60,000 feet and the planing mill capacity produced 50,000 feet daily. The brick and steel dry kilns were always up-to-date. There was also a large

Salmen Brick & Lumber Co on Bayou Bonfouca

shingle mill that produced 100,000 shingles daily and a cord wood mill that cut fifty cords daily.

The Salmen brick plant had a capacity of a quarter of a million bricks daily with the latest machinery equipped to handle pressed brick and building brick. The Slidell and Bayou Lacombe R.R. was laid for a distance of twelve miles to gain connection access with the Great Northern railroad west of Slidell.

The Salmen interests owned the largest mercantile establishment in the parish and maintained offices in New Orleans on Common Street.

From a meager beginning, the Salmen Brick Company rose to became a major plant manufacturing over a quarter of a million bricks daily.

Slidell Brick and Tile

E.J. Perrilloux and J.D. Kitchen established another brick-works known as *Slidell Brick and Tile* and was located by today's Northside Plaza.

The "Bise House" located on West Hall Avenue was built in 1890 by Dr. Smith, the only doctor in town at that time and also practiced in New Orleans. The home site had been occupied prior to 1890 by two homes which had burned down. The 2-story "Bise House" had two large chimneys with its first level built of concrete and brick, and its yard and patio was paved with brick.

After the house was sold to Mrs. Henry Keller, it was then sold to the Slidell Brick & Tile Co., presided over by William Heyl. He was followed by the Weston family who occupied the residence from 1911 to 1974.

Another early brick-works was reported on June 21,1890, by the *St. Tammany Farmer* stating; "a brickyard now running, (located) about two miles south of the station, is owned by Messrs. McCaren and Sons."

St. Joe Brick Works

Originating the next year was another brick-works, the St. Joe brickyard, located near the town of Pearl River. After arriving from Germany, Peter W. Schneider acquired the St. Joe Brick Works in 1891, later

St. Joe Station was located north of Slidell on the Northeastern Railroad. It became the site of a brick works in 1889, and by 1894, boasted 200 inhabitants, two stores, one barroom, a wheelwright, one blacksmith, and the brick manufacturing plant – owned and operated by Colonel P.W. Schneider renaming it Schneider Brick and Tile Company.

During its development period, the Schneider Brick and Tile Company employed two hundred men. The daily capacity of bricks and tile was 170,000 per day. A special feature at its plant was the Haig Continuous Kiln, which was the largest kiln of its kind in the United States.

Renamed the St. Joe Brick Works, Inc., it is the oldest family brick manufacturer east of the Mississippi River making colonial molded face brick using wood molds. Today, Peter Schneider, a descendant of the Colonel, continues management operations of St. Joe Brick Works, Inc. in Slidell and at Mandeville.

Shipbuilding

Presumably, the first signs of shipbuilding in St. Tammany began in 1805 as indicated by registrations at New Orleans.

These included the schooner, *Gourmand,* followed the next year with the *La Redoubtable* out of Bayou Bonfouca. Years before the Civil War, Francois Pichon was repairing and building boats.

At Bonfouca, the major ship builders during the late 1800s, were Lucien and Joseph Pichon.

John Faciane, known as Slidell's boat builder, completed:
1895 - the *JJ Clarke*,
1898 - the Rough Rider,
1900 - the *Katie M.*
1903 - the St. Tammany,
1904 - the *Harry P.*, 1906 - the *Carrie*

1907 – Boat building on Bayou Vincent – photo courtesy John Doherty

From these small beginnings, Slidell developed into a prominent home of shipbuilding which early on became a major contribution to economic life.

Salmen's Shipyard

In 1895, Salmen built a small shipyard which by 1914 had became the Slidell Shipbuilding Company, a stock company. The principle owners and officers were Fritz Salmen, Albert Salmen, and Andrew D. Canulette.

It was first conceived to maintain its growing fleet of barges and boats – the Salmen shipyard serviced its fleet of schooners that pursued the ocean route to Nicaragua where rough mahogany timber was loaded and brought back to Slidell for milling.

The shipyard later became owned principally by the Canulette family and then expanded, becoming the Louisiana Shipbuilding

Corporation. Under government supervision in 1916, Louisiana Shipbuilding during World War I specialized in composite construction of steel framing and wood planking – employing up to 1,500 men.

In 1917, a 229-foot wooden ocean-going vessel was built there. Also reported for the year, were vessels built for the Norwegian Line that included the *Baltic I. Baltic II. Baltic III,* and *Baltic IV.*

Ship workers, numbering 1,500 in 1919 - fulfill a government contract specializing in composite construction of steel framing and wood planking during World War I.

1919 Shipyard employees

In 1920 the plant, then operated by A.D. and F.N. Canulette and G.O. Salassi, moved the facility down the bayou and renamed it the Canulette Shipbuilding Company, which later became the J & S Shipyard, and finally the Southern Shipbuilding Corporation.

During World War II, this shipyard built tugboats for the U.S. Army – and net-tenders for the U.S. Navy, employing 1,900 laborers.

Slidell's shipyards were extremely busy during the war, but they suffered the same fate as those in Madisonville when the war ended. Government contracts were canceled and hundreds of employees were laid off.

A Ship Launching at Bayou Bonfouca by Canulette Shipbuilding workers in 1943.
1900 laborers were employed during the World War II war effort program.

> *Still remembered are the famed boat builders, the Baham and Galatas families,*
> *who had cultivated the refined art of wooden boat building for over a century.*

The Southern Shipbuilding facility was issued two Compliance Orders by the Louisiana Department of Natural Resources in 1984 and 1987. In August 1992, it was discovered that the levees around the sludge pits had failed, and 325,000 gallons of materials were released into Bayou Bonfouca. The LDEQ issued a third Compliance Order to Southern Shipbuilding, directing it to stop all unauthorized discharges and to comply with pollution control laws.

The site was identified to the EPA in December 1992. An investigation conducted by the EPA determined that the north sludge pit was releasing material into the bayou. In 1993 and 1994, the EPA initiated two removal actions at the site to pump down water levels within the sludge pits and treat the discharge waters. In 1994-95, the EPA and USAGE installed sheet piling around the levees.

The Southern Shipbuilding Corporation filed a petition for bankruptcy and ceased operations in 1993. The property is currently owned by Equity Development Systems Limited (EDS) in New Orleans, Louisiana.

The site was added to the National Priorities List (NPL) on May 10,1995.

A third Five-Year Review Report was completed in September 2010. Annual inspections are planned to continue until a 2015 five-year review is completed and will address the site's short-term protectiveness of public health and the environment.

Remedial Activities

- The site is in the operation and maintenance phase awaiting a Ready-for-Reuse proposal.
- The Louisiana Department of Environmental Quality (LDEQ) and the site owner maintain the site.
- The landfill cap is inspected once every year and the remedy is evaluated every five years.
- Discussions on reuse are being conducted between the city of Slidell and the current owner.

Built at Bonfouca

CrossRoads

Slidell is exceptional in being one of the few cities in the United States which has three major interstate highways intersecting. The city is a focal point by being a significant Crossroad community infused by a major highway system and a waterway network. The core of the city is situated on what is virtually a peninsula bordered by Lake Pontchartrain, the Rigolets channel, and the Pearl River Swamp basin. Slidell is ideally postured at the nearest high ground north of New Orleans and is located safely away from the dominant hurricane prone coastlines.

First Settler Roads

First the French with the founding of New Orleans in 1718, followed by the Spanish – and then the American migration following the Louisiana Purchase in 1803.

Early settler migrations following the War of 1812 and the Civil War, discovered loneliness, illness, and frustrations. Along the Military Roads from Georgia and Tennessee occurred the mass migration of thousands of families led by fathers and mothers with pride and generally deep religious convictions who were willing to undergo poverty and hardship in the hope of building a better economic life for themselves and their children.

What they found

On the West side of John Guzman's Plat was the Joseph Laurent property – acquired by Vincent Rillieux, the namesake for Bayou Vincent; in 1825, the land was acquired by Barthelemy Martin.

Another neighbor was Francois Rillieux, holding lands that extended to the Pearl River on the East side of John Guzman's Plat.

During the earliest days, most or all transportation was carried on by waterways that included Bayous, Rivers, and Lakes; which resulted in communications with settlers along the north shore, across the lake to New Orleans, east to Pearl River and Bay St. Louis communities. This created marriages producing children and more marriages that eventually populated the area in addition to new migrants from other areas.

Early Local Foot Travel
Roads, Ferries, and Bridges

Early on, **Madisonville** was an important port that provided bricks and other products from the towns along the Tchefuncte River that was shipped to New Orleans.

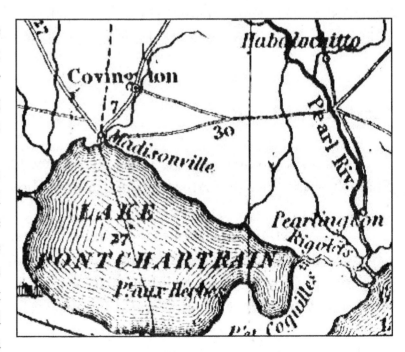

Madisonville was founded in 1800, being called "Coquille" because of the abundance of shells in the area. In 1810 the town was renamed in honor of President James Madison. Situated below Covington, it became a terminus for roads and a ferry site that crossed Lake Pontchartrain to New Orleans.

The Laurent Plat situated between Bayou Liberty and Bayou Bonfouca shows significant activity by way of ferries and roads prior to 1850.

1. Old Ferry

2. New Ferry crossing Bayou Liberty

3. Road to Mandeville

4. Road northward to a French settlement

5. Road to Pearl River

6. Road to Lake Pontchartrain

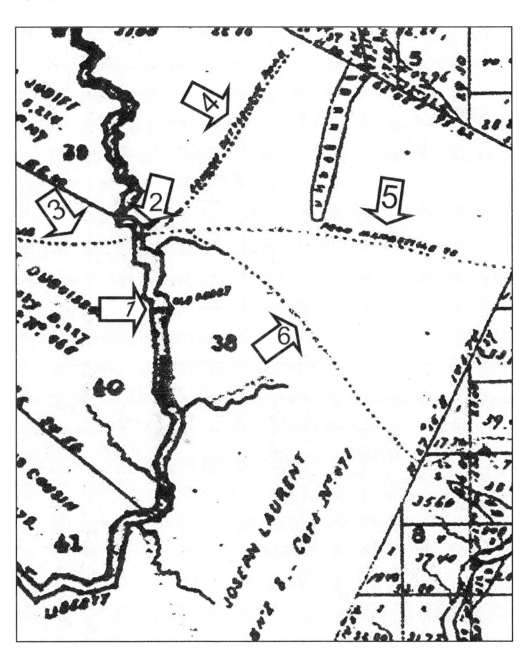

The adjoining area on the East shows a continuation of trails that became roads that have continued to exist today.

7. Bridge crossing Bonfouca

8. Road to Pearl River

9. Road to the Rigolets

10. Connecting Road

11. Road to Lake Pontchartrain

12. Ferry crossing Bayou Bonfouca

13. Guzman Hospital

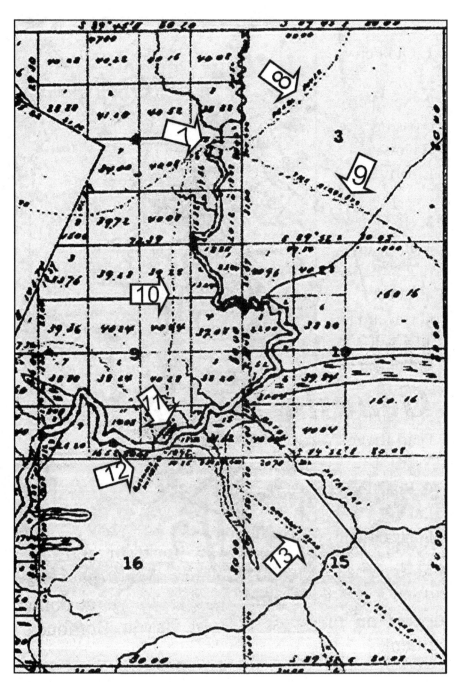

John Guzman held the largest land area which adjoined the Laurent property to the East. The Guzman family was industrious, having a supply house with boating and marine supplies, a general store, a ferry service, a sawmill, a brick plant, and a tar mill; in addition to trading horses and cattle.

In 1806, shipbuilding along the bayous was beginning to take hold; the Guzman boatyard began catering to lake trade.

Between 1811 and 1840 numerous schooners had been built by various designers.

The Military Road ending at Madisonville was constructed by U.S. Army troops in the years 1817 through 1820, which was originated by Gen. Andrew Jackson as quick access to New Orleans from Nashville. By legislative act, road maintenance was enforced upon the residents of Washington and St. Tammany parishes who lived within five miles of the roadway.

By 1850, the major roadways of the parish were in place. The rudiments of Highways 21 and 25 were established along with other roads between the existing towns. From Mandeville, the road ran east to Bayou Lacombe and on to Slidell. From Slidell, a road ran northeast to join the West Pearl River Road, and another ran southeast to the Rigolets. These developments were already in place before Slidell's existence.

Methods of transportation had developed very slowly until the railroad construction in the 1880s. There were no other outlets to the north or south. Winding trails, impossible in bad weather, led toward Covington and Indian Village at Pearl River. The streets of the town were either deep in dust or deep in mud. It was still natural for most of the populace to use boat travel on the waterways.

In the period before 1900, roads were constructed and maintained by the people who lived within proximity. The Police Jury created road districts and appointed overseers in each district to call out the residents to perform maintenance for a set number of days each year. With population growth, these roadways gradually expanded.

Horseless Carriages

With the advent of the first automobiles on the Mississippi Gulf Coast, due to the absence of roads between New Orleans and the coast, it was necessary to have purchased cars transported by rail. Automobiles were being sold and bought — but with no roads to travel on, it didn't take long for motorists to form organizations with the prime motive of having roads of quality built.

On December 1,1906, Louisiana autoists incorporated the "Motor League of Louisiana." Many of the well-to-do Orleanians had for decades shared second homes at places along the Lake northshore and Gulf Coast Mississippi. They wielded their influences politically and financially throughout Louisiana and Mississippi.

A prime mover for the Motor League was P.M. Milner who promoted an experiment and in order to show exactly what could be done in the matter of road construction. Gentilly Ridge, the old trail leading from New Orleans to Chef Menteur was chosen for the "test" improvement.

The estimated cost of the improvement was placed at $30,000 and the Motor League endeavored to raise the money among its members. The Mayor gave his assurance that if the road was built, it would be maintained by the city, as its eighteen miles are within city limits.

Governor Jared Sanders assured them assistance with Convict Labor providing the League covered all expenses.

On February 21, 1910, work on the roadway was started and the first formal inspection took place on April 17th. In just about two months, working six days a week, the convicts had dug ditches and graded and crowned roads for a distance of about four miles, from Gentilly Road to Michaud Station, and they had given positive assurance of the success of the great undertaking.

As a trial run, state and city officials drove in motor cars over the four miles of recently constructed surface at a lively clip, and the new road proved to be solid and well drained.

Road Expansions in Slidell

On September 15, 1913 a group of Slidell citizens petitioned the Police Jury to build a road from the southern city limits to reach the northern bank of Lake Pontchartrain. This was a Parish constructed road since there was no state highway system at the time.

The Pontchartrain Road was designed to run parallel to the rail line that had been completed in 1883 with a projected cost of $5000. The police jury provided $4000 and the remainder was accessed from the citizens of Slidell.

Howze Beach Road

In 1915, the St Tammany Parish Police Jury constructed Howze Beach Road, naming if after John Howze who later became a Jury President. It ran in a southerly direction from what is now Old Spanish Trail and ended at Howze Beach on Lake Pontchartrain, a distance of five miles from Slidell.

In July of that year, Howze gave a party in celebration of completion.

In following years summer camps and cottages were built and a boat channel with docking slip were added. By 1921 the police jury had given permission for the construction of a wharf and lake house and the East Pontchartrain Ferry Company began operating ferries and steamers.

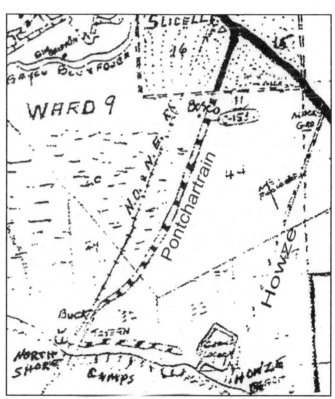

The Roads in this 1940's sketch appear as Dark for Paved and Dotted for Gravel.

Night time cruises to the Rigolets became popular for the younger set.

Over time, the ravages of tide and storms destroyed the Howze Beach resort, but Howze Beach Road remains today.

Road Development on the Gulf Coast

Before the 1920s the only way for vehicles to get to New Orleans was by ferry across Lake Pontchartrain. This route was greatly shortened when roads were laid and ferries were installed at the Rigolets and Chef Menteur and the Pearl River tributaries. Regardless, the trip to New Orleans from the Coast was still two hours on a winding shelled road. Once in Slidell all roads were dust and driving north of the city was hazardous and long even when gravel was laid to Bogalusa and Covington.

A coastal road from the Bay of Biloxi to the Bay of St. Louis had eventually been laid to replace the tracks that were part of the Coast Trolley service from Biloxi to Pass Christian in 1911.

Early on, a shell beach road existed from Waveland to Bay St. Louis.

> *In December of 1915, Motor enthusiasts from Alabama, Mississippi and Louisiana met in Mobile to developed plans that evolved into a transcontinental drive over newly developed road routes beginning at St. Augustine, Fla. ending at San Diego, Cal. that took place with a motorcade in 1925, and was officially launched in 1929.*

On June 2, 1917, the *St. Tammany Farmer* reported that a highway routing from Chicago to New Orleans was under study to determine local impact. Those involved were considering a connection for Robert Road to the Rigolets ferry. (*The "connection" is the current Louisiana Highway 433. LA 433 spans 14.8 miles and known at various points as Thompson Road, Bayou Liberty Road, Pontchartrain Drive, Old Spanish Trail, and Rigolets Road.*)

Road Conditions

Lumberman Horatio Weston recalled the road conditions and travel routes used by touring cars in 1917. Roads were dirt or gravel; and a typical route from Mobile to New Orleans was called Route 701 which was then a distance of 164.2 miles.

Including driving time, and waiting for ferries to arrive, and loading time, it usually took more than a day to make the trip. The Pascagoula Ferry took an hour and a half to sail across. Once landing, the continuation route included Ocean Springs, Mississippi City, Gulfport, Long Beach, Pass Christian, DeLisle, Rock Bayou, Fenton, Kiln, and Logtown and then at the fork, a plank road was maneuvered to the Pearl River Ferry. That crossing then took two hours.

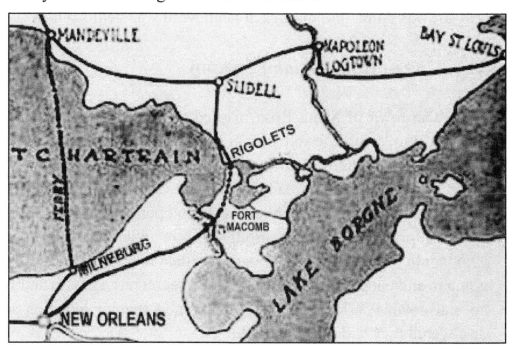

The route continued through Slidell, Lacomb, and Mandeville where yet another ferry station was located. The Ferry across Lake Pontchartrain took two hours to Milneburg and before finally proceeding to New Orleans.

On another occasion, Weston recounted, "I recall my trip from Logtown to New Orleans in 1926 when I went to register at Tulane University."

"It took four to five hours. From Logtown there was a cable ferry in service at the Pearl River, then on to Slidell and to the Rigolets where a shell road led to Chef Menteur; and then a cable ferry to New Orleans," he continued.

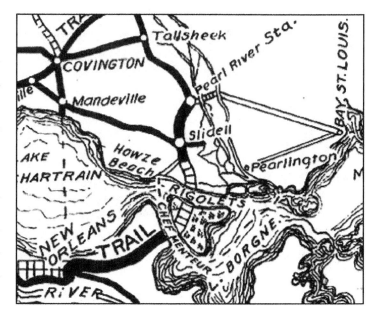

In 1912, Weston had taken over the Weston Lumber Company at Logtown following his father's death. Being community minded, for thirty years he was a member of the Hancock County Board of Supervisors, in Mississippi, serving as its President most of that time. During his presidency, the Hancock County concrete seawall was built; and the Beach Boulevard was dedicated in 1929.

The King of *Honey Island* Swamp

The town of Santa Rosa marked the Mississippi part of the *Honey Island* Swamp, now a wildlife refuge, but previously for many years the refuge of pirate bands headed by Pierre Rameau.

Pearl River with its many hidden entrance passages provided sanctuary for the most dangerous gangs of criminals ever to operate in the Gulf Coast area.

Before a road was cut through, *Honey Island* was headquarters for this gang who would make raids in fast boats into the Gulf and even into New Orleans itself, going in and out through little known and secret passages, to and from their hideouts up and down Pearl River. They maintained several hideouts so that if one was discovered they had others to go to.

Pierre Rameau was born and reared in Scotland and came from a good family, but sought an easy way to make money and became a brigand and a pirate. His real name was McCullogh. In New Orleans he maintained one of the city's finest homes under the name of Col. Loring, who passed as a mine owner and operator from Mexico.

"Old Spanish Trail" promotions

In mid-February 1916, newspapers reported about the bill introduced into the United States Congress to create a national defense highway running from Los Angeles across the nation through the Deep South to Jacksonville, Florida. The bill did not detail the route through Mississippi and Louisiana, but the "Old Spanish Trail Highway Association" manifested its influence to direct the routing from Mobile to New Orleans.

U.S. Highway 90

Work on Highway 90 progressed rapidly in 1928 when, on January 30, 1928, the first automobile passed over the five-mile long Watson-Williams Bridge across Lake Pontchartrain at Slidell. A month later, the first car passed over the Bay of St. Louis Bridge leading from Henderson Point to Bay St. Louis.

It was a great day for Bay St. Louis in 1928 when the ferry across Bay St. Louis was replaced with the wooden bridge across the Bay – built at the cost of $752,610.65 of creosoted pilings and timber. This project was the result of the hard work and energy of Horatio Weston of Logtown, then president of the Board of Supervisors. The bridge suddenly transformed Bay St. Louis from an isolated resort town to becoming the open western portal of the entire Mississippi Gulf Coast.

This also resulted in greater automobile traffic crossing Lake Pontchartrain to and through Slidell to make access to Gulf Coast destinies.

On May 10, 1928, officials dedicated the Harrison County twenty-five-mile-long step seawall protecting Highway 90 – at that time, the seawall was the longest concrete seawall in the world.

And, on August 14, 1928, "Old Spanish Trail Highway" managing director Harral B. Ayers dedicated the East Pascagoula River Bridge. This last event, heralded the first ferry-less ride from New Orleans to Mobile, and it marked the completion of a modern American highway that was not "old" or "Spanish" and which followed no historic trail."

Honey Island Swamp

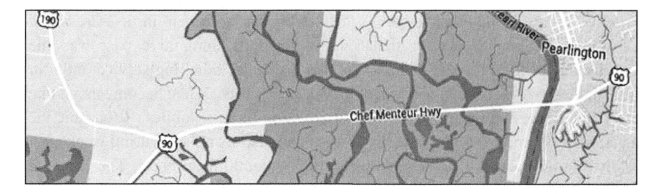

Eventually with the laying of the Honey Island Road, many hours of time were saved in traveling back and forth from the Gulf Coast; even though it was a gravel road where many hazardous accidents occurred. (*The road was cut from Pearlington through Honey Island Swamp to the intersection of Hwy 90 and Hwy 190*)

In 1935 the Louisiana-Mississippi Short-Cut Link from Pearlington to the Rigolets eliminated twenty-two miles off the former distance – from the Mississippi Gulf Coast to New Orleans. A ferry was put into service at Pearlington that cut the trip to the Coast to three hours.

Horatio Weston had taken an active interest in promoting the Old Spanish Trail short line road from the Gulf Coast to Slidell and the Rigolets; and through his efforts, the Bay St. Louis Bridge was built in 1928.

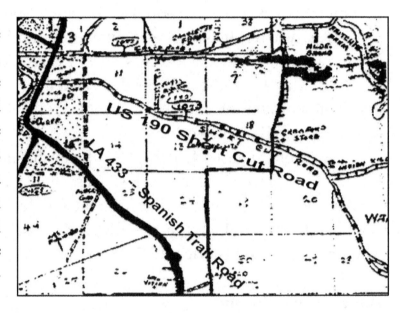

This was followed by the Highway 11 Bridge in 1928, with a toll of $3.50. The Rigolets bridge was completed in 1930 offering a second route from New Orleans, thus establishing Slidell early as a Crossroad. The impact upon Slidell was just as meaningful then as the opening of the Interstate System in the mid-1960s.

"Early on," stated Charles Fritchie in his UNO Courseworks, "Slidell began to ripen in its Crossroad evolvement. An instance of transcending from its diminutive past was the significance of the *Triangle Station*. As this major gas pumping service outlet in Slidell, the Triangle Station was *where all the action was*. It had become much like the Train Depot had been prior to the introduction of automobiles. It became the major stop-off and meeting place for tourists and visitors alike. During weekends, easily 50 to 100 cases of Coca Cola were sold by youthful car hops. The *Triangle Station,* had its beginning as a two-pump station, but with increased traffic, added a weather-free service canopy and three more gas pumps."

Slidell became a major stop-over for the *Old Spanish Trail* celebrations and motorcades which journeyed from St. Augustine, Florida to San Diego, California. The cross-continent drive also dedicated Highway 90 as a cross-country transportation route. The Highway was named the *"Old Spanish Trail"* for that purpose alone. However, this resulted in many cities maintaining that name as it routed through their corporate limits.

At that time, roads north of Slidell were in distressful condition.

Tree Surgeon Carl Glass

"I was about 4 years old when I moved to Gause Blvd. in the 50s. Then, the gravel street was just wide enough for two cars and often my dad used to pull aside to let the other car pass by."

"One evening my mother looked out the window of our house and said, 'I wonder who is driving by at this time of night?' .., she looked at the clock, it was 6pm."

"We use to leave our front door open and the screen door unlatched even when we left for a couple of hours. My dad was a grocer, if a strange car passed by he would jump in his car and follow them to their destination -- one case in mind was to Mr. Hingle's. When my dad got home he called Mr. Hingle to verify that he had visitors. "Everybody looked out for each other!"

Gause Blvd was widened in 1968.

Highways U.S. 11 and U.S. 90 became the first nationally paved roads to serve the city. This enabled tourism to become one of Slidell's newest and foremost industries.

U.S. Highway 90 in Louisiana (US 90) runs through southern Louisiana for 297.6 miles, serving Lake Charles, Lafayette, New Iberia, Morgan City, and New Orleans. Much of it west of Lafayette and east of New Orleans has been supplanted by Interstate 10 (I-10) for all but local traffic, but the section between Lafayette and New Orleans runs a good deal south of I-10.

The current US 90 route has replaced almost all of the original Louisiana section of the San Diego/St. Augustine Old Spanish Trail. (*"Old Route 90" from New Orleans to Pearlington was built in 1924.*) For a number of years, it was also designated Louisiana Highway 2 until the 1955 renumbering took hold.

U.S. Highway 11 runs from New Orleans along the railroad line that brought many travelers through Slidell who were on their way to the Mississippi Gulf Coast and Alabama. U.S. 11 ran through the middle of town along Pontchartrain Drive and Front Street, while U.S. 190 came down Fremaux Avenue from the east. The only traffic light was at Front and Fremaux at a time when the railroad depot's primary purpose was to conduct train traffic.

U.S. Route 190 is an east west United States highway in Louisiana and Texas. It evolved from the shortest of intrastate routes in 1926 to a length comparable to a main Interstate Highway route, leading from the swamps and pine forests of Louisiana to the West Texas desert.

In 1937, U.S. 190 took over the original route of U.S. 90 from Slidell to the Rigolets Bridge (along current U.S. 11 and LA 433) when that highway assumed its current routing into Mississippi.

U.S. 190 was given its current eastern terminus at U.S. 90 in the 1940s, following what is now U.S. 190 Business (Fremaux Avenue) through Slidell until the 1970s when it was shifted onto Gause Boulevard.

Louisiana Highway 433 (LA 433) is a state highway in Louisiana that serves St. Tammany Parish. It spans 14.8 miles in a west to east direction. It is known at various points from the West as Thompson Road, then Bayou Liberty Road– and East of Pontchartrain Drive, it

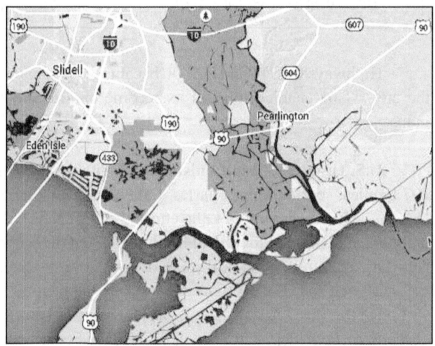

Current 2014 Map of Slidell area showing major highways.

is known as Old Spanish Trail, and Rigolets Road.

A number of the roads that run east from Front Street and the Railroad, such as Gause Road and Brown's Switch Road, were originally light rail lines that ended at the Pearl River Swamp.

Fremaux Avenue was extended to Salt Bayou opening a recreational area at Apple Pie Ridge Road for swimming and fishing.

In 1973, Third Street was widened, and in 1975, it was renamed in honor of one of Slidell's Police officers killed in the line of duty. It is now called *Sergeant Alfred Drive* for the slain African-American policeman.

In 1971, **Interstate 10 (I-10)** was opened into Mississippi that provided a vital link with the area which included the NASA complex. In the mean time, the stretch of Interstate 12 was in progress of completion to Baton Rouge, providing a vital link with that area. Cross country travelers were welcomed by the inclusion of the huge Union 76 truck stop terminal at 1-10, now the Interstate Travel Center.

The Interstate 10 interchange brought about a major transformation with a proliferation of businesses being developed. This resulted in the need for beautification ordinances to prevent the previous helter-skelter appearance along Slidell's main thoroughfares.

Since the opening of the complete Interstate System, north and south, east and west, considerable population increases and subdivision developments have taken place. Property values rose and residential homes could not be built quickly enough, speculative construction had also risen sharply and new businesses thrived. Commercial chains and franchises became apparent and are here to stay.

Along with new constructions taking place, payrolls were increased. And real estate developed with the first lot sales at Eden Isles.

For nearly half a century, until the completion of Interstate 10, U. S. Highway 90, or the "Old Spanish Trail," along the Mississippi Gulf Coast remained the highway link between New Orleans and Mobile. After the completion of the interstate the portions of Highway 90 inside the coastal towns became local traffic thoroughfares and the appellation "Old Spanish Trail" virtually disappeared except for an occasional sign marking a street or a business.

The "Old Spanish Trail" is making a comeback - with a goal of reviving tourism in cities and towns along the way. Plans are being made to have re-enactments of the motorcades that took place beginning in 1925 and officially rolled from Florida in 1929;— in celebration of a Centennial of events.

Bridges – Hwy 90 (*Chef Menteur Hwy*)

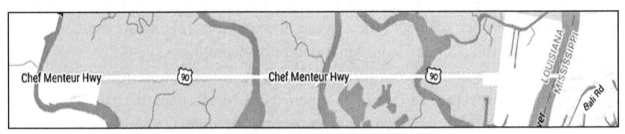

East Pearl River Triple Span Swing Bridge. On entry from Mississippi read "Hello Huey" and on exit from Louisiana read "Goodbye Huey" as a point of humor.

Two-lane truss swing bridge built in 1926, crosses East Pearl River into St. Tammany Parish.

Pearl East Middle

Pearl West Middle

Triple-pony-truss bridges cross each of the three middle-Pearl tributaries.

A two-lane lift bridge crosses over the West Pearl River.

Traveling southwest, U.S. 90 reaches the original Old Spanish Trail Louisiana 433 junction that ties into U.S. 90 just east of the Rigolets Bridge. This highway travels northwestward 6.4 miles to Interstate 10 and Slidell.

The Fort Pike/Rigolets Bridge was constructed in 1930. Paralleling to the north is a new fixed high-level bridge for U.S. 90 which was begun in October 2004 at a projected cost of $20 million. The Rigolets marks the eastern edge of the city limits of New Orleans. The bridge was planned in 1927 and opened to traffic on June 9, 1930.

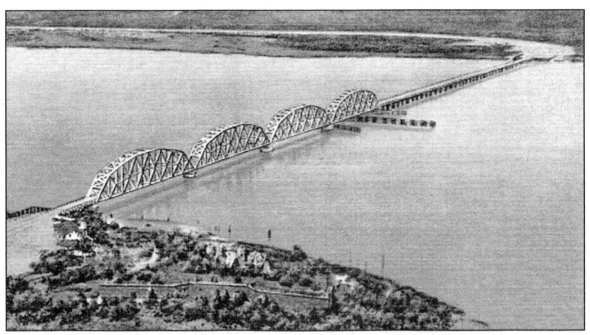

1950s View of Fort Pike and Rigolets bridge that opened in 1930.

2007 — Fort Pike with view of new Rigolets bridge in upper distance.

When the **Chef Menteur Bridge** opened in September 1929, with the Rigolets bridge, a free route was provided between New Orleans and Bay Saint Louis, Mississippi. Plans for a crossing here first arose as early as 1918.

U.S. Route 11

US 11 is a north south highway extending 1,645 miles across eastern United States. Its southern terminus is at U.S. Route 90 in the Bayou Sauvage National Wildlife Refuge in eastern New Orleans. US 11 was created in 1926, terminating just south of Picayune, Mississippi at the Pearl River border with

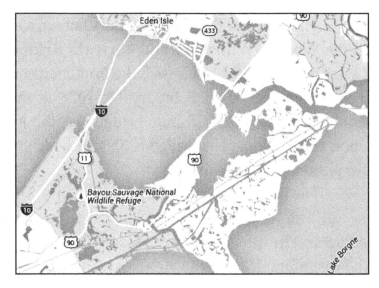

Louisiana. It was extended through Louisiana after the construction of the Maestri/Five-Mile Bridge.

Maestri/Five-Mile Bridge was billed as the longest concrete bridge in the World.

Maestri/Five-Mile bridge – paralleling the railroad bridge.

The **Maestri Bridge** (originally known as the **Pontchartrain Bridge** and later as the **Watson-Williams Pontchartrain Bridge** and the **Five Mile Bridge**) carries U.S. Route 11 (US 11) across Lake Pontchartrain between New Orleans and Slidell. The bridge opened on February 18, 1928 as the first permanent crossing of Lake Pontchartrain. The 4.78-mile bridge was the longest concrete bridge in the world upon completion. The bridge is 35 feet wide and has two bascule-type draw spans for passing vessels and barges.

The bridge was originally a toll facility, but Governor Huey Long was opposed to toll bridges and offered to have the state purchase the bridge from its private owners. The offer was rejected, so Governor Long constructed two free bridges to the east along U.S. Route 90 across Chef Menteur Pass and the Rigolets Pass.

With a free alternative, the toll bridge faced financial ruin by its investors Eli Tullis Watson and George Elliot

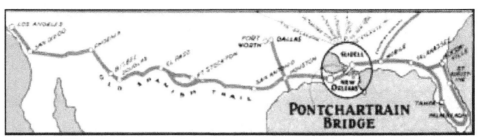

The bridge was touted as the longest concrete bridge in the world.

Williams and was sold to the state in 1938 for $940,000 (*thus, the Williams-Watson Bridge*). Following the purchase, the bridge's name was changed to the Maestri Bridge, named after Robert Maestri, the mayor of New Orleans. U.S. Route 11, formerly co-signed with U.S. Route 90 across the Chef Menteur and Rigolets Bridges, was re-routed onto the Maestri Bridge around 1941.

In 2005, Hurricane Katrina virtually destroyed the I-10 Twin Span Bridge to the east. However, due to its sturdy construction, the Maestri/Five Mile Bridge was largely undamaged and was the only route to New Orleans from the East until the I-10 Twin Spans could be temporarily fixed.

The Maestri/Five Mile Bridge was closed for $5.7 million repairs in 2012 to rehabilitate the bridge's railings.

State Highways
433
1091
Military Road
U.S. Highways
Hwy 11
Hwy 90
Hwy 190
Interstate I-10
Interstate I-12
Waterways
Lake Pontchartrain
Bayou Bonfouca
Bayou Paquet
Bayou Potassat
Bayou Vincent
Bayou Liberty

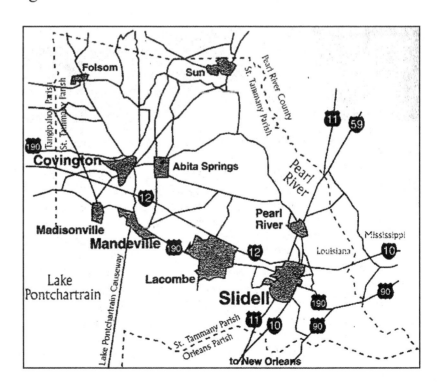

Leadership at the CrossRoad

An Evolving Olde Towne
As related by Pete Pravata

Pete Pravata remembered Front Street as the central part of Town during the late 1800s to mid-1900s. According to his recollections, the street basically started at the ice house at its north end. Heading south from there he remembered Harry Hoyle's Saloon and a two-story building located next door. Both of these buildings fronted the depot.

Just down from there was Edward's Restaurant (Old Slidell Garage and Ford Dealer) and a gift shop. Both Hoyle's and Edward's later burned down.

Continuing southward, Pravata referred to the intersection of Front and Teddy Avenue as Cornibe's corner where a package liquor store was located with *Cornibe's Livery Stable* located in the rear.

Crossing Teddy Avenue there was a two-story building which housed *Scat's Hamburger Joint and Bar* with rooms-to-let upstairs (This building was later replaced by the current two-story brick structure now housing the East St. Tammany Chamber of Commerce).

Pravata also remembered the large two-story *Commercial Hotel* on the southeast corner of Fremaux and Front streets operated by Mrs. S.H. Lott.

Next came the old *Triangle Square* followed by *Alphonse Sharp's Building* (he operated a taxi service and then later *Sharp's Coffee Shop.)* Still further down was *Gardner's Furniture Store* which was located Levy's Furniture Store and Currie's Bar now stand today. Near the next corner was *Mr. Landry's place of Entertainment*, followed by the Saraille place and next door was J.W. Decker's two-story home.

The *Langston Drug Store* Corner before the 1920s, was a private home. It later became a favorite pharmacy/soda shop, but had to be razed in 1981. It had been operated by Joseph Calvin Langston, Sr. until 1941, when his son, Langston, Jr. took over.

Pravata also mentioned that the *Bank of Slidell* and the *Masonic Building* were just north of the Philip Haddad home and store which were located at the corner of Front and Robert.

Just across Robert Street was the *Charles Biondo Fruit Stand* and home. Pravata referred to it as the *White Kitchen corner*.

The next major intersection that Pravata recalled was *Salmen's corner* or Commissary, with the Salmen home located just across Cleveland Avenue.

And the last intersection on Front Street is what Pravata called the *Conoco corner* (referring to the gas station that once occupied the spot). He said that was the area where the Liddle home had been located. Old maps indicated that it was Liddle Avenue which intersected with Front St. (today called Pontchartrain).

According to Pete Pravata's news column of July 18, 1971, the town's energy center was composed of *Dr. Polk's Drug Store,* Mrs. *McDaniels' Store,* Walter *Abney's Bakery, Levy's Market* was next door, across the street was Sam *DiMecili's Fruit Stand.* Around the corner was Andrew *Carollo's Store and Fruit Stand* across the street was the *G.A. Mire Store* and in the mid-block was Pete *Lalumia 's Picture Show* and across from there was Uncle Pete *(Pravata's) Candy Store* next to the *Champagne Store.* Behind the *Slidell Bank* was Mrs. *Jahrus' Open Airdrome* Picture Show. In the *DiMecili Building* was Ben *Giordano's Shoe Store* and the *Slidell Savings and Homestead* was located in the *Carollo Building* where the *Haas 5 & 10 Store* was later located.

In 1929, J.B. Spence from Mississippi opened a service station and café at 2859 Carey Street (later replaced by the St. Tammany Paint and Color building.) While expanding, Spence opened the *Curve Inn* at Front and Pontchartrain streets which was later sold to Wayne James. A few years later, Spence started a new restaurant which was also very successful and was sold to Sam Bosco in 1943.

E.N. Haas is shown here in his 1900's office at New Orleans. E.N. with his brother S.J., were raised at "the Kiln," Mississippi. E.N. had been very successful with the timber and kerosene business in Hancock County, but in 1906, with the down-sizing economy, a hurricane, governmental interventions, and the death of his wife, caused E.N. Haas to move to an area just northwest of Slidell where his homestead became known as *Haaswood,* as it is still called today.

A school building had been built there which in 1912, was converted to a lumber store, and years later converted to a general merchandise store managed by his two sons, Michael and Arnold. Other retail outlets were opened in Slidell such as the *Haas 5 & 10-Cent Store* in 1950, a first of its kind in Louisiana, and the *Haas Fabrics Store* was opened in 1962 as a one stop sewing center.

At that time, Willie Rousseaux's milk cows were pastured in the area bounded by Highway 11 and Carey and Kostmayer streets.

In 1928, the Hwy 11 bridge (also known as the Watson-Williams Toll Bridge) crossing Lake Pontchartrain was completed and brought increased traffic and further expansion to Slidell.

In 1929, the Stock Market crash began to show its affects on Slidell's economy.

City Expansion

From 1925 to 1938, Slidell started providing the infrastructure for water lines, sewerage, paved streets and the first Fire Truck. This opened the doors for subdivision expansions with some of the early developments promoted by Onesime Faciane and Pete Pravata.

In 1954, Faciane bought the Bonfouca Hunting Club that he converted into the 300-acre North Shore Beach Subdivision. His son-in-law, Eddie Carr, was in charge of dredging the marshlands that were part of another 1400 acres purchased for further development by Faciane.

The Carolyn Park Subdivision was named for Pete Pravata's first daughter, also naming its main street "Maris Stellar," an exalted tribute to his daughter for having become a nun. All the other streets were named for his favorite saints in keeping with his profound Catholic faith.

In 1963, West Hall was paved, part of which was paid for by Pete Pravata as it provided him an easy access to his Carolyn Park subdivision.

Leadership Heritage

Pete Pravata
Long active in Community programs

Pravata was an activist and promoter for community development as it pertained to roads, highways, bridges, etc.

Telling it like it is!, that's what people knew about Pete Pravata. His Christian morals, patriotism, common sense, and business success melded to make him a devoted political servant. He constantly urged others to get in the stream of action for the betterment of Slidell.

In a persuasive and firm manner, Pete, although limited to eighth grade education, became a newspaper columnist for the Sunday editions of the *Sentry News* starting in May 1971. That decision became the story of his life as well as a history of Slidell, as he related it.

His folks arrived from Palermo, Italy and had first settled in Pearlington, Mississippi where Pete was born in 1904. After moving to Slidell, Pete's first job was shining shoes at age 7 in his dad's barber shop located in the rear of *Polk's Drug Store*.

They eventually moved the shop and added a fruit stand located near the "old" depot south of the old Baker's Hotel (later known as *Slidell Hotel and Bar*). With his brothers, he helped develop an ever increasing newspaper distribution business which included the American Weekly, the Times, the States, and the Picayune.

Across from the "old" depot was *Harry Hoyle's Saloon* and next door the *Joe Pravata's Fruit Stand and Barber Shop*. Mississippians would drive over to buy liquor and cover the basket with fruit to conceal the contents during their return home.

Pete Pravata, life long resident of Slidell started selling cars at age 19, eventually owning his own new-car dealership for many years. He was a promoter for fire prevention having been one of the members of the "Human Bucket Brigade" in addition to his brothers and the taxi drivers and other employees. In 1926, better fire prevention equipment was employed and in 1952 the Slidell Fire House was dedicated and manned by a Volunteer Fire Department.

At the early age of 12, he learned respect for fire when the family business burned down including the *Headley Restaurant and Rooming house*. Mr. G. Neuhauser built a new building for them as his dad expanded into a 4-chair barbershop and housed other businesses which included Slidell's first taxi service which the eldest son, Lucian operated.

In the meantime, Pete, and his brothers established a peanut vending business along with other enterprises at the "old depot" across from the Ford Dealer and Garage. When the "new" depot opened, their peanut enterprise expanded so much that they were hiring 20 to 25 young boys of their own age at 20% commission. But, when Neuhauser built another building away from the Depot on Fremaux and Second Street; having relocated to the new building, the move became a disaster to the "Peanut and Paper" vending business. Pete learned the lesson of Location, Location, Location.

Following World War I, Pete's father moved their businesses back to the Depot area by purchasing "Triangle Square." His barber shop was where Cornibe's Barber Shop is now located. To Triangle Square, they added a mechanic shop, a pool hall, and a sandwich shop. By 1921, gasoline was added. As Slidell grew and traffic increased, their businesses expanded. The Pravatas added more gas pumps, an auto wrecking business, and ambulance services. They became the largest one-stop-super-service-station between New Orleans and Memphis.

The Triangle Service Station was the energy center and communication link for Slidellians and out-of-towners. This photo depicts the expansion of the station.

"The New Orleans business people and bankers (returning from weekend homes upstate and the Coast) ... had no way to get daily news until they hit Slidell Depot on Monday mornings. I would pile several hundred papers on the pavement, and they would actually fight to get a copy of the Times-Picayune," related Pravata.

Pete cherished the lasting friendships that were established with the "peanut sales crew" while growing up in Slidell, however, the "peanut and paper" business was eventually dropped. With the changing economy, the *Triangle Garage* started hiring young boys and men to pump gas, wipe windshields, check tires, check oil, fix tires, and to serve drinks. Pete realized that just as the railroad depot was the early nerve center, the Triangle Garage's auto traffic became the new "action center." Pete claimed that the Triangle Station, which was open 24-hours-a-day, became the *"Civil Defense Post"* for all emergency calls wrecks, fires, and general catastrophes needing ambulance services.

> *Telling It Like It Is!* was Pete Pravata's way of getting Slidellians to become aware of municipal needs in the expanding Community.

In 1927, with 400 light bulbs strung across its front, Triangle Motors was the brightest spot in town. In 1929, the cost of a gallon of gasoline was 12 cents.

Pete was also proud of mastering calligraphy (Spenserian Script) which he used extensively and was called on by many of his friends to make special invitations. At 19, he established his own auto dealership.

Onesime Faciane
A progressive and prosperous man.

Onesime, pronounced O-neh-ZEEM, was born in 1890 in the Bayou Liberty area and quit school after 5th grade to work in the Salmen businesses. During World War I, Onesime was general foreman for the Louisiana Shipbuilding Company and later became superintendent when the Canulettes bought the shipyard. In 1919 he opened an automobile dealership at the southeast corner of Carey and Robert streets. After he closed down the dealership in 1926, he opened a hamburger and sandwich shop on Front Street.

As a shipyard shop foreman, Onesime Faciane shows operating equipment to others.

As he became successful, he changed the name to *White Kitchen* and adopted the famed logo with an Indian kneeling at a campfire. He also did well by selling his special barbecue sauce throughout the South.

This photo shows the 1926 opening day of the *White Kitchen Cellar.*

This was the precursor to his White Kitchen chain of three restaurants that followed.

He continued his operations on Front street by building the massive two-story building which became the White Kitchen. Increased automobile traffic took place following the opening of Chef Menteur bridges and free ferry service.

In 1933, he built the White Kitchen at Short-Cut (Hwy 90), followed by another in New Orleans at the Claiborne and Poydras intersection.

Civic Activist

When Onesime Faciane served as a city councilman he pushed for sewerage and waterworks development – while serving four terms as mayor pro-tem.

He was also instrumental in bringing REA electricity to the surrounding area of Slidell by personally signing up many of the farmers and laborers. If they didn't have the required deposit, he put it up for them. He was well known for his generosity.

Homer G. Fritchie, Sr.
A Mayor for more than 3 decades

Perhaps the longest sustained mayoral administration in Louisiana's history, was that of Homer G. Fritchie. He served 32 years as mayor from 1930 to 1962 — often without opposition. Slidell benefitted from his ability and efficiency as an administrator and his dedicated love for the welfare of its citizens. With cautious foresightedness he monitored the city's growth while enhancing the status of the town for which he made many personal sacrifices.

Slidell was then a slow growing community as it approached the crossroads of expansion and development. Fritchie began his administration during the struggling Depression years of the 1930s and bridged the gap to Slidell's entry into the apex of space technology. The transition, although difficult at times, enured to the betterment for all Slidellians.

He was born in New Orleans, the son of Gustav and Mary Louise Fritchie; and as a young child, he occasionally stayed with his maternal grandparents, the Sollbergers; even having enrolled for a short stint at the Slidell grade school on College Street.

Following the death of his father in 1910, the family, including his mother and three brothers, were taken in by Mr. and Mrs. Albert Salmen, Homer's aunt and uncle. His mother, Mary Louise Fritchie was sister to Mrs. Albert "Elise" Salmen whose parents were the Sollbergers. At the age of 15, he once more enrolled in school at Slidell and worked at his uncle Fritz Salmen's brickyard. Receiving wages of 50 cents per day, working from six in the morning to six in the evening, his first job assignment was stacking bricks in the steam-dryer. After graduation in 1913, he entered Tulane University armed with a hard-earned engineering scholarship.

He quickly learned what it meant to be a daily train commuter as he traveled to the New Orleans Union Station to transfer via the St. Charles street-car to Tulane campus. Following his graduation in 1917, equipped with a Mechanical and Electrical Engineering

Homer Fritchie served eight consecutive terms as mayor — 32 years in all.

Degree, he was drafted into a U.S. Army Field Signal Battalion and served duty time in France.

Following his discharge in 1919, he became Chief Engineer for Salmen Industries and when faced with the cutting away of prime timber in St. Tammany, he was sent to Nicaragua, where the Salmen interests had expanded. There, he stayed until 1924, and returned to marry Nellie Bousquet and started his own engineering business, his first project being in Meridian, Mississippi.

On return to Slidell, he and his brother Gus, Sr., a lawyer, established "Fritchie Brothers," a real estate partnership which accumulated significant property investments including the rights to the unsold portion of the Guzman Tract. As a consulting engineer, Fritchie also specialized in the design and construction of creosote plants among other projects.

The Banana Republic It was the observant Homer Fritchie who, while in Nicaragua on lumber business for the Salmen Interests, had made Standard Fruit and Steamship Company investors aware of the vast banana plantations in Central America. When the forest lands were depleted of timber, the remaining 99-year Salmen lumber lease was conveyed to Standard Fruit.

In 1930, he was once again drafted, but this time by the two opposing political factions in Slidell who prompted his candidacy for mayor. During the height of the Depression, he immediately confronted Slidell's outstanding municipal debt exposure of $40,000. Undaunted, he, the City Council, and the Bank of Slidell rolled up their sleeves and worked their way through the dilemma to bring about economic stability.

Of the period from 1900 to 1945, former Mayor Fritchie commented that, "the population of Slidell remained around 3000, . . . (and) when I first became mayor, we had two policemen who furnished their own cars, and a street crew of six men." By 1954, the municipal census showed a growth to 5500 residents. With an eye to the future, Mayor Fritchie instigated the blanket ordinance for subdivision regulations and provisioned for water lines and sewerage systems. This vital infrastructure was already in place with the advent of NASA and I-10 highway construction. Fritchie always gave due credit as he explained that, "One of my happiest experiences of citizen and civic group cooperation was with the Priscilla Club and the Slidell Women's Civic League."

He served as an elder in the Presbyterian Church, and as a Mason, as well as a founding member of, or having held office in, the Lions Club, the Chamber of Commerce, and numerous Camellia societies.

In 1939, Homer purchased the old Fritz Salmen residence, which became a fine home for his then enlarged family of four daughters and one son. The home is now a Slidell heritage landmark.

To the grievance of family and all Slidell citizens, at the age of 82, Mayor Fritchie died on September 22, 1977. Lifelong friend, Mrs. Elizabeth Levy, stated, "He was a considerate Christian gentleman, generous and gave a lot of land for community projects – including the First Presbyterian Church and Trinity Presbyterian Church, and part of the land used by the Slidell Little Theatre, all of which were given by Homer and his brother, Gus A. Fritchie, and, in addition, he started a number of community organizations and clubs."

A.B. Plauche, former principal of Brock Elementary School, remembered him as a strong supporter of Slidell schools and that "he served as mayor for a dollar-a-year."

Former city councilman R.E. McDaniel in regarding his own tenure, 1958-1962, stated, "We had a $90,000.00 budget to operate the city, I never served on the council when the city was in debt . . . due to his (Fritchie's) superior management."

When Fritchie died, former mayor, Frank Cusimano placed a wreath on the city hall doors with a note which read, "Closed in honor of Homer G. Fritchie, Mayor of Slidell from 1930 to 1962."

Cusimano stated that, "Fritchie was a fine gentleman and a great man . . . I can look back now, and know that his thinking about this city and his philosophy of what it should be – have come true."

A Memorial to Homer Fritchie

Fritchie Park

Community Development

The City Halls

Each of the three domiciles of Slidell's city government still remain standing and continue to render a useful and worthy civic function.

• *(1889 - original Slidell jail and mayor's office was built for $275 at present location of 1907 two-story reconstruction - now Slidell Museum.)*
• In 1907, the "first" City Hall was erected as a two-story building on First Street, initially housing all the facets for running the city's services. Upstairs included the Mayor's office which doubled as a courtroom on Mondays and opened up to a large room for council chamber meetings. Downstairs was the Jail in the center, the Fire Engine House on the right, and the Water Works Department on the left. When the Police Department was moved into the Council Chambers, in January 1953, a construction bond issue was passed
• In 1954, the second City Hall was opened with twice as much space as the first (located where the new auditorium was built in 2012). Through the years, as the city continued its growth, renovations were made to accommodate needed variations. The first public library was also housed at this facility. By promotion of another bond issue, the Police Department was moved to its own station and jail located on Sgt. Alfred Drive.

Frank Cusimano was the first mayor to establish a "Mayor's Office" after moving into City Hall and relocating the Public Library to new premises.

• In 1973, the third City Hall, and current site, was established on Second Street where the former "Our Lady of Lourdes" school building was located.

The old "Sisters Convent" was also converted for use by the city's Purchasing and Permit departments *(Now, the G.O.S.H. Museum)*.

The clustering of these city halls and their continued ownership by the City of Slidell, either by wisdom or circumstance, has resulted in city government anchoring itself within Olde Towne and shoring up *Olde Towne* businesses and the local finance district of this quaint downtown.   As a unique Municipal Heritage Center, these three city halls epitomize the cycles of growth of very determined and resolute City Fathers.

Slidell has a Mayor-Council form of government. The governing council is responsible, among other things, for passing ordinances and adopting the budget. The mayor is responsible for carrying out the policies and ordinances of the governing council, for overseeing the day-to-day operations of the government, and for appointing the heads of the various departments. The council is elected on a non-partisan basis. Council members and the mayor serve four-year terms and are limited to two consecutive terms. Seven of the council members are elected by district. The mayor and the two remaining council members are elected at large.

Slidell Mayors
2009 Freddy Drennan
2001 Ben O. Morris
1985 Salvatore "Sam" Caruso
1976 Webb Hart
1962 Frank N. Cusimano
1930 Homer Fritchie
1928 Alonzo Badon
1924 A. D. Canulette
1920 G. A. Baker
1916 Alonzo Badon
1914 T. J. Hand
1910 P. J. Gardere
1904 F. A. Bourgeois
1900 O. L. Dittmar
1898 F. H. Sadler
1896 W.O. Wilder
1894 C.H. Lilon
1892 C.F. McMahon
1890 J. Cherry
1888 S.H. Decker

Katrina 2005

Hurricane Katrina caused catastrophic water and wind damage to Slidell. Approximately 51% of the city's land mass was inundated with up to 5 feet of storm surge causing flooding to approximately 5,600 residences and 700 businesses. After a slow start, substantially all residential and commercial rebuilding is now complete.

The city suffered extensive damage to its administrative buildings, equipment and infrastructure. Ten structures including city hall, the council chambers and the building that housed the jail and police administration were ruined by Katrina flood-waters. The jail, police administrative building, gymnasium, city hall and two administrative buildings were repaired or rebuilt within the first five years.

In March 2010, with bands playing and bright spotlights shining, Slidell and St.

Tammany leaders cut the ribbon on the $5.4 million Slidell City Council Administration Building.

"We've came a very long way since the disaster of Katrina," Council President Lionel Hicks told the large crowd gathered on Second Street. "It's just such an honor to be here."

The official opening of the building coincided with the city's first "Olde Towne Alive" block party of the year, rendering a real festive atmosphere as Hicks and Mayor Ben Morris cut the ribbon to the cheers Slidell residents.

The storm had destroyed the council chambers in City Hall and several other public buildings, forcing the city government to work out of a set of trailers on Bayou Lane.

The new building houses the City Council offices and its Chambers, the City Attorney, and Departments of Finance, Data Processing, Risk Management and Personnel.

In 2013 – FEMA provided $770,103.00 towards construction of the Slidell City Hall. FEMA had been charged with providing public assistance funding and grants to rebuild infrastructures destroyed by Hurricane Katrina.

As stated by Mayor Freddy Drennan, "Hurricane Katrina roared through the area – Slidell's progress on the road to recovery has been so remarkable that it's difficult for those unfamiliar with our community to notice the remains of Katrina's detritus in our city."

Center Entranceway

Post Office

The first post office was established on January 7, 1884 with Jacob F. Hufft as postmaster, which reportedly was located at the train depot.

Local citizen, Jeneva Gardere had recounted two later postmasters, A. J. Harding and Paul Gardere. She recalled, "I can also remember back to 1910, when I'd drive to the post office with a horse and surrey and pick up mail at the office in back of Mr. Polk's drugstore. Upstairs was the telephone company."

In 1999, Postmaster Anthony Milazzo stated that, "the station is no longer adequate to serve the needs of postal customers in our community."

-150-

In 1940, the Slidell postoffice was housed in the back of the Neuhauser Building on the corner of Front Street and Fremaux Avenue. The Postmasters were Ernest Jemison, Carson Miles, and Charles Block.

"There were no city routes in the early days because there were no street names and addresses," reminded Claude Lyon.

It wasn't until the 1950s, that city delivery was started when the Lions Club took on the project of naming streets and mapping out house numbers.

The next move was in the early 1950s, when the postoffice was located on the corner of Pennsylvania and Front streets. Residents were served by acting Postmasters Claude Lyon and Ethel Cullerton who were followed by Postmaster William Bulcao in 1958.

The post office was moved during the 1960s, to the corner of First and Bouscaren into a leased building providing 6,500 square feet. William Strecker became Postmaster in 1967, and was followed by Frank Gerald in 1981. When this post office building was vacated, it was sold in 1988, and became "The Regency."

In 1982, the fifth post office location was established in its present quarters on Second Street, while a second post office to serve the city was opened as the Westside Slidell Postal Station on Highway 190 in July 1988.

In order to handle the growing volume of mail, in 1998, a third post office facility was being reviewed to serve the eastern sector of the city. Slidell's 1999 population was estimated at 32,000 with an equal amount in the adjoining outskirts.

2015's Post Office locations are at: 1950 2nd St, Slidell, LA 70458; 1897 Gause Blvd W, Slidell, LA 70460, and 2250 Gause Blvd E, Slidell, LA 70461.

Postmasters since 1946

Name: Title: Date Appointed
Ernest S. Jemison Postmaster — Charles D. Block Acting Postmaster 09/30/1946
Charles D. Block Postmaster 06/16/1948
Claude E. Lyon Acting Postmaster 06/30/1951
Mrs. Ethel R. Cullerton Acting Postmaster 03/08/1957
William A. Bulcao Postmaster 07/24/1958
William I. Strecker Acting Postmaster 04/30/1967
William I. Strecker Postmaster 04/04/1968
Louis D. Guillory Officer-In-Charge 06/28/1981
Frank J. Gerald Postmaster 11/28/1981
Norbert T. Galivan Officer-In-Charge 07/28/1989
Glen Boquet Officer-In-Charge 01/11/1990
James F. Taylor III Postmaster 02/10/1990
Stuart A. Schayot Officer-In-Charge 04/26/1995
Alan Cousin Sr. Officer-In-Charge 07/24/1995
Anthony J. Milazzo Postmaster — Rachel F. Cousin Officer-In-Charge 10/13/1999
Bernard J. Moschitta Officer-In-Charge 01/13/2000
Steven Swartz Officer-In-Charge 05/12/2000
Earl J. Champaign Jr. Officer-In-Charge 09/05/2000
Earl J. Champaign Jr. Postmaster 12/16/2000
Edward A. Van Vrancken Officer-In-Charge 01/31/2006
Gregg P. Felger Postmaster 06/24/2006
Richard J. Palisi Jr. Officer-In-Charge 03/07/2007
Donald R. Hotard Jr. Officer-In-Charge 05/10/2007
Doland G. Pichon Officer-In-Charge 03/17/2009
Ray E. Phelan Officer-In-Charge 05/11/2009
Nickolas S. Piazza Postmaster 08/29/2009
Michael F. Hubin Officer-In-Charge 04/25/2010
Ray E. Phelan Postmaster 08/14/2010

Fire Fighting

According to Pete Pravata's records, the Volunteer Fire Department started as a "Bucket Brigade" in 1923, until a fire truck was purchased in 1926. From their business at the *Triangle Garage,* the Pravatas played a significant part in its founding. Of Pete's brothers, Carol was Fire Chief and Joe performed all necessary mechanical services, and Pete, with some of the employees, filled the ranks of firemen workers.

At that time, the city's fire truck was stored at the *Triangle Garage* service station. On one occasion the building caught fire while the fire truck was parked inside. Needless to say, due to quick action on the part of the volunteer firemen, the truck was saved. The Engine was a 1926 American LaFrance 500 GPM pumper – later stored at Central Station when it was constructed.

During earlier times, the Volunteer Fire Department when alerted that a citizen reported a fire, a volunteer would run to the *Carroll Building* on First Street to push a buzzer that sounded the alarm signal. A coded system was contrived. If the alarm sounded twice, the blaze was in the north end of town; three buzzes was for a mid-town fire; and four buzzes for the south end. When volunteer firemen heard the alarm, they would race to the engine house at city hall on First Street and take off to the area indicated by the buzzer coded sounds. Upon arriving at the predestined sector of town, they would then look for smoke.

On another occasion, the costly grammar school building fire of February 1951 brought out support fighters from Covington and Picayune, but to no avail. Very few classrooms were saved.

B.T. Carroll was appointed the first official fire chief of the organized Slidell Fire Department.

In 1964, while Pete Pravata was a commissioner with the St. Tammany Fire Protection District #1, he contributed part of his property in the Carolyn Park subdivision for use as a fire station west of the Southern railway tracks, located on Carroll Road off Hwy 190. Dedicated in September 1966, the Fire Station was named for Peter D. Pravata.

> **Pete Pravata**, life long resident of Slidell started selling cars at age 19, eventually owning his own new-car dealership for many years. He was an eager promoter for fire prevention having been one of the members of the "Human Bucket Brigade" in addition to his brothers and taxidrivers and other employees. In 1926, better fire prevention equipment was employed and in 1952, the Slidell Fire House was dedicated and manned by a Volunteer Fire Department.

The Slidell Volunteer Firemen's Association became very active and recruited newly motivated members. Mr. Emile Oulliber was elected President of the association and appointed a committee to form a Fire Protection District as defined by the State of Louisiana. On January 17, 1952, the Police Jury of St. Tammany Parish approved the creation of St. Tammany Fire Protection District No.1 and defined its boarders. A vote of the public confirmed the creation of St. Tammany Fire Protection District No. 1 on June 18, 1952. It is from these beginnings that St. Tammany Fire Protection District No. 1 was created to protect 60 square miles of the greater Slidell area.

> **Volunteer Chiefs**
> Carl Pravata 1926-1937
> B.T Carroll 1937-1952
> **Paid Chiefs:**
> Jim Decker 1952-1957
> Gayle Van Gilder 1957-1974
> Spencer Deyo 1974-1978
> Edward Poppler 1978-1999
> Albert Lee (Acting) 1999-2000
> Milton Kennedy 2000-2004
> Larry Hess 2004-2013
> Dave Kuhn (Interim) 2013- 2014
> Chris Kaufmann 2014-Present

The Central Station was built in 1952 for $42,000.00 housing three trucks. Slidell's two auxiliary fire stations were built in 1966 and 1968, each having two fire trucks.

Volunteer companies included the Slidell Volunteer Firemen's Association, the Bayou Liberty Volunteers, the Kingspoint Volunteers, the Northshore Volunteers and all City of Slidell employees. Chief Poppler eventually required the volunteers to merge.

Katrina

During Hurricane Katrina and the aftermath, even with four of the district's seven stations severely damaged due to the flooding, firefighters continued to staff their stations. They worked out of apparatus bays and slept in RV's until station renovations were completed. In less than one year, each of the seven stations was completely renovated.

The headquarters building on Old Spanish Trail was sold and the property at 1358 Corporate Square was purchased to house the Department Headquarters including the Fire Chief, Chief of Administration, the Information Technology, Fire Prevention and Administrative staff.

Flood waters in Olde Town Slidell had poured into the A.J. Champagne Fire Station 11 at 322 Bouscaren St. —
This photo shows renovations as appeared in 2008.

Longtime Slidell firefighter Chris Kaufmann was sworn in as fire chief of St. Tammany Parish Fire District No. 1., replacing Larry Hess, who retired after 10 years as head of the department.

Kaufmann was sworn in during January 2014 ceremonies at the fire district's newest station on Johnny F. Smith Avenue.

Police Department

Former Mayor Homer G. Fritchie related that, "In the early days, the entire Police Department consisted of two men. One day-man, and one night-man."

"There was no official police station, so when people had trouble, they called the *White Kitchen* on Front Street which had a panel of six lights in front of the building, five of them were for girls (car hops) and the last one for the police. The policeman on duty would drive by and if he saw the light on, he would go in and find out what and where the problem was."

By further comment on the security warning system, John Swenson added that, "An immediate response to an emergency just wasn't possible, you had to hope whatever your problem, you could wait a while."

Katrina

The devastation wrought by Hurricane Katrina spared no one – even those who protect and serve the community. FEMA funded the rebuilding of the Slidell Police Department, bringing the facility to pristine condition.

Municipal Auditorium

A new Civic Building had been built in the 1990s at a cost of $110,000.

The main auditorium was used for all civic events and Teen Town activities. The building also provided offices for the mayor, tax collector, secretary and other city officials.

Many organizations held their regular meetings in the conference rooms.

Katrina

Following the hurricane, the city government fixed up the building as well as possible in order to provide a continuance of community events on an interim basis.

In the meantime, Mayor Ben Morris refused to accept FEMA recommendations to renovate the existing building and erect a concrete wall around it for future storm protection. Mayor Morris sought firm resolve with FEMA to get agency approval to pay for demolition and reconstruction of the auditorium.

Ultimately he secured FEMA's cooperation before he left office in 2010.

The new structure replaces the former auditorium that was built in that same location in 1953.

Ribbon Cutting Ceremony and Gala celebrated the opening of the new Slidell Auditorium

The new Slidell Municipal Auditorium made its debut at a ribbon-cutting ceremony in April 2012, marking a long-awaited milestone in the works since Hurricane Katrina nearly seven years prior. Sizeler Thompson Brown Architects designed the new 22,166-square-foot, two-story multipurpose community facility situated across from the new City Hall on Second Street. The total construction cost for the new auditorium was $8 million, with approximately $7 million funded by FEMA and the balance assumed by Slidell.

The *"Arts, Camera, Action!"* Gala, hosted by Slidell's Friends of the Arts organization marked the grand opening of the facility.

During the ribbon cutting, Slidell Mayor Freddy Drennan stated "Is there any other word to describe this facility than "absolutely amazing?"

The new Auditorium accommodates a wide range of activities ranging from Mardi Gras Balls and receptions to trade shows and school graduation ceremonies. The main auditorium seats up to 1,400 for a performance or up to 600 for a banquet. Meeting/ Activity Rooms are also provided, and have moveable partitions to allow for a range of functions from meetings to a use as dressing rooms.

The facility is designed and sited to form part of the new Slidell Municipal Complex in "Olde Towne" the Historic District of Slidell. Courtyards and plazas were developed as part of the integrated complex to host communal fairs and other activities.

Ronnie Kole, world famous pianist from Slidell, commented, "I have traveled the world doing concerts and shows and I didn't expect the Slidell Auditorium to equal the many performing arts centers that I've performed in ... The acoustics are wonderful and totally unexpected."

Slidell City Court

Slidell Cultural Center

The original building which housed the Slidell Cultural Center on Erlanger Street was formerly the public library. It was donated to the City of Slidell in 1989 by the St. Tammany Parish Police Jury for specific use as a cultural center. A public meeting room was added in 1991 which accommodated hundreds

of community group events every year. Seasonal cultural crafts and features of interest were always on display.

In March 1979, the *Mayor's Commission on the Arts* was established and during the years since, has undergone several name changes and evolutions. In 1985, it was called the *Commission on the Arts.* later, the *Department of Cultural Affairs,* and most recently, the *Department of Cultural & Public Affairs,* adapting to and taking on new charges in being responsive to citizen needs in a growing eclectic society.

The first director was Judy Hagan, followed in 1981 by Suzanne Parsons who had administered to many growth changes that had taken place. In 1985, *"Bravo!"*, a quarterly newsletter, was published to announce cultural and public matters of interest.

As part of the original structure, a Commission on Arts consisting of eleven members is appointed by the Mayor. There is also an Advisory Board. These volunteers provide leadership and expertise in addition to recommending public policy regarding the city's cultural outlook.

The year of 1999 served as the 20th year anniversary and Mayor Sam Caruso was the recipient of the *Bravo! Award.*

1999 Commission on Arts
Stephen Cefalu
Nick Kooney
Ric Davis
Dorable Dangerfield
Beth Gendusa
June Green
Graydon Hass
Dr. Elizabeth McBurney
Martin Needom
Nancy Rhodes
Dr. Russell Westfall

1999 Advisory Board
Ray Alfred
Janet Bernard
Judy Bolt
George Dunbar
Leo Ehrhardt
Elise Fritchie
Darlene Haik
Marie Ricca-Lasecki
Claudette Songy

Bravo! Award

The Commission on the Arts first began to honor individuals and organizations in 1988 with the BRAVO! Arts Award, recognizing outstanding contributions to the arts and cultural activities in Slidell and St. Tammany Parish.

Past recipients have included Mayors Salvatore A. "Sam" Caruso and Ben Morris, Ronnie Kole, Darlene Haik, John Perkins, Suzanne Parsons-Stymeist, Allen Little, George Dunbar, Nancy Rhodes, Carol Wolfram, Kevin Davis, Kathleen DesHotel, and Kat Bergeron.

In January 2013, Alex Carollo, a City of Slidell media specialist, was promoted to director of Slidell's Cultural and Public Affairs department.

The Department of Cultural & Public Affairs consists of two divisions:

The City boasts its own Concert Band, Civic Chorus, Youth String Orchestra, a cultural arts center, an historical museum, a theater, and an excellent library system with two branches.

The Cultural Affairs Division is responsible for fostering the arts, humanities, and cultural and city-sponsored civic events of Slidell. It operates the Slidell Cultural Center, the Slidell Museum, and the Slidell Mardi Gras Museum. It coordinates festivals and various events throughout Olde Towne and promotes local and national talent. Under the guidance of an advisory board, Slidell's Commission on the Arts, the division creates programming designed to showcase the power the arts to enhance the quality of life for our residents and visitors alike.

Slidell's Technology and Cultural Arts Center opened April 2011.

The Public Affairs Division is responsible for the dissemination of information, including the activities of the administrative and legislative branches.

Elected officials joining Mayor Drennan for the opening event were Senator A.G. Crowe, Representative Kevin Pearson, Parish President Kevin Davis, Parish Councilman Al Hamuei, members of the Slidell City Council, Police Chief Randy Smith

Duties include, press releases, managing the city's website and social media pages, public service announcements, press conferences, tourism and coordination of the above efforts with private partners.

Keep Slidell Beautiful *(located at 2700 Terrace, off Old Spanish Trail.)*

KSB is a Slidell government organization that became an official Keep America Beautiful affiliate in March 2007. KSB focuses on litter prevention, beautification, community improvement and waste reduction in the. Partnerships are developed through education and participation in programs and activities to improve the city's physical environment. KSB has worked with the mayor and city council to enact ordinances to improve the quality of life for residents.

Slidell Beautification Committee – 2014
Council Member, Kim Harbison, Councilwoman-at-Large
Council Appointment, Margaret Tingle, Chairwoman
Chamber of Commerce Appointment, Tammy Mitchell
Greater Slidell Council of Garden Clubs, Liz McHugh
Parks and Recreation Appointment, Jennifer Drennan

Slidell Senior Citizen Center

Following Katrina, seniors who had been gathering every day at the former Cousin Street center were displaced first to Macedonia Baptist Church and later welcomed by Mount Olive African Methodist Episcopal Church, both in Slidell's Olde Towne district. In 2009, while former Mayor Ben Morris was still in office, the city awarded a $2.2 million contract to demolish the damaged senior center and rebuild it. FEMA agreed to provide $1.83 million for the project with the city providing the difference.

A new 10,000-square-foot facility at 610 Cousin St. that replaced the former Council on Aging St. Tammany building was dedicated in March of 2012.

Slidell Cultural Center
City Hall Art Gallery

Airport

With the construction of the Pravata Airpark, Slidell gained its first airfield. During the height of World War II, on 200 acres of land, Pete Pravata, almost singlehandedly graded the field by using an auto-wrecker to tow railroad cross ties pulled behind it for leveling.

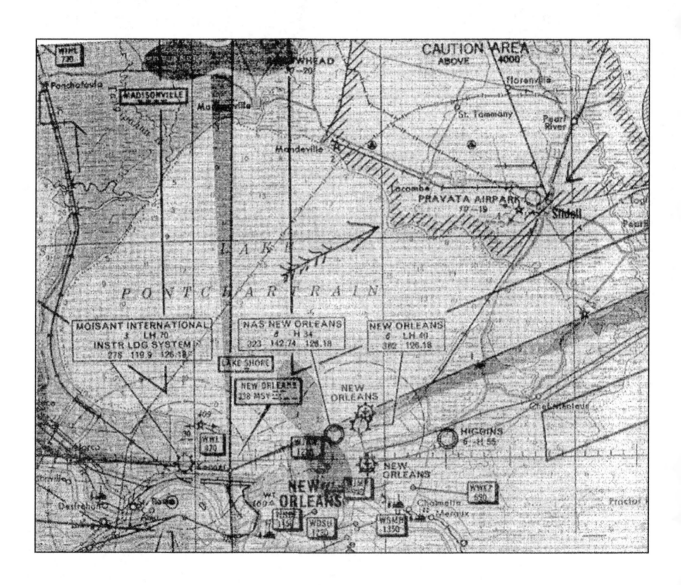

Civil Air Patrol

Realizing the necessity for preparing youth during their most retentive years for work that would help develop their future, far-sighted men such as Pete Pravata, sponsored organizations that would conserve and utilize youth power. The Civil Air Patrol program was structured to include Air Scouts and Wing Scouts, as well as CAP cadets. Through such groups, highschool students were encouraged to enroll and train in the use of flight equipment and airfield operations which included the Link Trainer and radio equipment.

After 15 years of service, Pravata finally closed down the airfield on August 20, 1959 due to the lack of continued local support. The closing left Slidell without an airport while other communities were stimulating the growth within their communities with renovations and expansions.

Civil Air Patrol 1948 Officers
Pete Pravata - Flight Commander
Earl Farmer - Assistant Commander
Rev. M.S. Robertson - Chaplain
Stanley Samrow - Adjutant
Philip Haddad - Supply Officer
Robert Toumier - Personnel Officer
John Pastoret - Training and Operations
Robert Warner - Communications Officer

Municipal Airport

The Slidell Municipal Airport is located approximately four and one-half miles northwest of the City of Slidell. The Airport consists of 350 acres with a 5,002' asphalt runway, and is lighted with medium intensity runway lighting. The Slidell Municipal Airport is home to one fixed-based

operation, 33 private hangar facilities, a National Weather Service Station, the Mosquito Abatement District #2 flying operations and Skydive N'Awlins. The Airport also supports two aviation organizations: the Experimental Aircraft Association and the Civil Air Patrol.

For the 12-month period ending April 15, 2008, the airport had 112,000 aircraft operations, an average of 306 per day. At that time there were 86 aircraft based at the airport.

Of several awards, the airport was recognized as Louisiana's Outstanding Airport for 1994. In 2015, the Slidell Municipal Airport received a federal grant of nearly $420,000 for taxiway sealant application.

> **Airport signals new positioning**
> *"An airport is as important to a community as a seaport, a railway station, or a major highway. The airport will become increasingly more important in the future. "*

"We are very pleased to receive this funding which will play a critical role in keeping our municipal airport safe and growing," Airport Manager Richard Artigue said in a news release.

Health and Hospitals

There appears to have been no early organized public health and emergency care system in Slidell. Most early hospitals, other than company run clinics, were organized by volunteer ladies groups such as the Circle of King's Daughters. These organizations spread nationally after the Depression years, and if Slidell didn't sustain one, then emergency treatment would have been at New Orleans' Charity Hospital.

Early practicing doctors were, Dr. Smith starting in 1890, and Dr. Joseph Polk in 1898; followed by Dr. A.L. Dubourge, Dr. J.A. Harper, Dr. J.G. Smith and Dr. O.E. Parker. One of Slidell's first nurses was Miss Janie Dunham, born on Pearl River and raised as a youth at Pearlington. After her father's death, her mother took her young family downstream to Gause Landing where they were transported to Slidell by ox-cart in 1885. Soon after arrival, her mother operated a boarding house with Jane helping out and tending to the other children. Urged to attend nursing training at Touro Infirmary, she was signaled out for her service and courage during the yellow fever epidemic of 1887. Following graduation in 1889, she remained in New Orleans until 1917 when she was employed as head nurse for the local Slidell shipyard. With the influenza epidemic of 1917, she took charge in supervising the conversion of the 3-story highschool at the present Brock School location. This was probably the first full-scale hospital in Slidell. Janie returned to New Orleans in 1921.

Today, Slidell has two acute-care state-of-the-art hospitals, a short-term psychiatric facility, and several long-term care facilities. Having over 200 practicing physicians representing virtually every medical specialty, eliminates the need to travel long distances for medical care. Two ambulance services provide both emergency and non-emergency transportation, enhanced by the 911 system.

Slidell Memorial Hospital

In 1956, a handful of interested citizens gathered at the city auditorium to discuss the feasibility of a community hospital. This resulted in a 30-bed hospital which opened in November 1959 known as Slidell Memorial Hospital. The gravel covered Gause Boulevard site, originally named East Hall Avenue, was donated by Mrs. Robert A. Jahraus.

> **SMH Medical Staff Executive Officers**
> Dale MacCurdy. M.D., President
> Vasanth Bethala. M.D.
> A. Foster Hebert. M.D.
> Thomas Hall. M.D.
> Esteban Romano. M.D.

Chartering physicians were Doctors John L. Kennedy, Richard R. Howard, Henry T. Cook, John C. Roberts, Louis A. Polizzi, Charles E. Farmer, and A. V. Friedrichs. The first Administrator, Thomas L. Qualey, reported 1,261 patient admissions for 1960.

> **SMH Executive Staff – 2000**
> Monica Gates. Chief Executive Officer
> Carolvn Greene. Chief Financial Officer
> Harvey Ganong. Chief information Officer
> Mark Diamond..Associate Administrator
> Kirk Soileau. Associate Administrator

The Candy Stripers volunteer group was organized in 1961, followed by the opening of the first blood bank, the first Nurses' Aid class, the 500th birth delivery, and an employee count of 120; all reported for 1962.

In 1964, a 21-bed rotunda was completed in addition to a 3-bed intensive care unit, an auxiliary power unit, employees' dining room, and supply storage facilities. This was followed by Dr. John Kennedy's request for a new 250-bed building due to the impact by the NASA population. This resulted in an 81-bed addition in July 1966 and SMH Accreditation in 1967. In 1977, 50 new beds were added with an increase of a 14-bed intensive care unit on the third floor level.

By 1988, a more sophisticated 182-bed community hospital had evolved to become a fully operational state-of-the-art facility with numerous specialty departments in force. A fitness Center, delivery rooms, a cardiology department, rehabilitation therapy department, a chemical dependency treatment program, a medical staff library, subsidiary clinics and other community services. These improvements had been put in place for the expanding citizenry.

A new 3-story, 54,000 square foot addition to Memorial Hospital celebrated the hospitals' 40th anniversary in November 1999. The modem medical office, 11-acre site adjoins the Defense Information Systems Agency will include parking for 600 cars and shuttle will transport across Gause to the main facility.

The new facility will house certain aspects of outpatient hospital functions in serving the growing need for managed care, and preventive and primary care programs.

In order to provide total medical care to Slidell and surrounding area residents, expansion has been aggressive in the last few years, engaging a staff of more than 1,000 full-time employees.

In 2013, expansion included 29 new beds to the Emergency Room and 38 specialized cardiac rooms to Cardiac Care.

Slidell Memorial Hospital celebrated its 55th anniversary in November 2014. "As a 229-bed acute care community hospital located in the heart of Slidell, La., we provide access to the latest treatments and technology and expert physicians."

The Economic Development Pioneer Award 2015
Slidell Memorial Hospital has been an asset to the community since opening in 1959.

In 2013, SMH made more than $30 million in capital improvements and increased payroll over $2.7 million as they added 38 full-time jobs. SMH is very involved in community events, hosting monthly lunch & learns and providing free medical screenings to more than 1,000 members of our community.

In 2013, more than 15,000 community members attended SMH seminars and health fairs. Each year, SMH also hosts major health education events, such as the Slidell Memorial Hospital Women's Health Alliance Fall Seminar, the Breast Health Symposium, the nationally recognized Fit as a Firefighter Camp and A Day for Girls' Health.

In recent years, SMH has expanded to include a Regional Cancer Center, a state-of-the-art facility that can treat 95 percent of all cancers right here at home, and an innovative Heart Center and Emergency Department to meet the needs of the citizens in our region. Each of these facilities utilizes technology that is unsurpassed in Slidell.

In addition to improving the quality of life in our community, Slidell Memorial Hospital has supported and participated in economic development as a pioneer in Slidell.

NorthShore Regional Medical Center

Opened in 1985, the 165-bed hospital has about 750 employees with a medical staff numbering over 250 physicians. Medical services include Obstetrics and Gynecology services, Neo-Natal Intensive Care, The Women's Center, Outpatient Diagnostics, Joint Care, Sleep Disorders, Pain Management, Pediatrics, a Surgery Center, and a Rehabilitation Center.

This 100-acre healthcare center offers a wide range of primary and specialized care services through two multi-specialty medical office buildings, a medical office park, an ambulatory surgical center, and a 15-bed inpatient rehabilitation unit.

Southern Surgical Hospital

Southern Surgical Hospital (SSH) is owned by local physicians, in partnership with Cirrus Health. Stealth surgery is performed in the integrated, image-guided suite, the first of its kind in the nation.

Specialties: Bariatrics, Cervical/Lumbar Spine, General Surgery, Neurosurgery

Facility Details: 57,000 square feet 6 operating suites, 2 procedure rooms 37 inpatient beds, 5 ICU beds, 2 sleep lab beds, 2 pain treatment rooms.

In 2015, Southern Surgical Hospital celebrated 10-years in the Slidell community. Remarkably, nearly half of the original 80 employees who started work there were still on duty. The 10-year-employees were assembled for a picture to commemorate the event.

(*Front row from left*) Nicole Brouillette, Theresa Becnel, Judy Adams, Angela Darby, Michelle Donnell, Amanda Fallon, Kelly Stein, Linda Rasnic, Phyllis Pavack, Pat Johnson, Louisa Brown and Juana Plaisance.
(*Second row from left*) Karen Causey, Mark Boeck, Lorraine Woods, John Guillot, Betty Kellar, Alice Hendrix, Kathleen Sturcken, Teri Lucas, Chanel Moten, Barbara Devoney, Brenda Fino and Debbie Johnson.
(*Third row from left*) Adrianne Urbano, Carolyn Griffin, Max Moseley, Jim Lovelace, Emily Fairchild, Brandi Darte, Joyce Hemelt, Kim Hendricks, John Nethery, Jason Ball and Mark Grush.
(*Photo courtesy of Slidell Independent*)

School System

As early as January 1891, there was an attempt to establish a pay school with Mrs. E. Gill hired as a teacher to 21 children. However, in time this endeavor failed due to a lack of continuing financial support. Later, Mrs. Gill returned from New Orleans once the Society of the Holy Name guaranteed her salary. The school was called St. Aloysius, and was open to all denominations at no cost, and was kept open ten months a year.

During these early years, education depended on private school masters. Such a person would travel from village to village, spending a few months in each locality. Also, some ladies would offer lessons in their private homes.

Quoting from a 1935 booklet prepared by Slidell High School; "It appears that the Linton family led in the establishment of one of the first of these private schools, using a small room on Bonfouca Street (now, Bayou Lane). Later, they built farther up the bayou on the location of what (was then the Heslin home). The school was directed by a Mrs. Spence, who divided the work according to grades, and gave a certificate to those completing the work offered. In time other schools were directed by Miss Mamie Powers at her home, and by Mrs. H.W. Rousseaux in what later became the Bourgeois home."

"During 1892, the Salmen Company interests established a private school in its community building located on College and Cleveland streets. Classes were offered under the direction of Miss Ellen Olsen followed by Mrs. Scotty Hughes."

The public school movement met with the usual difficulties. "While the Parish was offering salaries for teachers, there was no money provided for buildings or supplies.

This building still stands at original location.

Private buildings were used for a number of years and local citizens gave their time and money to supply other necessities."

"The first public school of record was established near the Henry Crawford place just off the Indian Village Road, which was then outside the city limits. Its one room was managed by Miss Mamie Rheams and later by Miss Amicker."

"The first elementary public school within the town of Slidell occupied the old Knights of Pythias Hall in the lower part of town (on Louisa Street, now Carey Street, near Mayfield). Six grades were taught in two cubicles formed by draping a curtain across the meeting room. The first elementary school principals were Mr. E.B. Shanks and Miss Sarah Hughes, assisted by Mrs. Bessie Simpson."

New School construction adjoining the Old School

A public school for Negro children was established about two blocks north of today's St. Tammany Junior High, near Fourth Street.

The origins of the first public high school began after 1900, with the addition of a high school curriculum to the elementary program. A four-room wooden building was purchased at the corner of Carey and Brakefield. It became Slidell's first public school. W.W. Fenton was principal from 1904 to 1908, followed by Dr. R.S. Crichlow, graduating its first senior class, in 1908; consisting of Ella Scogin

(Lee), Violet Holdsworth, Mollie Guzman, and Lena George (Scogin).

In 1910, Fritz Salmen and V.G. Neuhauser led a campaign to raise a $20,000 bond issue for construction of a new three-story brick building to accommodate 300 students. It was located at Carey and Brakefield streets, with C.E. Hooper as principal. In 1911, he succeeded in making it the only accredited high school in St. Tammany Parish.

In 1915, H.N. Baker took over as principal and established the school's first athletic program. By 1918, with work force increases during World War I, the school was enlarged to accommodate the influx of new students. Through the efforts of Mrs. D.G. Neuhauser as its first president, the Parent-Teachers Association was inaugurated.

In 1924, a new high school was completed where Slidell Junior High now stands at Third Street between Main and Pennsylvania avenues.

The Slidell Sun, in July 1924, stated that the New High School would be a modern facility complete with an auditorium and moving picture booth.

The former high school was designated Slidell Grammar School, which by 1939 was in need of extensive repairs. While classes continued to be held in neighboring buildings, a new grammar school was completed by 1942 with grades first through seventh.

1925- Slidell's first motorized school bus with Mr. Welsh and children, Lenwood and Mary.

Glynn H. Brock was principal of the grammar school in February 1951 when it caught fire. While being repaired, students were again distributed throughout parts of the town – at the Masonic Temple, the Scout Hut, the high school, the gym, and in the few saved rooms of the burned school. The American Legion, through an invitation by Commander A.G. Hinyub, also offered the use of its new building facilities.

The name of the school was changed in 1972 to memorialize Mr. Glynn H. Brock, who served as principal from 1932 to 1951.

On August 29, 2005, Brock Elementary School was severely damaged by Hurricane Katrina. Students were taught in modular trailers until the new school was opened on December 9, 2008 at the original Brakefield Street site.

Former school teacher, Laura Crawford, moved to Slidell as a child in 1905. After teaching 48 years, she recalled that her classroom population jumped from 35 students to 57 at the end of the 1961 school year. This was due to NASA employment in the area.

A long range study in 1998, revealed that the St. Tammany school system was expected to continue averaging close to 750 new students a year for at least five years. 1998 Parish enrollment figures were 31,954. In 2014, 38,193 students enrolled.

Slidell is known for having an excellent school system providing for the children of the city and neighboring communities.

"A sound education promotes community excellence," as is reenforced by Irma Cry, Executive Director for the Chamber of Commerce in 1998. She further stated, "I think most importantly St. Tammany has the best educational system in the state. To a lot of people, that's a major concern. And some of the cultural activities in the city make a difference to people as well."

Public schools in Slidell are operated by the St. Tammany Parish Public Schools. There are three public high schools in Slidell: Northshore High School, Salmen High School, and Slidell High School, and two private high schools: Pope John Paul II High School and First Baptist Christian School.

Salmen High School's football team won the 4A State Championship in 1994 and 1995. The girls' basketball team and baseball team went on to win state championships in 1996, bringing a total of three state championships to Salmen High School for the 1995-96 academic year. The football team garnered the state championship in 2001. Northshore High School's baseball team was the state champion in 2009, and the Northshore girls' swimming team were champions in 2009 and 2010. Slidell High School's power-lifting team finished as national runners-up in 2000. In 2001, the Tigers won the USAPL national championship, and followed it up with a third place finish in 2002.

2015 School Directory

Salmen High - 9 - 12 – 300 Spartan Drive
Slidell High - 9 - 12 – #1 Tiger Drive
Northshore High - 9 - 12 – 100 Panther Drive
Slidell Junior High - 7 - 8 – 333 Pennsylvania Avenue
St. Tammany Junior High - 6 - 8 – 701 Cleveland Ave
Clearwood Junior High - 4 - 8 – 130 Clearwood Drive
Boyet Junior High - 7 - 8 – 59295 Rebel Drive
Carolyn Park Middle - 4 - 6 – 35708 Liberty Drive
Little Oak Middle - 4 - 6 – 59241 Rebel Drive
Mayfield Elementary - Pre-K - 6 – 31820 Hwy. 190W
Honey Island Elementary – 500 S. Military Road
Florida Avenue Elementary -PreK - 6 – 342 Florida Ave
Cypress Cove Elementary - PreK - 1 – 540 S.Military Rd
Bayou Woods Elementary - PreK - 3 – 35614 Liberty Dr
Bonne Ecole Elementary - PreK - 6 – 900 Rue Verand
Brock Elementary - PreK - 5 – 259 Brakefield Street
Alton Elementary - PreK - 5 – 38276 North 5th Avenue
Abney Elementary - 1 - 5 – 825 Kostmayer Avenue

Private/Parochial schools
St Margaret Mary School, Robert Blvd.
Pope John Paul Ii Catholic High School, 1901 Jaguar Dr.
First Baptist Christian School, 4141 Pontchartrain Dr.

Houses of Worship

Early Worship

Local membership in various denominations of Christian churches was established between 1885 and 1900 according to historian Charles Fritchie. The white Protestant churches are presumed to have met first in a community building erected by the Salmen family on College Street located just below Bayou Potassat. As is evident, the early churches predominated within the area that today is known as Olde Towne.

The first Methodist Church building was at Guzman and Second streets, while the first Catholic Church was established at First and Bouscaren streets. The first Baptist Church building was on College Street, north of the Salmen building,

Through the years, the spiritual community of greater Slidell created strong and enduring churches to represent its various faiths.

Early Preaching
The World, the Flesh, the Devil were to be put under fire by the traveling preachers. The religious message was crudely lashed out with pulpit pounding and shrill emotions to meet the crudities of the place and time. Meeting tents were erected where services went on morning, afternoon, and night for weeks at a time. In between services, the women had cake contests and cook-offs providing food for sustenance while picnicking around the revival camp meeting. From these preacher sojourns, began the seed and stirring for higher spiritual and intellectual realizations.

During the late 1890s, a circuit rider named Kelly established the Methodist mission. In 1895, a new Methodist Church was built by Horace Rousseaux and Gus McKinney in the building just north of Salmen Park.

A Baptist Church was founded under the ministry of Brother O.D. Bowen, across the bayou from the Grammar School.

This was followed by the Presbyterians with John M. Williams, who provided space for other church congregations to worship for a number of years. The Episcopalians and Lutherans held their meetings in the Presbyterian Church until they were ready to build their own.

St. Peter's Catholic Church was founded about 1843 in Covington with missions established at Bonfouca, Bayou Lacombe and Chinchuba, – all were served by Father Adrien Rouquette.

In 1853, Rev. Timothy Flint, a Presbyterian minister, described the people as being, "poor and indolent, devoted to raising cattle, hunting, and drinking whiskey. They are a wild race, with but little order or morals among them"

Our Lady of Lourdes Catholic Church

Catholic Mass on the north shore was first performed during the 1850s, in private homes, or at the general store, by priests who commuted from New Orleans, or by committed missionaries who arrived by horseback. Reportedly, Slidell's first Catholic Mass celebration took place about 1885, at the home of Mrs. L. Lawler, mother of three daughters; Mrs. Kate Abel, Mrs. M. McDaniel, and Mrs. Mary Dubourg.

Father La Vacri supervised the first church building on a land grant just south of Old Town Hall.

The Our Lady of Lourdes cornerstone was laid on September 14, 1890, and a dedication Mass took place on November 24, 1891. The first Lourdes church had been built fronted by a tall iron crucifix which also served as its steeple. While in the adjoining school hall, Miss Eva Petrich served as the first teacher.

A 1915 Hurricane destroyed the church complex which was replaced with a new church, school, and convent that housed the Sisters of the Benedictine Order.

On July 8, 1917, the new enlarged, Our Lady of Lourdes Church was dedicated on the same site as the first.

Further school expansion took place with Father Bru and Father Pugh as they completed a new school at the south end of Slidell at its present location during the early 1960s.

First Baptist Church

The Slidell Baptist Church was organized with eleven charter members in its small wooden church that still stands today on College Street. That site was donated in 1892 by Fritz and Rosa Salmen, in whose home the first services were conducted. In 1910, the First Baptist Church moved to Carey and Robert Street with 92 members on land donated by the Neuhauser family (4141 Pontchartrain Dr).

It remained there until 1974, when the newly renovated structure was gutted by fire. With renewed spiritual energy, the congregation went about raising over a million dollars to finance its new First Baptist Church which

graces 20 acres of land at Pontchartrain Drive that was donated by Mrs. Rosa Salmen.

Pastor Hoyte Nelson established the priority for a Family Life and Education Center to house the pre-school, bible school, and family activity programs, which was opened in 1979. Alongside is a 3-acre lake that provides a charismatic setting.

First United Methodist

The church was originally formed on September 26, 1887, with 12 people following an exhilarating revival. Their first meetings were held in a building near the Salmen Brick and Lumber Co. – and a sanctuary and parsonage were erected at First and Guzman streets.

The congregation moved to First Street in 1905, with a later addition of an education building and parsonage.

In 1957, the church bought its current site at Sgt. Alfred Drive and Erlanger streets, across from Griffith Park.

The imposing architectural structures consist of the church, educational, and social buildings situated within a full-square-block.

The First United Methodist Church celebrated its centennial on September 20, 1987 with the placement of an official Louisiana Commemorative Historic Marker. As a part of the celebration worship services included a marvelous musical presentation upon its anonymously presented Zimmer pipe-organ. The organ,

433 Erlanger Street, Slidell

valued at $150,000, reportedly took two years to build.

First Presbyterian

1041 Ninth Street

With three members, on March 19, 1899, Evangelist John Williams organized the First Presbyterian Church. On November 26, 1905, the newly constructed church doors were opened to worship. Active groups at its Ninth Street location are the "Women of the Church" and "Men of the Church."

Mount Olive AME Church

2457 Second Street

The African Methodist Episcopal congregation conducts services in one of the oldest existing church buildings; located at 444 Guzman Street in Slidell.

The church building was moved from the corner of First and Bouscaren streets in the 1960s having previously been built for the Our Lady of Lourdes Church.

Aldersgate United Methodist

360 Robert Blvd.

As early as 1966, the New Orleans Board of Missions for the United Methodist realized the need for a church in the rapidly growing community and took the opportunity to purchase land on Robert Road. Their plans came to fruition in 1976, when a task force directed by Bishop Finus Crutchfield assembled to select a name for a new church and obtain temporary worship facilities and a parsonage.

Thus, Aldersgate United Methodist Church was born on June 27, 1976, followed by a charter service on October 3, 1976, by Bishop Kenneth Shamblin. With further growth, the first anniversary was celebrated in June, 1977, by moving to their present location. In 1979, the education building was added and in 1981, a 500-seat sanctuary was completed, followed by the multipurpose John Wesley Center, and in

1997, the Susanna Wesley Building. From its modest beginning, Aldersgate has grown to become one of the largest United Methodist churches in Louisiana.

St. Margaret Mary Church
1050 Robert Blvd.

A new parish was established by Archbishop John Patrick Cody in 1965, and was handed to Father Timothy Pugh even as he continued parallel duties as Pastor of Our Lady of Lourdes. In 1970, Father Richard Carroll was appointed Pastor following the death of Father "Tim."

In 1966, a school board was established in conjunction with the opening and operation of the new school plant. Mass was conducted in the school cafeteria until the first Mass was offered within the shell of the new church building that was erected in 1976. This was completed for Christmas of '76 with formal dedication by Archbishop Harman in January, 1977.

St. Genevieve Catholic Church
58203 Hwy. 433

Historic St. Genevieve was built in 1852 on property donated by Mrs. Anatole Cousin, who was an aunt of the famed poet-priest, Adrian Rouquette. The old church underwent renovations in 1914 and continued to offer Masses until 1958. The church was then moved to its present site on Hwy. 433.

St. Genevieve Chapel- Bell Tower

St. Genevieve was destroyed by Hurricane Katrina. A modern building was completed in 2012.

Like a number of churches in the Slidell area suffering Hurricane Katrina's wrath, St. Genevieve was heavily damaged.

St. Genevieve held its first Mass in the new building in January 2012

Starlight Missionary Baptist Church
2100 Second Street

Starlight Missionary Baptist Church of Slidell had its beginning in the year of 1878, and has continued to serve the needs of the Slidell community.

The land on which it stands was purchased in 1891, having its original church building destroyed by fire in 1920. In March 1947, the cornerstone was laid for the new church at the corner of Second and Bouscaren streets. With its rich history, the church is centered in the heart of "Olde Towne," displaying its greatness and the sustaining power of God.

Christ Episcopal Church
1534 Seventh Street

    With its start in 1906, Christ Episcopal first operated as a mission station served from its home church in Covington. In 1953, a plan of growth was inspired by Pastor Frederick Franklin. In 1958, Mrs. Carrie Comfort submitted its petition for Parish Status following the relocation of the church to Seventh Street.

Bethany Lutheran

1340 Eighth Street

The church is located at 627 Gause Boulevard and recognizes 1927 as its anniversary year for celebrating Lutheran services at Slidell. Bethany Lutheran has an active Ladies Aid, Women's Missionary League, and a Laymen's League.

Calvary Baptist

1615 Old Spanish Trail

On Easter Sunday of 1959, many of the original 181 charter members held their first congregational meeting in a vacant building on U.S. 190. Beginning with the acquisition of an $18,000 home for its first pastor, Rev. David Irby, the

congregation continued aggressive growth and utilized the first 3-acre land gift by Mr. and Mrs. George Mackemoth, at Faith Drive and Old Spanish Trail, formerly Rigolets Road.

Grace Memorial Baptist Church

58516 Pearl Acres Road

Grace Memorial, founded in1968, is a growing, loving, Christ-centered church on the New Orleans Northshore in Slidell, LA.

Cemeteries

• Guzman *(Our Lady of Lourdes Cemetery)*

John Guzman was laid to rest in the family cemetery near the site of his birth, a plantation that was located near the former Slidell Vo-Tech School.

Now a Catholic Cemetery, the Guzman Cemetery was donated to the Diocese, in 1926, and renamed Our Lady of Lourdes. It is located on Canulette Road off Hwy. 433 from Hwy. 11.

Our Lady of Lourdes Cemetery
Established by the Guzman Family

Jean Gusman died 15 Sept 1858

Our Lady of Lourdes Cemetery

His wife – Marie Veillon died 18 Sept 1844

Father Francis Balay erected   this crucifix in June 1930.

● *Photographs by William Blackwell*

● *Greenwood Cemetery*

One of Slidell's hidden historical gems, Greenwood Cemetery, can be found in the square bounded by Second, Cleveland, Guzman, and Carey streets. Located in Olde Towne

Slidell, Greenwood Cemetery, normally protected among the draping limbs of live oaks suffered damage during Hurricane Katrina including pushed over tomb stones.

Newly organized, the Guardians of Greenwood cleaned and restored most of the burial plots. The group hopes to develop a comprehensive plot map which will identify who is laid to rest in the cemetery, information that currently is unavailable.

Greenwood Cemetery
Originally owned by the Salmen Brick & Lumber company, the cemetery was donated to the city of Slidell in May 1951. The three Salmen brothers, Fritz, Jacob, and Albert including their parents, John F. and Katherine Lienhard Salmen and other relatives are buried in Slidell's Greenwood Cemetery .

Fritz Salmen and his wife Rosa Liddle Salmen

Photographs by William Blackwell

First Marker – John Albert Salmen and wife Elise Sollberger
2nd Marker – Jacob Salmen died in 1908 due to atrain collision.

● Dubuisson Cemetery

Some of the graves date back to the 1700s and was named for the original donor, Francois Dubuisson. It is located off U.S. 190 West accessing Thompson Road (LA 433) to Riley Road, then Dubuisson Road.

> The Dubuisson Cemetery can be found by taking Thompson Road, then a right on Reilly Street to Dubuisson Road to Dead End.

Upon the markers, headstones, and tombs of the Dubuisson Cemetery, can be found the etchings of Slidell's early beginnings. The first Dubuisson, Francois Dubuisson deMontferrier, arrived from France in 1721. He had one son, Guilluame, and a grandson Francois Bernardo Dubuisson. In 1778, he married Anne Charita (Caridad) Krebs at Mobile, AL. Several of their eight children had been born at Mobile before the move to the Slidell area where Francois received his first land grant in 1803.

It is *this* Dubuisson who provided the grounds for the "Old Dubuisson Cemetery," where his headstone reads below:
(Note: Judge Ellis reported his death as 1821)

Francois Dubuisson
Died latter part of 1700s
Donor of this cemetery
Grandson of Francois Dubuisson de Montferrier

His offspring married into family names such as the Nicaises, Pichons, and Galatases of the Slidell-Lacombe area. In turn, their offspring espoused persons with more names such as Carriere, Laurent, and Cousin.

The Dubuissons are spread throughout Louisiana, Mississippi, and Alabama, with heavy concentrations in DeLisle and Pass Christian, Mississippi and the Slidell area.

Photograph by William Blackwell

Information Resources

Current Books

Dan Ellis 2nd Edition

Dan Ellis 1st Edition

Arriolia "Bonnie" Vanney

Newspapers

The first newspaper in St. Tammany was the *Palladium* which was published in 1832 at Covington by Joseph Davenport. The paper was sold in 1833 to John Mortee and was resumed under Davenport's direction in 1839. This later became the *St. Tammany Farmer* in the late 1800s.

In *"Pichon's Diary"*, Francois mentions on several occasions during 1873, reading the *"Gazette"*. However, this may well have been a New Orleans newspaper written in French and brought in from across the lake.

The first newspaper published in Slidell was the *"Bugle"*. It made its appearance in mid-1892, with B.B. Garrison as its editor. Reportedly, it was a short-lived venture, since no copies have been uncovered.

Two more newspapers appeared. In 1897, the *"Slidell Item"*, with Messrs. Johnson and Foote, proprietors; and in 1899, the *"Slidell Brick"* was published. According to Judge Ellis, one issue of the *"Slidell Brick"* survives. Its Editor was an elementary school principal named E.B. Shank.

In August 1902, E.F. Bailey released the first issue of the *"Slidell Advocate"*. In February 1903, the *"Slidell News"* began publication.

By 1908, Slidell was again without a newspaper. With more failed attempts to publish the *"Slidell Journal,"* this organ was followed by the *"Slidell American"* in 1912.

The *"Slidell St. Tammany Times"* provided complete area and local news coverage for many years. It has been considered very supportive in advertising, reporting, and photographing of all local events.

The *"St. Tammany Farmer,"* Covington's newspaper, has many documented reports of the Slidell area and is considered a good heritage source — and, further, has been captured on microfilm.

During World War II, Milton Walch and A.J. Lanoux, Jr. published a sports page which continued for a few years after the war's end, with Walch producing a weekly called the *Slidell Ozone.*

The Slidell Weekly News started during the 1970s and is printed twice a week covering the local and cultural community news. (*May have ceased publication in the 2000s*)

The *Times Picayune* established its own branch offices and news bureau in Slidell with printing to St. Tammany circulation. The Times-Picayune published its last daily edition on Sunday, October 1, 2012 – making New Orleans the biggest city in America without a daily newspaper.

NOLA.Com is now the online version for news to St.Tammany, the NorthShore, and to Slidell.

Both *The News Banner* and the *Slidell Sentry News* stopped printing in 2013, having began publishing in the 1970s as suburban growth created a new demand for newspapers in St. Tammany Parish.

The *Slidell Independent* began printing in 2009 headed by Kevin Chiri.

The *Inside Northside* was founded in 2001 by M and L Publishing as a bi-monthly

The New Orleans Picayune newspaper was originally founded in 1837, by Amos Kendall. Selling it at the cheapest monetary denominator, which was the Spanish *medio real,* worth about 6.25 cents in U.S. currency. However, the French Creoles nicknamed the coin a "picayune", which was a French Piedmontese coin, the *picaillon.*

magazine covering St. Tammany and Tangipahoa parishes. It offers its print version as well as online services.

The Chamber of Commerce during the 1990s distributed the *Slidell Visitor Guide* which is printed several times throughout the year, as well as the *Slidell Magazine,* a monthly publication. With the popular use of computers, online publications and blogs offer information on demand. The East St. Tammany Chamber of Commerce currently prints its annual "Business Connection" listing its membership, annual events, and significant data. The Chamber now can be found on FaceBook and at its website.

St. Tammany Parish Library

In late 1946, the Covington Business and Professional Women's Club sponsored a Parish Library with Lucille Glisson chairing.

A committee was formed to establish a Demonstration Library and on June 2, 1950, the first members of the St Tammany Library Board was created with Miss Lucille Glisson of

> **Early mayoral support of Public Libraries**
> Abita Springs - Mayor Jon Leveson
> Covington - Mayor Emile Menetre
> Folsom - Mayor S.B. Dyess
> Mandeville - Mayor M.L. Hoffman
> Pearl River - Mayor Luther Crawford
> Slidell - Mayor Homer Fritchie

Covington as President, Mr. Glenn Brock of Slidell as Vice-president, Mrs June Boyet of Pearl River, Mayor John Leveson of Abita Springs, and Houston Tulley of Madisonville.

A plan was submitted and approved by the St. Tammany Parish Police Jury on January 18, 1951, with an overwhelming reception by a score of mayors and the towns they represented.

In continuance with public acclaim, on May 5, 1983, a parish-wide building program was put forth with a call for a $6 million construction bond program which passed in 1984.

This resulted in the Robert Road Library site selection on January 18, 1985. An earlier Slidell Library had been temporarily opened on June 9, 1950, situated at the former city hall and later, housed in its own building located on Erlanger Street. In 1989, that building was donated to the City of Slidell by the St. Tammany Parish Police Jury for specific use as the Slidell Cultural Center.

The St. Tammany Slidell Branch is the largest library and most used, offering over 85,000 titles, including books, audio tapes, video tapes, and CDs. The reference collection is excellent and includes many business oriented titles. The Library offers special services and programs directed to preschool and school age children.

The St. Tammany Parish Library system is considered one of the best in the state, and one that all Slidell residents can be proud of.

In July 2014, Branch Manager Nancy Little presided over a ribbon cutting in celebrating the renovations and new furniture in the 22,000-square-foot building at 555 Robert Blvd. that houses the library's 123,000-item collection.

Library Staff members were most helpful during the first edition of this book in 1998

I want to tell you that we continue to use your Slidell book at least weekly. Someone Regularly needs information on Slidell and your book is the most informal and easy to use book written to date.

I am now working in the Covington Branch so my work address has changed.

Best Wishes for the New Year,

Becky Taylor

Becky Taylor

The Book Sack

The Book Sack is located right off West Hall in Slidell having its start in 1991. It is owned by Judd and Betty Kintner, and also operated by Mary Lou Hilts. The local business features everything from mystery, romance, novels, manuals, gardening, cookbooks, Biblical, classical and more. Judd started the business when he retired from U.S. Customs. His wife is a retired teacher from Pearl River Jr. High.

The Internet

When the first edition of this book was printed, the internet was used mostly to email and for those affluent individuals who designed websites. That was before Ipads, smart phones and the proliferation of lesser expensive computers that are now available in most households. My research in the 1990s was limited to library files, courthouse records, church records, available history books, newspaper archives, and individual interviews.

As of this revision, the introduction of FaceBook in 2007 and years following, has propounded into masses of information that only needs verification of authenticity since the preponderance of users may have faulty recall – yet there are gold mines of data that can be extracted from trusted sources that can more easily be authenticated. These are thrilling times for persons to delve into the past and to share with others.

Insofar as Slidell; the following Group links are informative and supply ample bits of treasures of "Yesterday" – complete with photographs and pro and con attributes by those who participate in nostalgia.

Slidell, Louisiana History, Photos, stories, legends and tall tales
　　　– and –　　　*You might be from Slidell if... .*

The Times Picayune *www.NOLA.com* amply imparts much information.

"Google" provides access to an immense pool of data – more so, if you select the most penetrating Keywords.

The Organizations

Early Organizations

Francois Pichon's Diary reported early organizations such as the Society of Local Friends as organized on October 8, 1881 and the Bonfouca Hunting Club which was organized on October 25, 1884.

Early Organizations
Bonfouca Tribe No.51
A.O.R.M. Fraternal Org
Order of Red Men
Woodmen Lodge
Columbia Woodmen
Knights of Pythias
Maccabees

Other early organizations were formed when some of the women of the town saw a need for religious and social life, which was the start of the *Ladies Aid Society* and various missionary societies. They sponsored gumbo suppers and ice cream socials as promotions for funds to support churches and schools.

In 1905, the *Slidell Progressive League* was formed as a forerunner of the Chamber of Commerce.

Fraternal societies were the Knights of Pythias, Woodmen of the World, Masonic Order, and the Improved Order of Red Man.

A fraternal and community hall was built by the *Improved Order of Red Men* at the intersection of Brakefield and Ciruti streets. Also, on September 26, 1910, the Knights of Pythias dedicated a larger hall on Robert Street between Front and Carey. The old Pythias Hall was located on Carey Street.

The Y.M.C.A. was organized in 1913.

On February 22, 1917, the Slidell Benevolent Association was organized with Dr. F.R. Singleton - President; W.L. Ellis, - V.P; F.F. Wigginton - Secretary, and C.M. Liddle - Treasurer.

During the Depression of the 1930s, the Knights of Columbus was started with the required minimum membership of Thirty-eight. It took two years to collect the initiation dues from men who at that time held meager jobs with meager income.

The organization was formalized on July 31, 1930, with Edgar Dubourg - Grand Knight and Peter Pravata - Financial Secretary.

Winners of Miss Slidell Pageant sponsored by Slidell JayCees	
1987	Sharon Schnior
1986	Stacy King
1985	Tina Rester
1984	Cindy Williams
1983	Diane Granger
1982	Davm Galatas
198 I	Rhonda Bradshaw
1980	Michelle Mauffray
1979	Starr Webb
1978	Patty Sullivan
1977	Patrice Lee
1976	Pam Hueshcen
1975	Kelly Lee Ratzliff
1974	Janet Krozac
1973	Michelle Martin
1970+	Marie D'Arcangeio
1969	Dianne Lirrette
1968	Kathy Lirrene
1967	Ginny Beelman
1966	Becky Joy
1965	Darlene Franklin
1964	Lynn Dugas
1963	Judy Vincent
1962	Frances Kaiser

Current Organizations

Even today, most civic organizations were established to perform welfare work for the town. The Kiwanis Club furnishes free milk to needy school children and gives them a party with gifts at Christmas. The Lions Club provides glasses and dental work during the year, and at Christmas the members pass out boxes of food. The Women's Civic Club supplies food and clothing throughout the year to needy families, and boxes of clothes and toys at Christmas.

The Lions Club was regrouped in 1949, with founding officers; B.P. Dunham, Joe Lee, Henry Anderson, Neil Ouiliber, and Dr. F.R. Singleton. An earlier Lions Club was presided over by Claude Schneider, in 1937.

The Retail Merchants Association had its beginnings in 1972, with Wesley McMillen as its Chairman.

Organizational gifts by Pete Pravata

In 1973, St. Tammany Association for Retarded Citizens (STARC) was given land for a school facility by Pete Pravata. The land was located next to other land gifts by Pravata – such as the Fire Department, Knights of Columbus, Slidell Little Theatre in 1965, Disabled American Veteran Post #25 in 1979, two American Legion posts in 1970, a JayCees Hall, and the VFW Hall site.

Slidell Noon Lions Club

The Slidell Noon Lions Club has lived by the service creed of Lionism since its founding in 1928. The club has remained active and contributes to the well being and growth of the Slidell community.

In the 1950s the Lions Club mapped out house numbers and placed street signs at corners.

•<u>Eye Screening</u>. Each year more than 1,000 pre-school age children have eye-screening in order to identify diseases and conditions that may be correctable or treatable. This service is provided at no expense to families.

•<u>Recycling Eyeglasses</u>. The club collects thousands of pairs of used eyeglasses each year and sends them for cleaning and classification before being distributed throughout the world.

•<u>Support of the Louisiana Lions Camp</u> for Handicapped and Diabetic Youth. The Noon Lions sponsor handicapped and diabetic youths each year to attend the special Lions camp in Anococo, LA at no charge to campers.

•<u>Community Involvement</u>. The Slidell Noon Lions Club participates in many community activities such as the Keep Slidell Beautiful Program and the collection of food items at polling places on election days for donation to charitable organizations.

Lions Clubs International is the world's largest service club organization with more than 1.4 million members in approximately 46,000 clubs in more than 200 countries and geographical areas around the world.

East St Tammany Chamber of Commerce

During the mid-1890s, Covington and Slidell were rivals in striving to become the leading business center of the parish. In 1895, with the need to build a new courthouse, the two towns battled it out to have the county seat located in their own turf. In the process, Covington won out and continues as the Parish seat of government.

Participating in that harangue, were the forerunners of the Chambers of Commerce, then known as the Businessmen's Progressive Leagues. Slidell organized its first formal association League in 1905.

In those days, it was not unusual to have turf battles of a political nature. Since then, wisdom has shown that working hand in hand all regions get their fair share and it has been proved that the "whole is better than all of its parts."

Short History Sketch

The *Slidell Chamber of Commerce* was organized in February 1962, when it became evident that a group representing the entire city was needed to cope with problem resolutions arising from the area's proximity to NASA installations and other prospective developments.

After a number of meetings, a board of 15 directors was elected with Thomas W. Tanner as president, and Joseph Franklin appointed executive secretary to manage the Chamber office which was then located on Second Street in the former principal's office of Our Lady of Lourdes School, which was later a location for city hall.

Chamber Presidents / Board Chairmen

2015	Bill Davis
2014	Joe DiGiovanni
2013	S. Michele Blanchard
2012	John Smith
2011	Sam Caruso, Jr.
2010	Bill Newton
2009	Jack Francioni
2008	Alan Hodges
2007	Daniel Schaus
2006	John Smith
2005	Theresa Risley
2004	Pete Weiland
2003	Martin Bruno
2002	Richard Goodly
2001	Dave Reed
2000	Marc Bonis
1999	Joe DiGiovanni
1998	Lydia Alford
1997	Bruce Clement
1996	John Case
1995	Becky Reeves
1994	Gil Ganucheau
1993	Alton Rock
1992	Dudley Smith
1991	Bobby Sherman
1990	Rick Swartz
1989	Tom O'Connor
1988	Warren Haun
1987	Suzanne Krieger
1986	Darryl Warner
1985	Brian Deese
1984	Rick Parr
1983	Dave Anderson'
1983	Charles Fleming'
1982	Tom Palmer
1981	Peggy Menard
1980	Randy Slone
1979	Paul McDonald
1978	George Reine III
1977	Joe Martinez
1976	Lynn Bartbelemy
1975	Dave Martin
1974	Ron Guth
1973	Robert Thome
1972	Larry Breland
1971	Dr. Ron Francis
1970	Dr. Jack Sewell
1969	Milton Parmelee
1968	David Cooley
1967	M.P. Schneider, Jr.
1966	Robert H. Abney
1965	Homer G. Fritchie, Sr.
1964	George Broom
1963	Gus A. Fritchie, Jr.
1962	Thomas W. Tanner

In 1984, the Chamber moved into its own headquarters building at 118 W. Hall Avenue.

Irma Cry was the Chamber's longest standing executive director from August 1981 to August 1999, and was succeeded by Jill Mack.

1999 Chamber Officers and Board
Seated: Lydia Alford, Past President; Gary Picou, Vice President; Andy Prude, Treasurer; Joe DiGiovanni, President; Dave Anderson, Vice President; and Marc Bonis, Vice President.
Standing: Warren Haun, Keith Gauchet, Frank Hoyt, Bruce Clement, Paul Dillon, Brenda Cormier, Denise Bryant, and Dave Reed. Not Pictured: Doug Welch.

The Current Chamber
East St Tammany Chamber of Commerce

The Slidell Chamber was then known as the "Chamber of Commerce of Greater Slidell Area." Recently, with the new accord since Katrina, the name has been changed to "East St Tammany Chamber of Commerce."

With the move from West Hall into its new purchased location, the Chamber has a most significant presence in the business community.

Purchasing the over 100 years old, 8,000-square-foot, Front Street building has significantly brought the building and the immediate area back into commerce.

On May 22, 2014, the Chamber officially did its own ribbon cutting at the new home at 1808 Front Street. Over 500 members joined the chamber at the Jazzin' Up the Chamber Raffle event. It was truly a historic day in chamber history. Many public officials were present. Entertainment was provided by Ronnie Kole and the Flatliners Band. CEO, Dawn Sharpe-Brackett, officially cut the ribbon.

The building at 1808 Front Street is living out the vision of the building committee. Chamber offices are located upstairs and various cultural tenants are situated on the 1st Floor, including: Sambola Gallery, Pottery Studio KLH, bAd NOLA, Caron's Creations along with many other local artists who display and sell their works at the mARTketplace.

The Chamber represents more than 1,100 businesses and 28,000 employees in the region, and provides more than 250 events per year to assist business development and growth in the region.

2015 Chairman of the Board

Dawn Sharpe-Brackett, Chamber Chief Executive Officer –
(since 2005)

East St. Tammany Chamber of Commerce Board of Directors and Officers — 2015

Main Street Program

In 1977 the National Trust for Historic Preservation launched the Main Street Program for the purpose of revitalizing and preserving downtown and neighborhood commercial districts. Trough the efforts of local director Sharon DeLong, the Olde Towne Slidell Main Street program became part of the large coalition of coordinating programs situated across America. The East St. Tammany Chamber of Commerce is in charge of supervising and maintaining membership.

Junior Auxiliary of Slidell

Facing Slidell's greatly expanding population of the 1960s, fifteen women who were interested in helping the needy and underprivileged of the city, had their first organizational meeting. This resulted in the formation of the Junior Auxiliary on November 30, 1965. As one of their first projects, the ambitious group charged themselves with augmenting instruction and equipment for the arts, crafts, and music appreciation to a special class of mentally challenged children enrolled in the Slidell Elementary School.

During the ensuing years various fund-raising and project activities were instituted to service needy children and aging citizens. One event is the annual Charity Ball which was kicked off in 1971. Other support activities involve: the "Nearly New" Thrift Shop, Booze'n Cruise You Lose, Noah's Ark, Shoe-Fly, Silver and Gold, Sooper Puppy, STARC, and Juniors in Service, to name a few.

Founding Members
Junior Auxiliary

Elinor Smith Anderson
Audrey Browne
Grace Fritchie Burkes
Ruth Cooley
Gail Dinjar
Betsy Boscoe Downs
Lois Ourso Farmer
Vemell Allen Duczer Guillot
Sara Statom Hollon Wyatt
Lynn Palmer Holmes
Gloria Schindler Miramon
Barbara Fox Nix
Gloria Downs Poole
Mary Ann Duezer deBoisblancPrivat
Charlene Williams Sewell
Kay Walker Fitzmorris
Barbara Wall Vivien
Ann Adams
Betty Jo Beadle
Juanita Biggs
Mary Beth Breisacher
Carol Breeding
Jerry Brown
Guerin Yerkes
Browne Mary Burk
Rebecca Contois
Maria Cottingham
Lou Cusimano
Connie Davis
Kitty Deal
Jean Duean
Beth Fleming
Katherine Franklin
Mimi Fritchie
Pat Fritchie
Jayne Gibbins
Virginia Grush
Elaine Landry
Pomeroy Lowrey
Mary Lou Mouch
Mary Mohr
Virginia Riffel
Gardner Schneider (Kole)
Naomi Wolcon

1974 Installation of Officers (left to right) Liz Gambrill, Margaret Fowler, Ben Alice Farris, Vernell Guillot, Jane Alford, Sylvia Stanton, (in front are) Stella Babington and Charlene Sewell.

In continuing their offerings, in 2014, Junior Auxiliary of Slidell volunteers worked 1800 hours and spent more than $25,000 to serve over 11,000 people in the Slidell area, with a primary focus on serving children.

Junior Auxiliary of Slidell Officers for 1999-2000 (Seated left to right) Janet Stinus, Kary Couvillion, and Nancy Jones.
(Stand L to R) Nancy McIntosh, Linda Kelly, Lee Oge, and Jane Kinney.
(2nd row Standing left to right) Darilyn Cuyler, Kayla Ray, Vicki Sievers, Kelly Trainor, Donna Slocum, and Suzanne Krieger.
(Not shown) Debbie Constans, Sandy Curole, and Lisa Clement.

Executive Board 2015-2016.
L-R Wanda Enright (Treasurer), Colleen Courtenay (Secretary), Barbara Gravois (President), Christie Stubbs (Vice President), Cheryl Backes (Membership Chair).

Ozone Camellia Club

Because of Slidell's longtime interest in camellias, the interest spread to form an organization which would assist members and others in growing camellias and to conduct Camellia shows. The Camellia Club was formed on February 1, 1951 under the guidance of Ernest Judice, Joseph Johnson and former Mayor Homer Fritchie. By the end of the first year, the membership expanded to 130 persons and many cities along the Gulf Coast started their own organizations.

The Centennial Camellia

Sam Zerkowsky of Tammania Nursery engendered the Centennial Camellia which he described as a sparkling dark rosy-pink which blooms mid-season.

It was chosen from an unnamed seedling and became the official camellia for the 1988 Slidell Centennial celebrations.

At some of their first shows, there were as many as 10,000 flowers and 150 artistic arrangements being judged. During the earlier years, there were significant numbers of large quantity Camellia growers and there were competitions for young girls to become members or queen of the annual court which became an energizing part of the show events.

In recent years the Camellia Club has limited its membership to 325 persons as it continues to honor those individuals who have made outstanding contributions in promoting interest in camellias and other group activities.

The year of 2015 Marks the Ozone Camellia Club's 65th anniversary.

The Ozone Camellia Festival is held on the first Saturday in December each year.

About 1,000 blooms are displayed and arranged by camellia growers from Louisiana, Florida, Alabama, Mississippi, and Texas – these include protected blooms (grown in hothouses) and non-protected blooms (grown in the elements).

Ozone Camellia Festival Court

Membership in the Ozone Camellia Club is not required, and anyone may participate in the festival.

The festival ball is held in the evening with the presentation of the Festival Court is held at 3 p.m. Both the afternoon flower show and court presentation are open to the public and free of charge.

Rotary Club of Slidell

On March 1, 1963, the Slidell Rotary Club, led by its first president, Dr. Robert Nix, was admitted into Rotary International. Of the original 25 charter members, Gus Fritchie, Jr. remained active through the years. The organization held their regular meetings at Bosco's Restaurant.

In 1967, the meetings were held at Pinewood Country Club and after several years, established their gathering place at the Ramada Inn, and later returned to the Pinewood Country Club.

The club formed an Interact Club with the school system in providing an annual college scholarship award; an annual OK Race; and an Octoberfest fund raiser was inaugurated. Its 1999 president, was Brenda Case who presided over a membership of sixty-one.

On March 27, 1984, a second Club was sponsored, called the North Shore Rotary Club.

In 2014, the club began collecting new socks and shoes for "Shoes for Orphan Souls". Shoes are part of the largest humanitarian aid projects sponsored by Buckner International, a global Christian ministry dedicated to transforming the lives of vulnerable children, families and elders. The belief is that simple shoes can go a long way in preventing disease from hookworms and other

President Ron Davis, Past-President Bill Newton and Northshore Club President Sharron Newton

parasites, as well as protecting feet from injury. In many communities, shoes permit children to attend school who would not be eligible due to the lack of required footwear. Donations are distributed overseas, as well as in the United States, to vulnerable children and orphans.

The Slidell Rotarians celebrated their 50th Anniversary in June 2015 with a gala dinner affair.

Olde Towne Development

The Slidell Business and Professional Women was active in organizing the *Olde Towne* walking tour called "Historic Homes and Places" that was part of the 1988 Centennial celebrations.

The event was successfully chaired by Wilma Hoppe, Sandra Burks, and Sylvia Duplesis; along with its president, Gwen Wade.

The Olde Towne Merchants' Association has been an integral part in re-establishing the Olde Town area as historically significant and economically viable. The committed citizens of the association have sponsored many projects such as the St. Patrick's Day Parade, Olde Towne Maps, the Olde Towne Merchants Newsletter, Adopt-A-School program; and more, such as the Olde Towne logo that was designed by local artists, banners, olde style "period" lamp posts, and benches laid out on First Street, additional lighting, and *Olde Towne* was designated as part of the 13-parish Louisiana Scenic Byways route.

> **Olde Towne Merchants' Association**
> **1999 Leaders**
> Frank Jackson - The Soda Shop
> Brad Champaign - Aubert Insurance
> Eric Dubuisson - Slidell Cleaners

The Olde Towne Preservation District Advisory Commission was established to review building plans and to assist property owners interested in pursuing investment tax credits for historic rehabilitation. It also filed application for "National Certified Local Government" status in order to receive grants from State Historic Preservation Offices, in order to participate in nominations to the National Register of Historic Places, and to take part in statewide preservation programs and planning. It also maintains an inventory of existing businesses and buildings. Events sponsored include a Celebrity Roast and the *Olde Towne Cochon de Lait*.

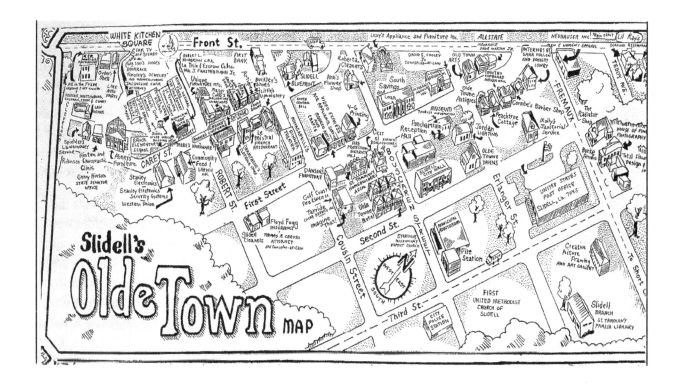

Its executive director acts as a liaison between the corporation and the community and develops working relationships with other associations and organizations interested in Olde Towne development.

On Sunday, March 15, 2015, the Olde Towne Merchants' Association presented the 42nd annual St. Patrick's Day Parade with large crowds in attendance.

"Our parade has more tonnage of vegetables than any other in Louisiana" stated Ronnie Dunaway, event committee member. This year's parade had 250 lbs of cabbage, 35,000 potatoes, 50,000 yellow onions, 35,000-40,000 carrots and garlic. "It is not unusual to see Slidellians dragging bags or carts of produce after the parade." said Dunaway.

Along with massive amounts of produce, parade goers can expect 25 super large floats, several marching school bands, dance teams, and a variety of Disney characters – totaling 50 units combined.

Slidell Little Theatre

Outstanding performances have been charted every year since its conception in 1962. Since 1963, Slidell Little Theatre has been producing quality plays for the enjoyment of the actors as well as the audiences. Educational Work Shops are also offered to generate new membership interest. Annual "Ginny Awards" are presented to outstanding cast and support members.

Slidell Little Theatre's first production was "The Matchmaker" conducted at the old Slidell Junior High School auditorium in June 1963. The Theatre company soon afterward moved their productions to the Municipal Auditorium until 1973, when it acquired the Nellie Drive building. This production site has undergone continued renovations and expansion throughout the years. Since moving into its current facility in 1994, the theatre community has grown significantly.

"Our ability to serve St. Tammany Parish is limited by our accommodation. To address the issue, the organization is embarking on a fund-raising effort to raise the funds necessary to expand. This expansion will provide the space to stage a broader range of productions so that we can offer the community a chance to see more diverse theatrical productions. Our goal for *The Next Stage II* is to enhance our facilities so that we can better fulfill our mission statement"

"To engage, educate and involve members of the community in high-quality theatrical productions."

Each season includes a variety of musicals, dramas, and comedies – with an occasional mystery, farce, or melodrama. 2015 is its 53rd season.

2015 Officers

Bill Saussaye, President; Tracy Gallinghouse, V.P. Marketing; and Roberta Hazelbaker, Member-At-Large.

Slidell Musical Arts Association

The Slidell Musical Arts Association was organized in 1984 as an all-volunteer concert band. It was comprised of professionals, novices, and students who perform several afternoon concerts each year.

Slidell Symphony Society

Symphony Patron Party

The Slidell Symphony Society annually provides more than 6000 students of St. Tammany Parish with special Children's Concerts, that are performed in-school and free of charge, by professional musicians. In conjunction with the Louisiana Philharmonic Orchestra and the Talented Arts Program, the Youth/Community Orchestra and the Lollipop concerts also provide musical and cultural enrichment.

For more than 50 years, since 1962, community enrichment programs have been sustained by the efforts of many dedicated men and women.

The first organizers, numbering only 15 ladies, enticed the support of local Parent Teacher Associations in bringing to Slidell these annual concerts. The New

**Slidell Symphony Society
Past Chairpersons**

98/99 Judy Bolt
1997- Don Hagan
1996· Nick Koaney
1995- Nancy Westfall
1995- Joan Newcomb
1994- Nancy Westfall
1993- Anice Bell
1993- Jane Halley
1992· Effie Ehrhardt
1992- Karin Kastanek
1991 ~ Claudette Songy
89/90 Mary EBen Kilanowski
88/89 R. Mary DuBuisson
1987- Janet Bernard
1986- Jean Caldwell
1985- Patricia Kooney
]984- Ersalene Hubbell
1983- Sharon Soulier
1982- Sharon Shirk
1981- Kay Miller
1980- Ramona Epperson
1979- Faye Hautot
1978- Diane Gustafson
1977- Greta Strange
1976- Jane Alford
1975- Benn Alice Buccholtz
1974~ Sara Hollen
1973- Lois Tanner
1972- Patsy Folse
1971- Gail Dinjar
1970- Nora Bailey
1969- Kay Fitzmorris
1968- Anne Flotte
1967- Mrs. Leake
1966- Barbara Nix
1965~ Elinor Anderson
1964- Gardner Schneider Kole
1963- Dorothy Tanner

Orleans Philharmonic Orchestra first performed at Slidell High, and later, Salmen High School was included.

The original founders were more than just organizers, they also provided labor and materials in staging the musical productions.

Through the years, with growth and changes, the Society moved from a private closed group to open-membership which now offers tax incentives to donors. Gaining co-sponsorship with the "Commission on the Arts," provided a new era in promotion and funding support. Symphony performances are held at the Slidell City Auditorium where a number of outstanding youth and adult concerts are staged. Annual *after-concert soirees* are considered the most esteemed of social community galas.

To fulfill this mission, each year the society brings the Youth Community Orchestra to fourth graders to introduce the concepts of instruments and an orchestra. It also organizes and sponsors free Louisiana Philharmonic Orchestra Concerts that are specially written and conducted for students in grades 1-12; teachers are given classroom learning materials to enrich the concert experience. And because it is never too early to spark the love of music in children, three free concerts specifically designed for preschoolers help instill in them an early appreciation for music.

Slidell Art League

The Slidell Art League, originally named "Lakeside Artist's League of Slidell", was formed in 1962 with nine charter members.

The mission of the art league is to create and cultivate the appreciation of art amongst artists and the community.

The art league is administered by a board of directors who meet monthly. The board is elected by the members annually and serve one to two year terms.

At the present time, the art league holds five major exhibits annually. These shows attract many artists from all along the Gulf Coast.

From its inception through 1979, the art league welcomed the courtesy of proving display space from many of the Slidell area businesses. From 1980-1986, the art league held exhibits in the Municipal Auditorium, and then at the Northshore Square Mall. Post-Katrina, the art league's home was the Slidell Train Depot. In 2010, due to cuts in arts funding, the art league closed the facility, but currently meets at Christ Episcopal Church, 7th & Michigan in Slidell. Art exhibits are also held at the Slidell Memorial Hospital, SMH Cancer Center, Summerfield Retirement Community, and the Cultural Gallery in city hall.

The Slidell Art League's biggest goal today is to expand the cultural economy in Slidell, so that artists continue to mature in the skills of art expression and the community continues to grow in its knowledge and appreciation of art.

STARC

STARC was founded in 1972 by Laura Delaup with two other mothers after her 8-month-old daughter, Heaven, was bitten by a mosquito and contracted encephalitis. The disease left Heaven developmentally disabled, and she became one of three original STARC participants.

Today, STARC's east and west divisions serve more than 700 individuals and their families in St. Tammany, Washington, St. Helena, Tangipahoa and Livingston parishes at any given time. As a private, nonprofit organization, STARC has helped thousands of people since it started nearly 35 years ago.

Steve Duvernay is STARC President for 2014-2015 term.

Senior Clubs & Organizations
AARP (American Asso. of Retired Persons)
Council on Aging
Happy Hour Club
ProAge at Slidell Memorial Hospital
Retired Teachers Association
Slidell Senior Citizen Center
XYZ Club

Pelicans – flock to Olde Town

Mardi Gras

The first celebrations of Mardi Gras in St. Tammany reportedly were at Covington, on February 25, 1879. With promotions in the *St. Tammany Farmer,* King Rex made his first pilgrimage by train, stopping at various depots along the route. "He arrived at Pontchatoula on the 24th, and from there, he was escorted to Covington where there was a day parade, a night parade, and a Grand Ball." During the formative years of carnival, Covington continued to play the host city, but included Slidell area memberships.

A children's Rex Organization was started in 1891, with J.L Smith reigning as King and Miss Adele Pichon his Queen. The following year, the Knights of Carnival Association initiated a parade and ball, with Ernest Pichon as King and Miss May Monet, Queen. In 1893, Julian Smith and Jennie Pujol presided, and in 1895, Jules Pichon and Frances Heintz reigned.

The adults eventually took over again in 1896, with a Rex parade consisting of eight floats. That night there was a Grand Masquerade Ball in the town hall with Charles Stroble as King and Bessie Norman, Queen.

A.L. Pichon and Rebecca Strain were King and Queen in 1897, followed by Leon Hebert and Philomene Pichon in 1898.

Anatole Decoudray rallied as King on two separate occasions, however, in some years Mardi Gras fever lost its early enthusiasm.

Carnival

In 1999, there were twelve organizations in Slidell that celebrated during the season. Five of them having Mardi Gras balls and parades, complete with floats, marching bands, and throws for spectators

Krewe of Slidellians

This krewe presents a 12-float parade in theme, as sponsored by the Slidell Women's Civic Organization. Founded in 1947, the Slidell Women's Civic Club was formed to foster service to the small community. The krewe is involved in numerous activities and community projects. It is dedicated to fostering civic, welfare, cultural and social interest towards civic projects such as: Keep Slidell Beautiful, Rainbow Childcare/My Girlfriends Closet, Relay for Life, Senior Citizen Nursing Homes, Caring Center, Mt. Olive Soup Kitchen, Habitat for Humanity, East St. Tammany Chamber events, and Women's Health Alliance, scholarships, SMH projects, and the Christmas Giving Program.

Mardi Gras – 1970
Pete Pravata and Mrs. Henry Mohr reigned as King and Queen Samaritan XXI.

The Krewe of Slidellians held its 65th Mardi Gras Ball Masque on February 7, 2015 at the Northshore Harbor Center lead by an exciting tableau presented by Ball Captain Carol Beech.

Queen Dawn Sharpe-Brackett and King Troy Brackett with Pages.

Their surprise 65th King and Queen Samaritans were Dawn Sharpe-Brackett and Troy Brackett. The Royal Court is chosen on a basis of community spirit and leadership.

Krewe of Selene

The All-Ladies Krewe sponsors an annual parade with 16-floats in theme. The most coveted throws are the hand-decorated purses.

t saP

*Queen Selene XVII Amanda Molaison
with King Selene XVII Paul Saunders*

Queens and Kings of Selene

I - Gina Bergens and Brent McCoy, II - Diana Boesch and Jim Lamz, III - Terry Becker and Al Schmiderer, IV - Terry Barrilleaux and Will Baird, V - Laurie Saucier and Robert Coniglione, VI - Julie Boesch and Dennis Cenci, VII - Kim and Will Hatcher, VIII - "Katrina", IX - Gail Ledet and Coy Faucheaux, X - Judy Judd and Royal Montz, XI - Lucille Bienvenue and Eric Haro, XII - Anita Price and Timothy Destri, XIII- Joyce Knight and Eric Williams, XIV- Peggy Goertz and Chad Domangue, XV- Maria Natal and Ronald Leon, XVI - Margaret Diaz and Kevin Walcott, XVII - Amanda Molaison and Paul Saunders.

Mystic Krewe of Titans

The krewe's annual parade rolls with 10 floats in theme. Throws include lighted wristbands, footballs, frisbees and T-shirts. The club was established in 2010 by a group of men desirous of riding in a night parade through the streets of Slidell. The Krewe is a family oriented organization sharing in the love for Mardi Gras.

Krewe of Dionysus

The 30th anniversary parade featured 17 floats in theme. Some of the more popular throws will be logo medallion beads, aluminum and wooden doubloons, the fourth edition of the Dionysus doll and wooden beads.

Dionysus was founded in 1985 by a group of Northshore businessmen with the intention of bringing the first all male Krewe to Slidell.

Mystic Krewe of Perseus

The krewe celebrates a 15-float procession in theme. Throws include plastic crabs and custom cups. The Krewe of Perseus was established in 1970. Parade day is on the 3rd Sunday before Mardi Gras Day.

Krewe Captain – Allen Little

Krewe of Bilge
Oak Harbor Marina –

Decorated boats parade in theme

The Krewe was formed in 1978 by a few local residents who costumed and decorated their boats to parade along the canals of the Eden Isles subdivision in celebration of the Carnival season.

The Krewe of Bilge celebrated its 38th year in 2015 with a membership of more than 400.

Krewe of Mona Lisa and Moon Pie est 1984

The walking krewe parades with decorated wagons, carts and other nontraditional vehicles in theme. Plus 56,000 MoonPies, Brass Bands, and the Red Beans & Rice Ball and King cakes. The coveted throw is the Moon Pie, which gives the group its name.

Krewe de Paws

Costumed dogs and their human companions march in theme.

Krewe of Troy

The Krewe of Troy was organized as a carnival and social club in 1983 by its Captain, Mike Moreau. Troy is a family oriented Krewe consisting of men and women. Its motto is "Fun". The Krewe of Troy's first ball was held in 1984, followed soon afterward by its first parade in 1986. Historically, this event signals the start of Slidell's Mardi Gras season with the

Captain - Krewe of Troy

Past Kings and Queens of Troy
Mr. & Mrs. Bob Lewis
Mike Moreau - Lorraine Woods
Bob Thorne - Pollye Tressamer
Darwin Reed - Brenda Holloway
Mr. & Mrs. John Fabey
Mr. & Mrs. Jerry Broussard
Rod Madlock - Ann Mazzola
Mr. & Mrs. John Stevenson
Darwin Reed - Emma Rogers
Mr. & Mrs. Bob Facio
Mr. & Mrs Sam Lewis
Mr. & Mrs. John Malinski
Mr. & Mrs. Donald Boudreaux
Darwin Reed - Brenda Holloway
Tom and Susan Ordone
Ron Koch - Helen Lacombe

crowning at the ball and the revelry of the first Parade.

Mardi Gras Grows

The Slidell City Council originally adopted a parade ordinance in 2013 – which had been the subject of years of meeting and study. That old parade ordinance established a three-week carnival parade season with a cap on the number of parades at eight and a cap on riders.

In mid-2015, the City Council adopted an amended parade ordinance that cleared the way for a new parading krewe. The amended ordinance now permits nine parades to roll or step out.

The new parade, the Krewe of Poseidon, will be a daytime parade with male and female riders – "There was a lot of interest by people in a co-ed, daytime krewe," Poseidon captain Ronny Kastner said. "We wanted to bring something more traditional."

Poseidon president Jack Hutchison said the krewe has 338 riders, much more than 120-rider minimum the city's ordinance calls for.

Krewe of Poseidon

Recreation – Past and Present

Marine Life

Slidell's geographical location makes it a natural for the outdoor family and boating enthusiast. Situated on the shores of Lake Pontchartrain and surrounded by winding bayous and fast-flowing rivers, provides an unlimited source of fun and frolic for enthusiasts for outdoor recreation. Boating and water skiing along the picturesque bayous and beautiful Palm Lake are zestful for the young at heart. For those interested in wild game, a profusion of waterfowl, quail, turkey, rabbits and deer are still to be found in nearby wooded areas.

For those whose pleasure is fishing, lakes and bayous offer a wide variety of salt and fresh water fish. The many bayous and rivers entering the lake are teeming with bass and perch. Speckled trout are abundant and there are large numbers of red fish, drum, and sheephead that gather beneath the bridges that link Slidell with New Orleans.

A sporting invitation for skin

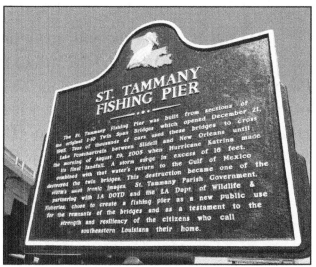

The St. Tammany Fishing Pier near Slidell is located at 54001 East Howze Beach Road, site of the Family Fishing Rodeo. The 2,900 foot pier is complete with crossovers, restrooms and fish-cleaning stations.

divers wishing to seek out large sheephead and jack crevalle can be an exceptional experience for those venturing out to the Lake Pontchartrain gas rigs.

The speckled trout fishing season is at its best during early spring. Large trout, weighing in at four to five pounds, gather to feed on the small croakers breeding in the lake at that time of year. During summers, large schools of smaller trout enter the lake along with shrimp being closely pursued by tarpon and Jack Crevalle.

Because of the Rigolets and Chef Menteur straits, the eastern extremity is of more interest than the western. A strong tide surges daily in and out of the Rigolets, and deep-sea fish swarm inside the narrow passage, which consequently is preferred to the lake itself by astute anglers. The crumbling walls and dry moat of Fort Pike are situated on the channel, closer to the Mississippi Sound than to the lake. This fortress was built after the War of 1812.

Just beyond Lake Catherine is the Chef Menteur which connects with Lake Borgne. This is the location of Fort Macomb, built about the same time as Fort Pike. It is equally in a state of ageing, crumbling ruins.

Entertainment

Pichon's Diary reported early dances at the homes of the Cousins and at Louis's in the 1880s.

During the 1920s, the only good times a young man had was to attend the two or three dances each year that were given at the Knights of Pythias or the Red Man Hall that was located at the site of the old Grammar School (Brock Elementary) on the edge of the narrow Bayou Potassat.

Out-of-town entertainment was sought after by traveling to Madisonville, Mandeville, Covington, or Abita Springs, where New Orleans visitors made their weekend vacation spots. A popular local group that traveled the

---

The Days of Lake Schooners
During the early 1900s, there were a number of excursion schooners still running across the lake on a regular basis. Notable, were the *Margaret.* boarding 2000 passengers and the *St. Tammany,* a sidewheeler capable of 1000 passengers. There was also the well known *Mandeville,* originally named the *Hanover* that operated for many years. And then, there was the *Margaret L.P.* which sank in March 1920. With the Great Depression of the '30s and the increased use of automobiles, the romantic ferry lake traffic came to an end. It was a great source of entertainment when passengers could enjoy the ride while dining, drinking, and dancing to the varied bands and orchestras of the time.

road, was the Parker Band. Dances were held every week end, in addition to several during the week. Pete Pravata's brother Carol chauffeured the band from Slidell to play at these towns.

A source of early entertainment was aboard the lake ferries, the "Steamer St Tammany" and later the "Susquehana," which made trips from New Orleans to Mandeville. Atop the ferries, dancing was the favorite sport for young adults during the lake crossing, and while the vessels were moored at Mandeville, dock-side dancing continued. Local folks joined in to attend the dances at the riverside.

The New Camellia in 1815

Bosco's

This famous landmark was a favorite lounge and restaurant. It still holds its place in nostalgia with fond memories by old-time Slidellians. The business was originated by J.B. Spence, after selling his *Curve Inn* restaurant and bar at the curve of Front and Pontchartrain.

Sam and Elizabeth Bosco bought out Spence in the 1940s and turned the tavern into the hottest dining and entertainment place in Slidell which attracted

Bosco's was razed in 1997.

many local folks as well as fans from New Orleans. Bosco's was famous for its seafood as well as being the in-spot for night club dancing. During the day, it was a meeting place for local business and political folks, and at night, entertainment for young and old.

Some local musicians known to play there were, of Jack Galatas (trumpet), Hal Gilder (bass), Francis Madison (sax), Sparky Penton (drums), and Joe Blackman (piano). Others who sat in were Nunzio Giordano, Oscar Davis and Ralph Rousseaux. Bands were also brought in from New Orleans and from Bogalusa, such as the *Rhythm Aces*. Jimmy Goldman orchestrated the bands and was a big attraction as the house-emcee.

Spence's Curve Inn

After J.B. Spence sold his Carey Street gas station and café, he built at the corner of Front Street and Pontchartrain Drive. Out front was a service station facing the well trafficked streets. Adjoining this was the tavern/restaurant and at the rear a two-story residence that became the family home.

Spence sold his "Curve Inn" to Nick Sansone who renovated and operated as the *St. Christopher's Curve Inn* for forty-seven years before it was gutted by fire on October 28, 1987. The local landmark was razed by bulldozing in 1988.

Miguel "Mike" Rodriguez
The Hot Tamale Vendor

The first "hot tamale" to be sold in Slidell was *The Rodriguez Tamale*. During the early 1950s, Slidellians were treated to the first Mexican style tamales that were sold every evening from a cart on the curve of Highway 90. The craving for tamales endured through a path of communities in south Louisiana as the pioneer tamale maker, Miguel Rodriguez, opened new virgin territories.

Mike Rodriguez, an emigrant from Costa Rica, arrived with his family, wife and nine children, at New Orleans during the early 1920s. In his home country he was a shoemaker and later a Lieutenant Colonel with the Costa Rican police department. Following a political revolution in 1917, he was exiled to Cuba, from where he made plans to emigrate his family to the United States.

Typical vendors cart

Having no formal education, little money, but a large family, he saw the opportunity to make tamales as a living and a means to keep his children home-employed and to send them to business schools or to college. The tamale making enterprise was good and he developed the idea of selling his products at major street corners throughout Orleans and Jefferson Parishes. He developed a unique *Hot Tamale Cart* that was transportable on two wheels, and with two extended wooden handle bars, enabled easy movement from one location to another. Two large pots of freshly made tamales would snugly fit into each of two paper-lined insulated wells cradled within the cart.

Some locations were brisk with sales where the cart would sometimes be permanently located by simply securing it to a post with a lock and chain. He engaged other vendors for whom he made tamales. One of these was Manuel who most people from New Orleans remember for keeping his beat at the intersection of Canal and Carrollton. Manuel, later made an agreement with Miguel to operate his own business using the Rodriguez recipe.

When four of Miguel's children wanted to pursue a college education, without hesitation, Miguel took them to the only nearby college, which was LSU at Baton Rouge. There, Miguel rented a house on Government Street where he opened a Mexican Restaurant and during the evenings would sell tamales from his Rodriguez Tamale cart at the corner of Florida Avenue and the cemeteries. He remained in Baton Rouge to see his last children graduate.

"Mr. Mike," as he was better known to Slidellians, spent his final years making tamales in Slidell and raising chickens in Lacombe. He is survived by many grand-children, great-grandchildren and their progeny. Many of the first and second generations of Mike Rodriguez, The *Tamalier,* learned to prepare tamales by cleaning corn shucks, cooking cornmeal and beef, rolling the ingredients by hand, — as well as taking their turns at street corner sales — including the author of this history book.

John Heller Griffith Park

Located on Second Street next to city hall, Griffith Park is named for Dr. John Keller Griffith, a local doctor that served in the U.S. House of Representatives from 1937 ti 1941. During WWI he served as 1st Lieutenant in the Reserve Medical Army Corps. He was a Royal Arch Mason and a member of Slidell Lodge #311. He died on September 25, 1942.

At the corner of Erlanger and Second is a well conceived municipal park complete with benches and a gazebo which attracts the local "take-out" lunch crowd.

Christmas Under the Stars is one of the featured events held there. The event was held in Griffith Park in Olde Towne every year from 1983 until Hurricane Katrina damaged the park in 2005. The program was then moved to Heritage Park temporarily, but has since returned to its original home in Griffith Park.

The Park is dressed up to greet Santa during the two week period prior to Christmas. The celebration of lights and music brings cheer and merriment to thousands of residents and visitors each year.

One of the favorite aspects of Christmas Under the Stars is its annual Parade of Trees display. Trees are "adopted" by civic organizations and schools throughout the area, which select a holiday theme upon which to base their tree decor.

Made possible by the City of Slidell, the community celebration is held for two weeks during mid-December. Besides viewing the decorated Parade of Trees, nightly there is entertainment that includes music and storytelling as well as visits by Santa and Mrs. Claus.

Fort Pike

(Due to State budget cuts, the park has been closed for an undetermined period beginning in March 2015)

This historical place of interest is located just a few miles from Slidell and is situated near the Rigolets Bridge where the canal joins Lake Pontchartrain to Lake Borgne. Before its closure, tourists visited the fort often. It had been a favorite picnic and outing spot for local people. The thick walls, storage rooms, and gun turrets still remain as it commands a view of the narrowed passage between the two lakes.

After the War of 1812, the United States built the fort in 1818 to protect New Orleans and the Gulf Coast against British or other invasion of the United States. During the Seminole Wars in Florida through the 1820s, the US temporarily held Seminole Indians here who had been taken prisoner. They were eventually transported to the Seminole Reservation in Indian Territory (now Oklahoma.)

The Louisiana Continental Guard took control of the fort in 1861, just weeks before Louisiana joined the Confederacy and the American Civil War began.

The fort was used during the Civil War and during prohibition as a liquor drop-off point. In later years, a band of smugglers stored their loot there. They would take the goods off ships in the Gulf of Mexico and bring them in through the lake aboard smaller boats without paying duty. Most of the gang was captured along with a large quantity of hidden merchandise.

When Union forces captured New Orleans in 1862, the Confederate forces evacuated Fort Pike. The Union reestablished control of the installation, using it as a base for raids. The fort was also used for training United States Colored Troops. These soldiers in the South included mostly former slaves. The USCT was established in 1864 becoming critical to Union success in the war.

All the bricks in Fort Pike's construction came from an early brick-maker in the Slidell area

The fort was abandoned by the United States Army in 1890 – with no cannon ever being fired in battle there. It was listed on the National Register of Historic Places in 1972 and has been maintained as part of a state park known as the Fort Pike State Historic Site.

Swamp Tours

Monsieur Cocodrie
M'su Cocodrie, pronounced *Ko-ko-dree,* is the Cajun word for Alligator.
"See ya' later~ Gator!"

Guided boat tours take visitors through the pristine Honey Island Swamp, consisting of about 38,000 acres preserved for the public as a Wildlife Management Area. This impressive swath of land is over 250 square miles, including some 70,000 acres of protected wildlife area. It includes a nature trail and an outdoor shooting range.

Reptile Jungle
No longer existing

Reptile Jungle in Slidell was owned and operated by the famous Arthur Jones who after opening Reptile Jungle, went on to became a millionaire when he invented the Nautilus physical fitness equipment system. Arthur was one of the first "Crocodile Hunter" types. He always filmed his travels and expeditions to later broadcast on the local television stations around the New Orleans area.

One of the many ads

Tammany Trace

In 1992, when the Illinois Central Railroad filed for abandonment of its outlying track corridors, one of these roadways was the former *"Lakeshore Railroad."* With spontaneous community response, **START**, the "St. Tammany Area Rails to Trails," successfully mobilized to pave the way for an exciting healthful recreation program.

The *Tammany Trace* is one of over 800 "Rails to Trails" projects in the United States. START was the first to initiate its project in Louisiana. The former roadway spanned 31 miles between Slidell and Covington.

It is now a year-round multi-use recreational facility which has been made accessible to wheelchairs, runners, walkers, bicyclists, roller-bladers, and horseback riders. The 10-foot-wide asphalt surface is paralleled by a separate equestrian trail stretches along much of its route. Horses share the main trail with other users only at bridge crossings. Needless to say, no motorized vehicles are allowed.

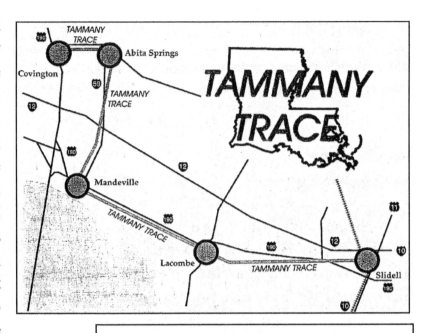

The Tammany Trace Foundation is a non-profit fund-raising arm which provides amenities such as restrooms, trail-heads, signage, bridges, and benches.

The first span opened on September 17, 1994 – and on November 25, 1996 – the 1.2 mile section in Slidell opened from Neslo Road to Sylve Road.

An annual fund-raising benefit known as *"Dancin' on the Trace"* offers food, drink, and dance music during the month of April.

Most of the corridor is 200-feet-wide as it traverses enchanting wetland areas as well as flourishing forests. Along the trail are 31 mostly hand-hewn log bridges Security is maintained by Rangers who remain on duty from dawn to dusk.

Trail head entrances are located at each of the historic towns of Slidell, Lacombe, Mandeville, Covington, and Abita Springs, where visitors experience the piney woods and moss-draped oaks that earned the area its Ozone Belt nickname.

Parks and Recreation

The Slidell Department of Parks and Recreation maintains 30 city park areas and is responsible for the Summer Recreation Program of Children.

Slidell's largest park is located at 1701 Bayou Lane, on the banks of Bayou Bonfouca.

Heritage Park hosts many festivals, fairs, concerts, and special programs throughout the year. The park features a large gazebo, Scogin Station, a childrens playground, splash pad, seven shelters, picnic tables, benches, walking/jogging paths, restrooms and a free boat launch.

The children's playground within Heritage Park was coordinated through the efforts of Gina Beck and Rene Legrand. The 20,000 square foot playground was accomplished by volunteers over a period of six days – April 9 - 14, 2002.

The playground initiative was funded by the community through individual donations, playground component sales, and engraved brick sales in addition to donations from civic groups, foundations, businesses and corporations.

The playground is designed to stimulate children's imagination, creativity, physical development and education. Included are unique features designed to accommodate and enhance experiences for physically challenged youngsters, including ramping areas, Braille signage and special surfaces to permit wheelchair accessibility throughout. The playground appeals to children of all ages.

Bayous and Creeks

Throughout Slidell are a number of bayous, streams and creeks which can be found just about anywhere in or near the city. During the city's history, bayous Paquet, Liberty, and Bonfouca have been used for commercial and industrial areas.

Residents and tourists also use these waterways for fishing as a sport that anyone can partake in.

A Bayou scene.

Bayou Potassat

This U.S. Hwy 11 bridge crosses what is known as the small bayou of Potassat, sometimes spelled as *Patassat* which meanders through Olde Towne.

The name is embedded in the bridge marker on Hwy 11 (Front Street).

Landmarks and Heritage

Olde Towne

Olde Towne offers an experience reminiscent of the late 1800s where beautiful old homes and nostalgia of an historic flavor attracts shoppers and tourists. Inner city marker signs designate the boundaries of Olde Towne. *"Antique Row"* in Olde Towne is the site of a street fair twice a year that draws a  crowd from around the region. Banners, benches, and lampposts were installed to enhance the historic flavor. *Antique Row* is where locals and tourists drop in to buy or browse for furniture, furnishings, lamps, linens, jewelry, glassware, silver settings, pictures, frames, and a rich and varied assortment of collectibles.

Some of the restaurants and lounges that abounded in past years have moved on while others have remained among the newer ones that have opened. An old favorite is the bicycle shop turned eatery known as KY's Olde Towne Bicycle Shop, another is the Old Town Soda Shop. Even though the area is at times seemingly transient, many of the homes and buildings are maintained in good shape, or are in process of renovations.

A significant facet to sustaining the central district has been through the continuing efforts of Slidell's governing officials who have kept the major civic buildings within the core of the district.

Further, encouraged by concerned groups, the Olde Towne Merchants' Association was formed and became an integral force in reassessing the future values of the original downtown. Realizing its historical significance and economic viability, project and event promotions have included St. Patrick's Day celebrations, Olde Towne maps, and a scenic by-way route complete with over-hanging logo banners and old style lamp posts and benches.

Annual Festivals & Events
St. Patrick's Day Parade
Spring Antique Festival
Heritage Festival
Fall Antique Festival
Artists and Craftsmen Fair
Christmas under the Stars

A priority mission has been to establish a setting of the late 1800s, by maintaining an historic flavor to attract shoppers and tourists from surrounding communities. Brochures include: a walking tour, tourism aides, a heritage home tour, and in-city marker signs which designate the boundaries of Olde Towne.

The Olde Towne Preservation District was established and a low interest loan pool for facade improvements was promoted. The corporation also implemented a tax reduction program to encourage new investment interests.

Annual events besides the St. Patrick Parade include the *Olde Towne Cochon de Lait* and a Celebrity Roast. In 1998, the City, the Rotary Clubs, Slidell Memorial Hospital, and the Times-Picayune inaugurated the Fourth of July *Heritage Festival* establishing a food and entertainment throughout the district held at Heritage Park.

Nostalgia for the Past

Some say, "Olde Towne has gotten quieter!" Before the 60's, Carey and Cousin streets were the center of town. It was easy to find Red Skelton's Amusement

Center, Haas's 5 & 10 Store, Polk's Drug Store, and the Acme Department Store.

Telephone operators were responding with, "Number, please?" There was the old George Hotel with the Jitney Jungle Food Store downstairs. The Arcade Theater was called the "Old Show," while the aging theater on Front Street was called the "New Show."

Car hops hung trays on the passenger side of autos as cokes and sandwiches were consumed at the *White Kitchen.* — And, there were Church Bingo games.

Nightlife at that time was mostly devoted to "going to the movies."

For a period of years, Olde Towne had transformed to being an all-night entertainment spot with the conversion of buildings to lounges and saloons. The old Jitney Jungle became known as *Minacapelli's Speakeasy.* Polk's became the *Time Out Lounge.* The McDaniel Building converted to

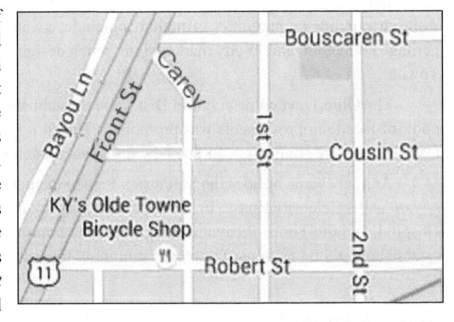

Dirty Harry's. The Acme Department Store transformed into the *Olde Towne Saloon,* while above the old dime store became the *Second Story.*

In the "80s, a city ordinance established a Sunday-2:a.m. door closing to arriving patrons. Only those locked in could remain. This has changed once more.

Points of Interest

The Salmen-Fritchie house was built by Fritz Salmen circa 1895. In 1939, it was acquired by Homer Fritchie, former Mayor of Slidell. In the early 1990s, his son Homer Fritchie, Jr. along with his wife Sharon restored the home to its original grandeur. For nine years, they operated the 6,500 square foot mansion as a lovely bed and breakfast furnished with exquisite antiques. The Salmen brothers were uncles (by marriage) to Homer Fritchie, Sr.

Historically known as Salmen-Fritchie House

The beautiful home, graced with many memories, provides a beautiful and tranquil escape to a gone-by era, now owned by Oliver and Shirley Patton who specialize in luncheon and event catering.

Commissary of 1880s

Just across the street is the brick two-story structure that served as the commissary for the Salmen Brick and Lumber Company. The commissary operated as a large department store offering items to the general public.

Former Commissary building as seen in 2000s

Located at the northern end of College Street is a house built in the early 1890s which served as the Salmen School House.

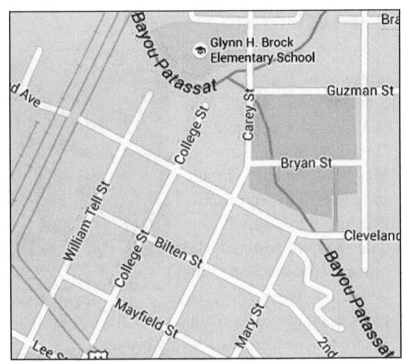

On the northwest corner of Cleveland and Carey Street is the Slidell Lions Club. It was originally built by A.D. Canulette, and caddie-corner at the southeast quadrant is the house built by Frank Canulette. Both gentlemen were the owners of the Canulette Shipbuilding company. The Lions Club began in 1928, and is the oldest service club in Slidell.

Nearby on Bilten Street is the Mayfield house which was built in 1898.

Greenwood Cemetery occupies a two-block area in Olde Towne. The land was originally owned by the Salmens and was donated to the city in 1951. The first known burial was Lee Liddle Salmen, the four year old son of Fritz and Rosa Salmen, who died in 1894.

Member Lions at their home on Cleveland and Carey Street.

Brock Elementary on the corner of Carey and Brakefield was built in 1941 as part of a WPA project. The school was previously called Slidell Grammar School.

Arcade Theater Bldg

On Carey Street, between Robert and Cousin streets is the Arcade Theater Building.

On the southeast corner of First and Cousin Street is the Old Town Slidell Soda Shop formerly known as Buckley's Shoe Store.

Old Town Slidell Soda Shop

KY's Restaurant located on the corner of Carey and Robert Street was formerly a bicycle repair shop.

Dr. P.R. Outlaw owned the building below circa 1908-1913. He used it as his office in the practice of medicine.

Prior name "Le Grande Maison" reception hall at 153 Robert Street.

First Street Antique Row

Cornibe's Barber Shop

Cornibe's Barber Shop is the oldest continuously operating barber shop in St. Tammany. (1932 First Street)

Louis Joseph Cornibe III was the son of Henry Cornibe, the first undertaker in Slidell. Louis Joseph Cornibe III, worked as barber for the previous owner Calvin Craddock for six years, before buying the barber shop business which he operated as *"Cornibe's Barber Shop"* since June 1960.

Craddock, the first owner, had built the quaint shop in 1932. In 1952, Lou Cornibe rented the 3rd chair in the rear when haircuts were 50 cents. He learned to work 12-hour-days.

Lou Cornibe in 1997

In 1984, he bought the shop and kept much of the original items including the gas heater that warms the place.

He installed an antique porcelain covered cast-iron bath tub with claw feet and word got around. A trucker dropped by and asked if he could take a bath and he did for a charge of 50 cents.

For many years until 1999, he prevented Bell South from removing the last remaining "dial-up" pay telephone in town. Louis Comibe was always amused by the many people who didn't know how to operate it.

Bobby Cockerham in 2015

Lou Cornibe passed away in 2015. His sons now own the shop with Bobby Cockerham managing and continuing to cut hair.

Monuments, Flags, and Memorials

The Flag Plaza
(*North of Train Depot*)

Facing the Depot

Flag Plaza and Monument
Dedicated Fall 2000

The Honorable Salvatore A. Caruso, MSW, Mayor
Reinhard J. Dearing, CAO

City Council 1998 - 2002

Alvin D. Singletary, At-Large — Kevin Kingston, Dist. D
Dudley D. Smith, At-Large — Marti Lavaudais, Dist. E
Lionel J. Washington, Dist. A — John E. Cerny Dist. F
Jerry Binder, Dist. B — Pearl Williams, Dist. G
L. Landon Cusimano, Dist. C

Davis Dautreuil, Council Administrator
Architect, NY & Associates
Contractor, Mc Donald Construction of Slidell
Sculpture, Bill Binnings

Facing Hwy 11

The Slidell Overview describes the founding, the railroad camp, naming the town after John Slidell, the early town layout and street naming, the creosote plant, brick making, and ship building. And its growth and expansion with NASA.

FLAGS OVER SLIDELL

I. THE UNITED STATES OF AMERICA	1810-1860; 1865-PRESENT	
II. THE STATE OF LOUISIANA	1812-PRESENT	
III. THE CITY OF SLIDELL	1888-PRESENT	
1. THE KINGDOM OF FRANCE	1682-1763	
2. THE UNITED KINGDOM (GREAT BRITAIN)	1763-1783	
3. THE KINGDOM OF SPAIN	1783-1810	
4. THE REPUBLIC OF WEST FLORIDA	1810	
5. THE REPUBLIC OF LOUISIANA	1861	
6. THE CONFEDERATE STATES OF AMERICA	1861-1865	

The Flag Marker at base of Slidell sculpture lists a time line of the flags that fly from the flag poles.

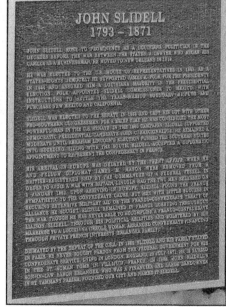

Historical sketch of John Slidell

View from the tracks lists time line of mayors — 1888-2002

Slidell Jr. High Donates Spanish Flag To City

A new Spanish flag was presented to Slidell Mayor Freddy Drennan by the Slidell Junior High School Spanish and Culture Classes in ceremonies October 17, 2014 at the Flag Plaza.

The idea came to Spanish Teacher Melba McDaniel as she passed by the flag plaza one day and noticed that the Spanish flag would be retiring soon. "My students have been studying about Spain and it's cultural impact in Latin America and in Louisiana, so I presented the idea of buying a new flag to Principal Patrick Mackin and students and they became enthusiastic about the idea.

The program opened with comments by Trevor Roy about Spain's influence in Louisiana. Tyler McManus described the Spanish flag symbols, and the flag was presented to the Mayor by Ahrieal Albert.

Mayor Drennan remarked that the ceremony was a wonderful event, and he was honored to be a part of the presentation. "I think it's great our students are studying Spanish history in our country. The Old Spanish Trail being one of the major thoroughfares through Slidell reminded the Mayor that this area was a part of Spain many years ago. "We have a lot of Spanish influence in our city, and that influence is growing," he said. "It gets overlooked sometimes, but our city has many historical Spanish cultural influences."

The mayor presented a Certificate of Appreciation to the Spanish and Culture Classes, thanking them for their contribution to the city.

The school band played the National Anthem and the Spanish National Anthem, while the Mayor and Tyler McManus raised the flag next to the statue of John Slidell.

Slidell sculpture by Bill Binnings

City of Slidell Flag

The flag of the City of Slidell is divided into three primary areas with light blue representing the broad expanse of sky for which the area is famous and below is a darker blue that represents the water and its influence on the city's development.

On the left border is a light green area that represents the land and forests. The basic colors are divided by stripes of

white, bordered in green, representing the three interstate highways that intersect in referencing the rapid growth and expansion of the city. Slidell is one of very few places in the United States where a Crossroad exists with three interstate highways intersecting.

The seal represents the City of Slidell, placed at the center of the intersection indicating its place at the "crossroads of the future." At the center of the circular seal is a corner of bricks representing the contribution of the brick industry in the early development of the area. The brick foundation is inscribed with the date of Slidell's founding. The brick cornerstone sits at the edge of the shore of Lake Pontchartrain surrounded by pine trees which are typical of the area.

The boat on the water represents the fishing, shrimping, ship building and recreational boating in the area. The rainbow over the lake represents the bright, colorful, and cheerful nature of the people and their appreciation of the natural beauty of the area. It also symbolizes the bridge crossing the lake with connections to the rest of the world.

In the foreground below the center of the seal are railroad tracks which represent the strong influence the railroad played on early development. At the bottom of the seal is a camellia for "Slidell, the Camellia City" – symbolizing traditions and appreciation for the area's natural beauty.

The top banner "Excellence" and bottom banner "Effort" with arrows leading upwards – symbolizes the community's work ethic of Effort creating Excellence. The arrows connecting these words represent the early Indian occupation of the area.

Encircling the center portion of the seal is a rope border symbolizing the strong bonds that tie the community together. It also represents the maritime and lumbering industries. Around the rope border are the city and state names identifying the city and its location in the nation. Circling the entire design is a rim of gold that symbolizes the continuous ring of life, the natural richness of the area, and the endurance of its people.

Shrubbery Landmark

Northward along Front Street, between Pennsylvania and Michigan avenues backed by the railroad tracks is a shrub greenery spelling out the name:

S -L -I -D -E -L -L

Garden Club Memorials

On the south side of the Depot in the green space near the Fremeaux crossing are several markers gifted by various Garden Clubs honoring deeds of past members and the members of the Armed Forces.

Blue Star Memorial Highway marker honoring the Armed Forces

City of Slidell
Bayou Liberty Garden Club
2002
In Memory of

Lettie M. Allen	Austin Anderson
Jewel Arceneaux	John G. Badon, Sr.
Lois Baker	Honey Beadle
Marra Lyne Bingham	Karl G. Briesacher, Jr.
Karl B. Briesacher, III	Martha Brown
Marcedes Burton	Bobbie H. Butts
Charles E. Carroll	Audrey R. Crawford
Anthony DiFranco	Fred De Villeneuve
Norman Dubuisson	S. W. Fertitta
Milton Fogg	Bill Folse
Dr. W. L. Folse	Mrs. Nettie Folse
Jane Ellen Francioni	Homer G. Fritchie
Nellie B. Fritchie	Ben Gibbs
Percy Honaker	Joseph B. Johnson
Dorothy Kennedy	Helen Kuehn
Marvin Landry	Bernard Larmann, Jr.
Elizabeth McDonald	Willis McDonald
Max Mercer	Josephine Miltenberger
Anna M. Moore	Robert (Bob) Moore
Elizabeth P. Moran	Forrest B. Moran
Malcolm Mundy	Donald Norman
Carl Penton	Frank S. Randazzo
Ralph Richardson	Amanda Robert
E.P. Robert	M. Peter Schneider, Jr.
Marinus W. Stilling	Edwige & John Switzer
William L. Temolet	Daniel & Stella Thomas
Jacob Thonn	Bob Van Tuyl
Alice Weller	Vivian Westmoreland
Josephine Williams	

This monument is located in the green space off Hwy 90, south of the train depot.

City of Slidell
Bayou Liberty Garden Club
2002
In Honor of

Joseph Pryor Anderson	Lester Boos
Robert (Bob) Cooper	Peter L DeMarsh
Mike Donovan	Louise P. Dubuisson
N. Eric Dubuisson	R. Marti Dubuisson
N. Scot Dubuisson	R. Marry Dubuisson
Terrance Flanagan	Norman Francioni
Veli Geissmann	Steve C. Kennard
Richard (Bud) Kennedy	Anthony J. Livaccari, Sr.
J.B. McKenzie	Dr. Donald W. Minton
Frank (Ralph) Moran	Marvin Norman
Walter Seymour	Val Terribile
Raymond B. Williams, Sr.	Arthur M. Zatarain

The City of Slidell thanks Joycelyn J. Kendrick and family for their generous donation of 60 trees that have been planted on the east side of Front Street in loving memory of pediatrician, and loving husband and father, Marvin E. Kendrick, M.D., April 16, 1931 - January 12, 2002.

Dr. Kendrick believed in John Wesley's Rule:

Do all the good you can,
In all the ways you can,
In all the places you can,
At all the times you can,
To all the people you can,
As long as ever you can.

(THIS RULE IS FROM FAVORITE POEMS FOR CHILDREN, EDITED BY HOLLY PELL MCCONNAUGHY)

9-11 Monument

Area residents and public officials gathered in Heritage Park on April 27, 2008 to memorialize the victims of the Sept. 11, 2001, terrorist attacks on America. The purpose was to pay tribute to the first-responders who put their lives in danger during the catastrophe. — And to pay homage to the 2,800 people who were killed in separate attacks on the World Trade Center, the Pentagon, and in the jet crash in Pennsylvania.

Slidell's efforts to build the memorial began in 2002 with gifts of a 2-foot section of steel beam from the World Trade Center and a chunk of limestone from the Pentagon. The City Council approved the project after the beam segment was given to the city by the Krewe of Bilge Carnival group.

In November 2003, architect Kieran Weldon of Fauntleroy and Latham submitted the winning design for the 9/11 monument.

Among those who spoke to the crowd at the site of the 9-11 Memorial Plaza were Slidell Mayor Ben Morris, City Council member Kim Harbison and New York City firefighter James Sands of Engine 10/Ladder 10 (located across the street from the World Trade Center). Harbison chaired the committee for the 9-11 monument.

On Sunday, September 11, 2011, Slidell Mayor Freddy Drennan, the Slidell City Council, Police Chief Randy Smith and the 9/11 Memorial Committee celebrated ***Slidell's Patriot Day Ceremony*** at Memorial Plaza in Heritage Park.

The ceremony included speeches by Mayor Drennan, Police Chief Randy Smith and St. Tammany Fire District No. 1 Chief Larry Hess.

"Ten years ago, as the World Trade towers collapsed, many heroes rose to the occasion," said Mayor Drennan. "We have not forgotten the sacrifices of the first responders and we honor the men and women who lost their lives or loved ones on that day. We also honor those who have served and those who continue to serve our country in the name of freedom."

9-11 Memorial in Heritage Park

Veterans Memorial Park

In 1988, a veterans memorial was dedicated (corner of Sgt. Alfred Drive and Cleveland) by Mayor Sam Caruso and the City Council. The memorial marker and flag was installed by the Slidell Elk Lodge #2321. The memorial is adjacent to the Henry J. Calamari Memorial Tennis Center and the Carl Hickman Baseball Field. These are all city owned properties.

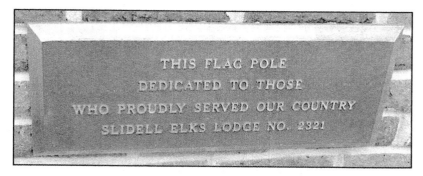

Hurricane Katrina Monument

The city of Slidell in August 2010 held a memorial ceremony at Heritage Park marking the 5th anniversary of Hurricane Katrina. The "Fleur de Triomphe," a 13-foot steel sculpture, was donated by former city resident John Doherty.

Mayor Freddy Drennan reflected upon the city's progress since the storm, followed by a prayer by City Councilman Bill Borchert and a moment of silence.

The sculpture is crafted from a 24-inch steel pipe, standing 13-feet 4-inches tall and weighing 1,200 pounds. It is crowned with a

City employees placed the sculpture.

curved fleur de lis, and at the 7-foot mark there is a hurricane symbol and a line depicting the water level reached in the area of the park in which the statue stands. "It will still be there standing strong for many years to come, even through the future storms."

City officials participating in the ceremony were: from left, Councilman Sam Abney, Slidell Police Chief Randy Smith, Councilmen Joe Fraught, Buddy Lloyd and Bill Borchert, Slidell Mayor Freddy Drennan, and Council President Lionel Hicks. – John Doherty's mother, Pat Taylor, stands at right.

Local Notables

Ronnie Kole— Jazz pianist

Ronnie Kole is consummate performer who is popular locally, nationally and internationally. The New Orleans-based musician spends much of his time abroad where his smooth sound and elegant persona lend themselves to refined venues and guest appearances with symphony orchestras. Kole is known as a piano man's piano man, being admired by many of his contemporaries in the business.

In November 2012, Kole was acclaimed by being inducted into the Louisiana Music Hall of Fame at the Slidell Municipal Auditorium.

His answer when asked, "Trying to say what my favorite kind of music is would be like asking, 'What's your favorite kind of wine?' Whatever is in my hand at the moment is what I like. I enjoy making music that sounds like chimes, an organ or any object," Kole said.

"I'm very happy to receive an honor such as this. It's a lifelong dream," Kole said.

Kole, a Slidell resident, performed at the induction for the large crowd and received a standing ovation after each performance.

Ronnie and Gardner Kole

Born in Chicago, Kole was afflicted with heart trouble as a child, resulting in his enrollment in the Spaulding School for handicapped. While there, he received support from local celebrities who made it a point to visit the school. In thankfulness for such encouragement, Kole became involved in charitable and civic organizations throughout his professional career. Some of his organizational positions were President of the Louisiana Easter Seal Society, President and Chairman of the Sugar Bowl, Chairman of the Louisiana Tourist Commission, 2008 President of the World Trade Center and 2009 Chairman of the Board of the WTC. He was also involved with the New Orleans Jazz Festival and the French Quarter Festival.

As a protégé of Al Hirt, Kole began his professional career on television, gaining exposure on the Johnny Carson Show. After a stint in Las Vegas, he followed Hirt to New Orleans as a musician in Hirt's Bourbon Street club. Later, his own club, "Kole's Korner," joined with Hirt and Pete Fountain's clubs in promoting traditional jazz.

Jazz on the Bayou

Since its creation by the Koles in 1993, "Jazz on the Bayou" has raised more than $1 million to support Easter Scals and STARC in New Orleans and on the Northshore.

"Jazz Girls," dressed in colorful Antebellum-style dresses, mingle with guests to offer raffle tickets for prizes.

Each evening after the end of the two-day event, a "private" concert is performed by Ronnie Kole on his

1940 Steinway concert grand piano in the Koles' living room.

John Doherty – Sculptor

John Doherty, a 1984 Slidell High School graduate, in addition to several metal sculptures, created and donated the *"Fleur de Triomphe"* to help the city commemorate the fifth anniversary of Hurricane Katrina.

The sculpture is crafted from a 24-inch steel pipe that stands 13-feet 4-inches tall and weighs 1,200 pounds. It is crowned with a curved fleur de lis, and at the 7-foot mark there's a hurricane symbol and a line depicting the water level that had been reached in the area of the Heritage Park in which the statue stands.

The "Fleur de Triomphe"

John Doherty, raised in Slidell, Louisiana, learned to work with steel at Southern Shipbuilding. Although having moved to Denver, Colorado in 1994, he was in Slidell the day before Katrina landed. As residents evacuated, he headed back to Colorado, later to learn of his hometown's fate.

Doherty created the steel fleur de lis sculpture while awaiting storm updates in early September of 2005. The endeavor was an outlet for his frustrations and concern for his family and friends in Louisiana. He viewed his "twisted fleur de lis" as a symbol of defiance, strength and resilience following Katrina, and he inscribed the symbol within his artwork as a show of support for his hometown.

The twisted curl atop the cylinder represents the extreme rotational forces exerted during Hurricane Katrina.

Notice the twists in Doherty's "fleur de lis"

When asked about his donations, Doherty replied, "It is my hope that young people in the future will look up at the water line inscribed on the monument and have respect for the devastation of powerful hurricanes. Additionally, I believe they should know about the extraordinary actions of the people in response to the storm."

"The idea came naturally for me. I grew up in Slidell and concluded that it was the least I could do when considering the countless volunteers that gave up their vacations to gut houses and clean up debris in Slidell and surrounding communities," he explained.

Ashleigh Austin

Ashleigh Austin's first book, St. Tammany Parish Postcards," was inspired by her own collection of vintage postcards. As a Louisiana native, she sought out cards that not only reminded her of home, but that also recorded local landmarks that have disappeared. "I am so grateful to all those early postcard photographers and publishers for having the foresight to capture pieces of history," she says.

Ashleigh

Ms. Austin was born in New Orleans, Louisiana. Her family later left the city, moving across Lake Pontchartrain to St. Tammany Parish when the author was nine years old. She graduated from Slidell High School and attended Southeastern Louisiana University as an English major.

Ms. Austin continues to explore and celebrate her Southern heritage through her writing and through her historical and genealogical research. Ashleigh Austin is also an accomplished singer. Her Web site www.ashleighaustin.com features many examples of her work.

Clarence "Gatemouth" Brown

Clarence "Gatemouth" Brown, the world-famous instrumentalist and Grammy Award winning blues musician, lived in Slidell from 1983 until shortly before his death in 2005, just days after Hurricane Katrina passed through Slidell.

Clarence "Gatemouth" Brown

Brown started crossing boundaries – both musical and geographical – at a very young age. He was born in 1924 in Vinton, Louisiana and raised in Orange, Texas. He learned guitar and fiddle from his father— a multi-instrumentalist who taught his son to play Texas fiddle music, traditional French tunes and even polkas.

Gate began his professional career at the age of 21 as a drummer in San Antonio. In 1947, he was in the audience at the Golden Peacock nightclub in Houston, when famed guitarist T-Bone Walker became sick and dropped his guitar onto the stage in the middle of a number. Gate leaped to the stage, picked up Walker's strings and laid into one of his own tunes, "Gatemouth Boogie."

In the last few years of his life, Gate continued his hectic touring schedule with performances across the U.S. as well as debut appearances in New Zealand and Australia. When asked by a *New York Times* reporter to explain his tours to such politically tense areas as Central America, Africa and the Soviet Union, Brown replied, "People can't come to me, so I go to them."

His knack for blending the various American music forms – jazz, blues, bluegrass, country, swing, funk and zydeco – coupled with his determination to bring his music to audiences around the world brought him praise from fans and the international media alike. *Newsweek* called him "a virtuoso talent." In 1982 he won a Grammy with "Alright Again!," a big-band record modeled after the sound of his old records.

The Museums of Slidell

The Slidell Museum

The Slidell Museum was originally conceived during preparations for the 1976 American Revolution Bicentennial commemorations. A committee was formed to seek heritage donations and materials depicting the history of Slidell for display.

Following that project, the City of Slidell refurbished the old Town Hall to house a museum to preserve the collection. As a result, photographs, maps, documents, books, magazines, newspapers, scrapbooks, memoirs, household items, and artifacts were collected for display within the cubicles which once served as jail cells.

Slidell Museum Curator

Dale Tidrick volunteered to assume Curatorship and began preserving and categorizing the many artifacts entrusted to his care. His experienced contributions were derived from being a former oceanographer with the Naval Oceanographic Office at the NASA facility where he compiled marine and administrative history. Tidrick died in 1996, leaving his mark on the Slidell Museum.

The Slidell Museum is situated in the preserved heritage building which once served as City Hall, Jailhouse, and Fire Station.

Slidell Museum – 1999 photograph

Following Tidrick's death, the *Guardians of Slidell History* was organized by Annie Rogers in 1997, as a volunteer group to keep the doors of the Slidell Museum open. The staunch volunteers were also interested in gathering family histories, cemetery maintenance, and gathering church historical records. GOSH volunteers maintained the Slidell Museum until 2001 when they assumed authority over their own museum on Second Street next to City Hall.

Jail Cells on 1ˢᵗ floor

The Slidell Museum has its own Curator and is open Tuesday through Saturday, 9a.m. to 4p.m.

The second floor has been stocked with Mardi Gras regalia with many precious items on display from past royal monarchs of Mardi Gras krewes.

Slidell Museum – located at 2020 First Street – 2015 photo

History of the GOSH Museum Building

Our Lady of Lourdes Catholic Parish

In 1892, the **Church building** was constructed at the comer of Bouscaren and First Streets. That building was moved after 1962 to serve as the Mt. Olive church on Guzman Street.

In the Fall of 1929, the **Lourdes school** was opened for classes, while the nuns were still living in private residences until 1932. Today, that main school building is also preserved and is located on Second Street, now serving as the Slidell City Hall.

In 1932, the **Convent building** was constructed to serve as the residence for the Saint Benedictine nuns, providing teachers for the school. They were an integral part of the first church-affiliated school established in Slidell, that of Our Lady of Lourdes Catholic Parish.

Transition – 1962

In 1962, Lourdes parish moved to its present location in South Slidell, and the original parish property, extending on Bouscaren from First Street to Second Street, was transferred to private hands.

The church building site on the corner of First Street including the western portion facing Bouscaren Street then became home to a new Slidell post office which later became a reception facility, and in the 1990s was established as Slidell's UNO and Delgado campus. This site in 2011 had a new building constructed upon it serving as the "Technology and Cultural Arts Center."

The Second Street Lourdes school portion was transferred for use as a private school from 1962 through 1965 and then became temporary home for Salmen High School during the 1965-

School cornerstone – rear of City Hall

1966 term. The buildings remained empty until acquired by the city in 1972 for conversion into a new City Hall and office space.

The third portion, the Nun's residence at the corner of Bouscaren and Second streets, was used for city offices as an extension of City Hall. When it fell into disrepair and was condemned to be demolished, it became the solution for a home for the G.O.S.H. organization (Guardians of Slidell) that was looking for a place to house their historic treasures. The suggestion to allow GOSH to use the restored building was tendered by Slidell City Councilwoman Pearl Williams and Councilman Lionel Washington, while urging the city council to allocate $67,279 from its supplemental budget for repairs. When the repair work was completed, a group of appreciative Slidellians moved in.

G.O.S.H. Museum – located corner of Second and Bouscaren streets – 2015 photo

The Story of GOSH
(Guardians of Slidell History) – *(A synopsis from the GOSH handout)*

When the Slidell Museum on First Street was opened in celebration of the United States Bicentennial in 1976, Dale Tidrick was the volunteer curator until his death in 1996. Carol Wolfram, a writer for the Times Picayune, wrote about his dedication to the museum.

One phrase in the article, *Museum Future Uncertain*, seemed to wave a red flag in front of a group of "native" Slidellians ... and at that moment an organization was formed ... Guardians of Slidell History (GOSH for short). These "old timers" didn't realize the tremendous job ahead, but were determined to collect, save, and restore memorabilia from the beginnings of this small town. Their goals were simple ... a museum to house these artifacts and people to volunteer in all areas of collection, restoration, and exhibition. Simple ... so it seemed ... but in the doing, quite an undertaking for this "older generation." They began with the election of officers and the usual duties of beginning an organization.

1999 Officers of G.O.S.H.
Annie Abney Rogers, Pres.
John C. Broom, Vice Pres.
Wesley Carroll
Blanche Carroll
Dorothy Murphy
Olive Bukao
Board Members
John Lamarque, Jr.
Marguerite Levy
Rosita Pastoret
Bea S. Penton
"Courier" Newsletter Editors
Margie Mayfield Packer
Carl Wayne Packer
Jan Ena Carr Pichon, Sec.

The Slidell Museum on First Street was the first priority. The building was renovated and thanks to a generous Mayor and City Council was reopened to an enthusiastic crowd in 1997. After a few years under the direction of GOSH, a permanent curator was found and the members of GOSH began looking for another site in which to display more artifacts.

The Our Lady of Lourdes Convent at Second Street and Bouscaren was scheduled to be demolished, and again "GOSH to the rescue." And again, thanks to the Mayor and City Council, the building was saved and beautifully restored. It was opened in March 2001 and dedicated as the GOSH Museum. In 2005, Hurricane Katrina had its toll causing a loss of some of the collection and needed rehabilitation to the building by the City of Slidell.

These volunteers who keep the place open perform a vital service as a clearing house of historic artifacts and documents. Many start off as history buffs with limited experience but develop a keen sense of heritage knowledge by spending time with treasured maps, photos, and documents. They learn from one another and are challenged by questions asked by the many visitors.

2015 Officers and Board Members
(Left-Right)
Adrian Inerarity, Treasurer
Elwin "Jimmy" Jones, Board Member
Leslie Mae Pittman, Membership Chair
Linda Hebert, Secretary
Steve Haas, Board Member
Sonya Soniat, President

The GOSH Museum contains photos, maps, artifacts, etc. that help to tell the story of Slidell. Visitors to the museum or greeted by the Gatekeepers to answer questions and speak of old times and new. The exhibits change every few months so that something exciting and interesting is an attraction for visitors. Permanent exhibits are located upstairs – complete with a nun's bedroom furnished as it was in the 1930's – and even a miniature exhibit from the Space Center. There are numerous GOSH publications that provide detail for the visitor's quest.

The GOSH Museum is located on the corner of Second and Bouscaren streets – open Thursday afternoons between the hours of 2 and 4.

The Rear of the GOSH Museum building has very interesting architectural facets.

A Poem by Hattie Robert

We took a long, last ride together.
Yet alone on the train we sped.
My heart was broken,
My thought's unspoken.
For he was in the baggage car ahead

Bells tolled in Forest Hills cemetery
Beneath the sod he was laid to rest.
I just cannot see
Why he was taken from me,
Yet they say God's ways are best.

Hattie Robert was born in 1898.
As a young woman, she had lost three boy friends.
*** — This resulted in her becoming a spinster.***
Hattie wrote this poem as a dedication to her lost loves.

John Slidell and the Trent Affair
A place at City Courthouse

A bronze plaque profile of John Slidell with an inscription hangs in the main courtroom of Slidell's City Court building completed in 1998. Those who have been curious about learning more about the historical event known as the *Trent Affair* can thank Slidell attorney Henry Hoppe III for his research contribution.

In the opening phase of the War between the States (Civil War) the Union blockade was in effect and had created grave concern to the European powers of England and France regarding commerce and access to open seas. Both, France and

England were hesitant to take open sides with either American cause, although both were prone to support the South. The United States already had in place a number of diplomats in foreign capitals, some partial to the Southern cause, others with the Federal cause.

Jefferson Davis appointed John Slidell and James Mason as special Confederate Commissioners to France and England.

Slipping through the Blockade to Cuba, they transferred passage aboard a British mail carrier, the *Trent*. A Federal warship, the *San Jacinto*, stopped the Trent at sea, boarded it, and took Slidell and Mason as prisoners to Fort Warren.

This incited the British who accused the American Federals of violating international law. The English demanded immediate reparation, an apology, release of the prisoners, and gave seven days for the problem to be rectified. Simultaneously, they sent troop reinforcements to Canada and made earnest preparations for war against the Americans.

The U.S. argued from a weak position because the right of "seizure at sea" was the very reason for the United States waging war against the British in 1812, and in this case, they were defending the same action they had previously taken offense to. Through level headed diplomacy on both sides, Slidell and Mason were released after nearly two months, during which time there was the real threat of war between the U.S. and England.

The originators of the inscription on the bronze plaque supposed what would have happened had Slidell and Mason been successful in their mission to bring France and England to the aid of the Confederate cause. However, instead, the *Trent Affair* resulted in England declaring neutrality, thereby leaving the South and the North, both, greatly dissatisfied.

In view of the fact that John Slidell never set foot on Slidell soil, he has been honored in many ways. The city was named for him. The railroad depot heralds his name. His bust sculpture appears at the Flag Plaza on Front Street. There is the John Slidell Park and the John Slidell High School among numerous other designations. – And the Trent Affair plaque hangs in City Court.

Economic Development

The Port of Slidell

Equity Development Systems Ltd. replaced the old Southern Shipbuilding sign with one of its own and cleared the area of much of its unsightliness. Off Bayou Liberty and Canulette roads, this site served as a shipyard for construction and ship repair from 1920, when it was moved from further upstream, until its closure in 1993.

The old shipyard after having been designated a superfund site to remove its toxic waste had been acquired and had been undergoing changes. The 54-acre facility was found clean by Federal and State environmental controllers and would be converted for use as a port facility for docking, cargo transfer, and storage with some ship maintenance and repair activity according to its new owner, Equity Development Systems Ltd.

Established in 1986, Equity Development Systems, Ltd., (EDS) is an internationally-recognized valuation, lending compliance, and collateral-asset management provider and, trusted mergers and acquisitions advisor and private-equity investor.

An EPA report issued in March 2015 stated that:
the site is in the operation and maintenance phase awaiting a Ready-for-Reuse proposal. The Louisiana Dept of Environmental Quality (LDEQ) and the site owner maintain the site. The landfill cap is inspected once every year and the remedy is evaluated every five years. Discussions on reuse are being conducted between the city of Slidell and the current owner.

NASA – *a welcome economic thrust*

In 1962, the year after astronaut Alan Shepard became the first American to fly in space, NASA opened a computer complex at the corner of Gause Boulevard and Robert Road. The 121,000-square-foot building housed room-sized machines that would support the manufacturing and testing of equipment related to NASA's various programs.

Gause Boulevard transformed from a tranquil two-lane road where cows had grazed to a major commercial highway. Slidell's signature pines vanished – replaced by sprawling subdivisions, shopping centers, and new schools.

Between 1960 and 1970, Slidell's population more than doubled to 16,000. By 1980, Slidell's population reached 26,700.

As NASA computers became smaller and less labor-intensive to operate, the computer complex became unnecessary. It closed in 1994 with a result of almost 170 jobs being lost in Slidell.

After NASA's exit, Congressman Bob Livingston led a successful effort to have the complex donated to the city. The Department of Defense then moved in and operated an information systems center there for about 10 years, starting in 1995. That brought about 300 well-paying jobs to the city.

> **NASA Computer Complex Acquisition.** Through negotiations by the City fathers, in December 1994, the federal government donated the $32,000,000 facility to the City of Slidell.

Now, Textron Land & Marine Systems' engineering and administrative divisions lease much of the complex for more than $1 million a year. Residents typically see the company's armored vehicles lined up at the entrance. However, the maintenance cost to the City of Slidell is approximately $1 million a year, leaving a narrow balance for profit to the city.

Textron Marine & Land Systems

Textron Marine & Land Systems is an American military contractor that manufactures armored vehicles, turrets, advanced marine craft, surface effects ships, and other weapon systems. It is owned by Textron, and was formed in the merger between Cadillac Gage and Textron Marine in 1994.

A new M1117 Guardian vehicle at the Textron Marine and Land Systems

Textron vehicle construction contracts began in New Orleans East, then extended to two locations in Slidell.

Textron operates in Slidell from its Gause Boulevard main office, as well as the Front Street and Stone Road facilities. (The Front St. location was formerly the site of Bernard Lumber Co., which manufactured factory-engineered homes.)

In 2015, Textron began beefing up its New Orleans staff to fulfill a U.S. Navy order for air-cushioned vehicles, known as ship-to-shore connectors (SSCs). The majority of hires were at the Slidell site, which began production on 500 tactical armored patrol vehicles (TAPVs) for the Canadian army.

Previously, Textron had announced a $84 million contract option from the U.S. Navy to build two additional ship-to-shore connectors. In 2012, the company received a $214 million contract with options to build up to eight craft by 2020. The Navy's SSC program calls for a total of 73 craft.

The renewed January 2013 lease with Textron was for $1.4 million, meaning the city would only benefit by $400,000 net.

Work on order for 500 tactical armored patrol vehicles for the Canadian army in 2015.

WorldWinds Inc.

WorldWinds Inc. has installed one of the most powerful computer clusters in the New Orleans area at Slidell's Gause Boulevard Complex. WorldWinds purchased the system to run storm surge simulations for historical and hypothetical hurricanes, which will be used by the Federal Emergency Management Agency to develop new flood zone maps. The complex, which once was home to a NASA computer complex, also houses Textron Marine and Land Systems.

In stark contrast to the previous huge computers, the new computer cluster purchased by WorldWinds, Inc. fits in two racks only six feet tall by four feet wide. It is housed in a basement computer room and only requires two WorldWinds' staff members to operate it. Hurricane storm surge simulations run around the clock, with much of the operation unattended. "Storm surge simulations that previously took days to run on old computer systems now take only a few minutes," explained Elizabeth Valenti, WorldWinds CEO.

Fremaux Town Center

Located on more than 80 acres at the southwest corner of Interstate 10 and Fremaux Avenue in Slidell, Fremaux Town Center will be roughly 635,000 square feet upon completion. With its interstate location and high-visibility, Fremaux Town Center is expected to become a regional shopping destination.

To provide construction funding to the Fremaux Town Center, the City Council approved levying a half cent sales and use tax by the city. The tax only affected purchases at the mall or Town Center for infrastructure improvements there.

Phase I of Fremaux Town Center opened in March 2014 with approximately 350,000 square feet of retail anchored by Dick's Sporting Goods, Michaels, T.J.Maxx, Kohl's and LA Fitness 1.

Stirling Properties and CBL & Associates Properties, Inc. (NYSE: CBL) officially announced twelve additional new tenants for Fremaux Town Center in Slidell, Louisiana. Anchored by a 128,000 square-foot Dillard's, the second phase of this development would include approximately 285,000 square feet of additional retail space, including previously announced tenants Red Robin, Zales, Francesca's and Aveda.

Northshore Harbor Center
– 10th year Anniversary in 2015
100 Harbor Center Boulevard

Joe Anderson was chairman of the East St. Tammany Events Center Commission from 1991-2004. The idea of the Northshore Harbor Center was created at a Slidell Chamber of Commerce Board retreat and Joe was present during that weekend. He is proud to have been with this project since it was just a brainstorm conception and he stayed to see it through the building's successful opening.

This large capacity events center completed in 2005, centrally located between New Orleans and the Mississippi Gulf Coast. The spacious 45,000 square-foot facility hosts nearly 200 events annually – from corporate retreats to large consumer shows, as well as banquets, sporting events, business seminars and more.

The Center states that their mission is two-fold: to be an economic development engine an enhancement to the quality of life for the residents of St. Tammany Parish.

The Center describes their location at the crossroads of three interstate highways is with easy access to more than 1,400 hotel rooms.

Slidell's New Growth

Into the New Millennium

Greater Slidell is located at the southeastern section of St. Tammany Parish in Louisiana's famous "Ozone Belt." Having grown from a population of 364 in 1890, corporate Slidell has become the largest city in St. Tammany Parish. As of the 2000 census, the city had a population of 25,695. 2010 population was 27,080. 2015 estimate is 28,000.

A Growing Population

Slidell's greatest growth began in 1962 when NASA located a computer facility in Slidell and built a new test facility twenty miles away in Mississippi. The Mississippi Test Facility became operational on August 29, 1965 and the employees of NASA and its contractors began to move into the surrounding area. Population spurted from 6,356 residents in 1960 to 16, I 01 in 1970. Thus, Slidell became one of the fastest growing communities in the nation as its population had more than doubled.

With the opening of the completed Interstate System of — I-10, I-12 and US 59, further population increases took place. Property values increased and houses couldn't be built quickly enough. Speculative construction rose sharply and new businesses continued to fare well. Commercial chains and franchises became evident and continued to remain in the thriving economy.

With the conversion of the Mississippi Test Facility to the National Space Technology laboratories in 1974, new employees with the Navy Oceanographers and the Army Ammunition Depot began to arrive in continuing to bolster Slidell's population.

Centennial Capsule

In 1988, a unique time capsule was designed and built by Martin Marietta as a space rocket above ground for permanent public display. Located at John Slidell Park, the rocket capsule is filled with documents, photos, and memorabilia of the City's 100th anniversary.

Economic Growth

— And, the city pursued its path to economic growth by encouraging more development of commercial enterprises. Shopping centers and shopping malls were developed. North Shore Square with five hub stores was built off US-190 and 1-12 West in November 1985. The Factory Outlet Stores complex was built off I-1 0 and Old Spanish Trail in July 1989.

For the most part, the population of Slidell is composed of two segments, permanent residents and those from New Orleans and elsewhere in the state who have summer homes near the lake and within the surrounding dense piney woods. Many of the new citizens are part of the major influx from other states, now working in the industries which have become established.

Its Geography

Slidell is abundant with forests and waterways. Vast amounts of acreage are owned by corporations which now benefit from reforestation programs in recycling the uses of timber and its byproducts. Even yet, timber continues to provide piling, pulpwood, and cut lumber.

The same rich and fertile soil that makes the pine trees grow tall is also ideally suited to cultivating many exotic and beautiful plants, shrubberies and trees. Greenhouses and nurseries are plentiful for exporting plants and flowers to other destinations.

Both salt water and fresh water surround the city of Slidell. These waterways are the Pearl River, some six miles to the east; Lake Pontchartrain, but a

> **Local realtor Ken Levy** had reminded that besides good schools and fishing, "the city is financially well-managed. The city government always ends up with a surplus, and it delivers city services to the people in an upright way."
>
> And realtor Jeff Breland stated, "I think people really like the small-town, suburban feel of the city. It's much more of a bedroom community than New Orleans. The schools are great, and it's very family oriented.

short distance to the south; and Bayou Bonfouca and Bayou Vincent, flow into the city limits as well as Bayou Potassat. Pearl River and Lake Pontchartrain, both, open into Lake Borgne, which flows into the Mississippi Sound continuing to the Gulf of Mexico.

Pearl River, with its net work of parallel tributaries, winds through the heart of the Honey Island Swamp to meet Lake Borgne. Picturesque Lake Pontchartrain is crossed by five bridges, and is surrounded by marshlands that provides a trapper's paradise. Moss-draped oaks line the banks of the bayous in Liberty, Paquet, and Bonfouca- Vincent – which empty into the lake. An 11-year ban on fishing was lifted in 1999, following a multimillion dollar federal cleanup which began in 1990.

Its Retirement Benefits

Slidell's location is also an alluring draw for seniors. It is but an hour to New Orleans; 30 minutes to the Gulf Coast beaches and casinos: and just an hour away from the State's capitol at Baton Rouge.

The spacious Senior Citizens Center, completed in 1994 – and reconstructed in 2008, is located at 610 Cousin Street. The Center offers many services including meals, transportation, recreation, and professional services which also includes income tax assistance and legal counseling.

The mild climate and ample rainfall supports all types of vegetation, inducing many seniors to maintain beautiful gardens — and there are many of them here. The annual Camellia Show is one of the largest in the South — and carries with it signs of Latin customs that have been culturally retained. Events such as the Camellia Show are celebrated with a queen and her court. Mardi Gras is another annual event that is heralded with the finery of majestic grand balls reigned over by the royalty of handsome kings and queens.

Safety and crime control is another of the numerous advantages in Slidell that gives comfort to newcomer seniors.

Its Government and Economics

In 1977, the city underwent a charter change which instituted district representation by seven councilmen and two at-large positions with a strong-mayor system of government. At that time, the City Planning Department was also initiated.

"Building a Better City"
Salvatore A. Sam Caruso, Mayor

Since May 4, 1985, Mayor Caruso every year has released one annual report after another, each showing excellent fiscal responsibility and factual provisions of unhampered progress and continued growth.

During his first mayoral year, he called into place a *"Priorities Convention"* which brought about a great turnout of citizens who were asking for services that could only be met by increased taxes. Therefore, in answering this call, in September, 1986, he led the way for a one-cent sales tax increase, which was supported by Slidellians. This was the doorway that resulted in a major upgrading and expansion of the city's infrastructure.

Immediately, capital improvement programs were launched to refurbish and strengthen the city's infrastructure which included drainage, sewerage, pumping stations, water towers, street paving, new construction, building renovations, land acquisitions, new equipment and replacement of old equipment replacements, computer and data processing, lighting and utilities, parks, recreation facilities, beautification, general repairs and improvements, and preservation and renovations to Slidell's heritage in Olde Towne.

In a specially prepared report, there were 322 capital improvement projects listed between May 1985 through June 1987 totaling $97, 654,618.00.

Referring to the elected public officials, public employees, and volunteers, in quoting from Slidell's 1998 Annual Report, Mayor Caruso stated that, "Because of their hard work, and the outstanding cooperation among my office, the Slidell City Council, and the Chief of Police, I can happily report to you that the city is in sound fiscal condition, that we have completed the largest series of capital improvement projects in our history, and that crime is down by 8% - again."

The legislative branch of government is the Slidell City Council, consisting of nine members, two At-large, and the remaining councilmen represent each of seven districts.

In 1999, the At-large members were Dudley Smith and Alvin Singletary, Lionel Washington was the first Negro councilman to be elected in Slidell and has served "District A" since the '70s. The newest councilmen elected in 1999, were

Jerry Binder, Landon Cusimano, Kevin Kingston, and Jack Cerny. The other in place councilmen were Marti Livaudais and Pearl Williams.

The city infrastructure is served by several departments such as Finance, Parks & Recreation, Cultural & Public Affairs, Planning, Permits & Inspections, Engineering, and Public Operations which includes Public Works, Public Utilities, and Wastewater Treatment. Other divisions include the City Attorney, Animal Control, Civil Service and the Slidell Airport.

In 1999, Chief of Police, Ben Morris was always quick to praise Slidell's cooperative citizenry for their support and assistance in keeping the city safe and making the task of crime prevention easier for his force of professional and dedicated personnel.

Ben Morris-Police Chief

Ups and Downs

The City underwent a temporary setback with near catastrophic conditions in 1995. Being completely surrounded by water — torrential rains, heavy winds, rising tides, faulty drainage, insufficient and over-taxed pumping stations, eroded and incomplete levee systems resulted in the Flood of '95. Since then, most of the faulty conditions have been resolved, new levees developed, and the completion of the Schneider Canal drainage plant with six pumps would have greatly deterred the circumstances of 1995. However, needless to say, with increasing populations, the development of new subdivisions, and more annexations, the cycle of needed improvements to solve ever new problems will always require a strong, solid panel of public officials who are willing to serve their constituency. Taking any page out of the past decade of Fiscal Reports is a good start in solving a crisis as Slidell faces its next Cross Roads. During each decade over the past hundred and more years, its citizens and its public officials have merged together to bridge the gap in finding an expedient solution. These strong character traits were to prove themselves with the more devastating blow by Hurricane Katrina in August of 2005.

The Cross Roads
Once More

Slidell remains on the brink of change – at the Cross Roads – and continuing in growing pains in seeking and implementing solutions to bridge the gap. Each of the mayors who administered for more than a decade, like Homer Fritchie for 32 years, Frank Cusimano for 12 years, and Sam Caruso for 12 years — each was confronted with aspects of change in an ever evolving society. Each has provided a bigger and better Slidell and a challenge to their following administrations.

With the additional one-cent sales tax increase in 1986, it is evident that the inflow of cash has enabled Slidell's economic course more in the intervening years than in any time prior.

The establishment of the UNO Campus became a reality. The Slidell Airport is positioning for a 10-million dollar master plan to cover the next 17year period. The airport has been well maintained since the city took over operations in 1990, and further strides have become evident since Laura Zaidain became its Manager in 1992.

Under the able management of Irma Cry, Executive Director for the Slidell Chamber of Commerce, volunteer participation and support by professionals and businesses greatly benefitted the city's growth. After 18 years, the challenge changed hands to Director Jill Mack.

Tourism continues to provide significant income to the city's coffers.

Organizations such as the Chamber, the Rotary Clubs, the Junior Auxiliary, and the Mardi Gras Krewes provide an advent of stimulation to the newcomer and visitors.

> **NASA Computer Complex Acquisition.** Through negotiations by the City fathers, in December 1994, the federal government donated the $32,000,000 facility to the City of Slidell.

G.O.S.H., in preserving and sustaining the city's historic values, provides an escalating increment of information and education in heritage tourism. Charles Fritchie, Jr. had written "Notes on Slidell History" as published by G.O.S.H. It is a significant contribution in compilation form of early facts of Slidell's historical development.

In keeping with electronic technology, an official web site was designed in 1999 — "About Slidell" ... a short history of the city and of St. Tammany Parish. It also provided like the new internet model, a "Newcomers Info Page" with all necessary information on utilities, vehicle registration and licensing, voter registration, taxes, media resources, organizations, libraries, overnight accommodations, school enrollment, food and entertainment, attractions, and festivals, and emergency information.

A Mayor during change and crisis
Mayor Ben O. Morris

Ben Morris was born in Knoxville, Tennessee and raised in New Orleans, but he has called Slidell "home" since 1976. He holds a Bachelor's Degree from Louisiana State University and a Master's Degree in Criminal Justice from the University of Southern Mississippi; and is a retired Colonel from the U.S. Army Reserve. Prior to taking office as Mayor of Slidell, Ben served for twelve years as Slidell's Chief of Police.

Slidell voters overwhelmingly re-elected Ben Morris to another term as mayor with more than 80 percent of the vote, a strong show of support from a city that suffered greatly due to Katrina. Morris has been credited with his strong leadership of Slidell during the crisis.

Hurricane Katrina
Report from the Mayor September 10, 2005

To the Citizens of Slidell

The Weather Service reports that Slidell had sustained winds of 176 mph and gusts of 190+ mph during Hurricane Katrina. In addition, Slidell was hit by a 23'-26' storm surge that devastated much of the city. This has been very difficult for everyone, but I want to report that we are making great progress thanks to the many city workers, police officers and firefighters, citizens and volunteers who have worked so hard over these last two weeks. Here is the latest:

Our water service is now operational and the drinking water in the City of Slidell is safe to drink and cook with. You do not need to boil your water first. Our sewer system is also operational.

Telephone service is back up and running; however, Charter Communications has still not recovered.

Clean up is still in progress, thanks to our city work crews and the efforts of over 400 United Stated Marines from around the country.

Security remains tight throughout the City of Slidell. Curfew is still in affect from 9:00 p.m. – 6:00 a.m. and is being strictly enforced. The Slidell Police Department is receiving assistance from police officers from across the nation, as well as the Louisiana National Guard and the Alabama National Guard.

Cleco continues to do a tremendous job. There are working lights now on major thoroughfares throughout the city and in some subdivisions. Considering the catastrophic damage to the system, it is absolutely amazing that we have come as far as we have.

Northshore High School is now designated as a Red Cross Shelter. It is fully staffed and operational. All of the city government buildings were severely damaged from Katrina. Because of the required repairs on these facilities, your city government will continue to serve you from trailers located in the large parking lot just north of Heritage Park.

We have queried our 325 city workers and police officers and have determined that almost half of our employees have had catastrophic damage to their homes and are basically homeless. These same employees continue to work hard every day to help restore the City of Slidell. I am so proud of their efforts.

We are fairly confident that there were no storm-related deaths or serious injuries in the City of Slidell. Between 300 and 400 people were rescued by boat during the storm by the Slidell Police Department, city workers, and volunteers. Those rescued were brought to shelters around the city. Those people who still remain in shelters are now in the Red Cross shelter at Northshore High School.

Feeding locations are open throughout the city including First Baptist Church on Pontchartrain Drive, Harvest Church in the John Jay Shopping Center, Grace Memorial Church on Pearl Street, and the vacant lot next to Starbuck's on Front Street. FEMA is handing out ice, water and MREs at the old Wal-Mart on Gause Blvd & I-10.

The West Slidell Post Office is open. They are also handling mail from the very-damaged Olde Towne location. The Post Office will begin limited mail delivery today. If delivery is not yet possible in your neighborhood, you may pick up your mail from the West Slidell Post Office. In addition, Social Security checks can be picked up at the West Slidell Post Office.

St. Tammany Parish schools have a target date of October 3 to reopen schools. Please continue to check their website www.stpsb.org for daily updates.

Many stores have reopened including Wal-Mart, Home Depot, Lowe's, Sam's and some grocery stores. Restaurants are also beginning to reopen. Banks have reopened, Hibernia, Whitney, Parish and CPB.

There have been many cities and communities from across the United States that are offering and providing assistance to our rehabilitation efforts. There are too many to list here, but I will properly thank each and every one in time.

Thank you to the citizens of Slidell for your assistance and patience as we all continue to strive to regain the quality of life that we had in this community prior to the arrival of Katrina.

Thank you and stay safe, **Mayor Ben Morris**

Hurricane Damages

Mayor Morris estimated that of approximately 10,000 homes, 4,000 were badly damaged by floodwaters and a total of 8,000 suffered either wind or water damage. Slidell's pumping stations are in disrepair and the biggest pumping station was knocked out completely. Several miles of subsurface drainage remain clogged and he hasn't received any federal help to fix those problems.

With concern for getting Slidell prepared for the next hurricane season, he stated, "No one has a clue what happened here. The state legislature doesn't. Our local guys know, but the rest of them don't know and most probably don't care."

Six months after Katrina —

Mayor Ben Morris showed grave concern for the federal government's lack of response to the clean-up, as he exclaimed,

"It's been six months and a lot of the houses are still in disrepair, abandoned. There are still a lot of people living in tents. There are more than 3,500 hundred that are still homeless in and around Slidell. The city's out money and Congress is (saying that) the city must pay a bigger share."

Hurricane Katrina —
Federal Government Assessment

Slidell suffered damage from the effects of Hurricane Katrina which hit the region on August 29, 2005. In various parts of the town, damage ranged from significant to devastating. According to maps in the Hurricane Katrina special issue of National Geographic, the storm's eye passed directly over Picayune, MS, less then 20 miles away. Reports say the town was hit by a huge storm surge and that there were approximately one-thousand dead fish in the city streets. The Olde Town and lake front areas of the city were hit especially hard with many buildings taking on 8 feet (very conservative estimate) of water from the storm surge. The storm surge completely leveled many of the houses in the large and prestigious Oak Harbor and Eden Isles subdivisions.

Most of old fishing camps that lined the lakefront north and south of I-10 were all but erased, with only the wood pilings remaining. Yet some areas, like the area around the intersection of I-10 and Gause Boulevard, have all but resumed functioning as normal. There have been a great number of teams of people traveling to the Slidell area in order to help with clean-up and repair. Thanks to their efforts, many families living in Slidell are able to resume living there.

The following photographs were lifted from several internet websites.

City Leaders – 2010

Slidell City Council and Officers – 2010

Mayor – 2014– *City's 43rd Inaugural Ceremony*

Touting Slidell as a great place to live and work, Mayor Freddy Drennan took the "oath of office" on July 1, 2014 for a second term. Taking oaths of office alongside him were Police Chief Randy Smith and the nine members of the City Council.

Drennan, a former police chief for the city, won the mayor's office in 2010 and was re-elected this spring when no one challenged him.

"I believe we have the best-kept secret in the South", Drennan said during his inaugural address before a large crowd at the Slidell Municipal Auditorium. "We're moving forward. We've got a lot of good things going on."

Drennan's inaugural address touched on the rebounding city and national economy. It closely mirrored the "State of the City" address he presented to the East St. Tammany Chamber of Commerce last week, during which he used a laser pointer to highlight slides of public works' projects and new businesses.

Drennan stated that 170 businesses have opened, expanded or relocated into the city since July 2013. "Our city is being looked at. Our city is being recognized, " he said. "Sales tax revenues have shown modest increases the last two years, after several years of declining numbers. And building permits show healthy growth as well," he said.

As the Executive Officer of the City of Slidell, the Mayor sets municipal policies and provides leadership, vision and direction for Slidell City Government. The Mayor is also the City's chief representative for all economic development projects and interactions among municipal, state and federal agencies. As Slidell's primary political leader, the Mayor is also the City's chief spokesman and public relations official.

Freddy Drennan was elected as Mayor of the City of Slidell in 2010 and re-elected in 2014. As Mayor of the City of Slidell, he is responsible for directing over 350 employees and managing a budget of approximately $40 million each year. Drennan has a long history in public service, protecting and serving the public for over 35 years, working for St. Tammany Parish Sherriff's Office, serving as Chief of Police for the City of Slidell from 2002-2010 and Chief of Police for Picayune, MS, from 1989-1996.

Drennan is married to Glenda Drennan. They have 4 children and 15 grand children. Drennan is an LSU graduate of the Law Enforcement Institute and the FBI Executive Development Program in Quantico, VA.

Awards & Accomplishments: Founder and chairman of the annual Freddy Drennan's Wild Game Cook Off for Community Christian Concern, which raises thousands of dollars each year to help local citizens; Founding chairman of Glitz & Glamour for the United Way; Active member of the Slidell Rotary, Slidell Lion's Club and Masonic Lodge #311; Member of First Baptist Church; 2004 Campaign Chairman of the St. Tammany Parish United Way; Elected in 2005 as Chairman of the Board of Directors of the Regional Organized Crime Information Center in Nashville, TN, which is made up of 14 southeastern states.

2006 president of the Southeast Louisiana Police Chief's Association Board of Directors of the 911 Board. In 2006, received a commendation award from Fire District 1; 2006 Slidell Republican Women's Leadership Award; 2007 King Samaritan of the Slidell Civic Women's Club; 2008 United Way Hidden Hero Award; 2008 Elks Lodge Distinguished Citizenship Award; 2011 Angel Among Us Award from the Hospice Foundation of the South; Serves on the Friends of the Harbor Center board; Invited as a national guest lecturer and trainer for FBI retainer in MO; COPS Conference in Washington, DC; Maryland Association of Chiefs of Police, Columbia University in S.C., CALEA in Colorado Springs, CO and at Fort Stewart, Georgia for the US Army.

Slidell Police Department

The Slidell Police Department is a dynamic and innovative department composed of over 100 officers and civilian employees who serve with pride and dedication. The department's efforts are supported by a contingent of community volunteers who donate their time to perform a variety of essential and valuable duties by serving as reserve officers. The department's focus is on reducing crime and maintaining quality of life for the citizens of Slidell. The Slidell Police Department became an internationally accredited law enforcement agency in 1995. It obtained this accreditation through the Commission on Accreditation of Law Enforcement, also known as C.A.L.E.A. This means the Slidell Police Department is held to a higher standard when it comes to our daily operations, training, and policies.

Through the dedication of all of the Slidell Police Department employees, the department remains highly professional.

Randy Smith was elected in 2014 to his second term as head of the city's police department, having first been elected in 2010.

"I take great pride in being entrusted with the honor and responsibility that comes with leading the Slidell Police Department. Just as my predecessors have, I will continue to seek and embrace changes that resolve the problems affecting our community in a forthright and effective manner. To accomplish this, the values and principles upon which the department was founded will continue to play a major role in how we serve the public and will be used as our parameters of future success. As this city continues to grow and the Slidell Police Department continues to move forward, we will maintain the highest standards of professional ethics and personal integrity," stated Chief Randy Smith.

Mayor Freddy Drennan
As the Executive Officer of the City of Slidell, the Mayor sets municipal policies and provides leadership, vision and direction for Slidell City Government....

L. Landon Cusimano
Councilman at-Large

Sam Abney
Councilman,
District-B

Sam Caruso
Councilman,
District-E

Kim Harbison
Councilwoman-at-Large

Warren Crocket
Councilman,
District-C

Jay Newcomb
Councilman,
District-F

Glynn Pichon
Councilman,
District-A

Val Vanney Jr.
Councilman,
District-D

Bill Borchert
Councilman,
District-G

Chief Randy Smith
The Slidell Police Department is a dynamic and innovative department currently composed of over 100 officers and civilian employees who serve with pride and dedication....

On the council, Landon Cusimano, Kim Harbison, Sam Abney (District B), Sam Caruso (District E), Jay Newcomb (District F) and Bill Borchert (District G) are returning to their posts after winning re-election. Glynn Pichon (District A) and Val Vanney (District D) are newcomers. Warren Crockett, who held the District C post from 2006 to 2010, – rejoined the council.

Judge James "Jim" Lamz, Slidell City Court

The Louisiana State Bar Association presented the Crystal Gavel Award to Judge James "Jim" Lamz, Slidell City Court, at a ceremony held at the Courthouse in Slidell. The Crystal Gavel Award recognizes outstanding lawyers and judges in Louisiana who have been unsung heroes and heroines in their communities, according to John H. Musser IV, 2012-13 president of the Louisiana State Bar Association.

Louisiana State Bar Association President John H. Musser IV (at left) presents the Crystal Gavel Award to Slidell City Court Judge James 'Jim' Lamz at a ceremony in Slidell City Court that was attended by hundreds of community members.

Figure 5*Judge Lamz received Crystal Gavel Award in 2012*

"Judge Lamz was chosen due to his outstanding work in educating the public and students about legal matters," Husser said.

The Crystal Gavel Award citation noted "Lamz has opened the doors of Slidell City Court to civic and community organizations so the public can watch and learn about the judicial process and the court's functions. Each year the Leadership Slidell/Leadership Northshore class, of which Lamz is a 1992 graduate, visits the court for an in-depth presentation on how the court operates and the roles played by lawyers, litigants, court staff and the Judge. He also gives a similar presentation to the Slidell Police Department Citizens Academy, which visits the courtroom each session. Locally, Lamz has become well-known for his efforts to brief and educate business, civic and community groups on the court's operations, jurisdiction and case trends.

His effort to educate the public on court issues is extended to children as well, including developing a special coloring book with his administrative assistant Kasey Coote. He engaged elected officials by getting them to participate in a "Judicial Ride-along" program which allows government leaders to witness case planning sessions and hearings to improve communications and raise awareness.

Lamz also was recognized for his public speaking concerning the important work done by Court Appointed Child Advocates (CASA) who offer unique insight that assists judges in deciding cases involving abused and neglected children. Lamz also has coordinated and appeared in public service announcements to encourage local residents to volunteer for CASA.

Lamz earned his law degree from Loyola University Law School.

Good Neighbors

North Shore as it was in 1940

Le Grande Lagoon

Rat's Nest Road

Pontchartrain Drive

1940 View

5-Mile Bridge

North Shore as it was in 1999

As described in first edition of "Slidell Camellia City."

Upon departing from the Highway 11 Bridge onto Pontchartrain Drive, the first business encountered in 1999 was *Gilbert Cousin's,* with his signs listing such services as: boats, motoring, live bait, beer, ice, and tackle.

1999 – Gilbert Cousin's next to Tite's Place

Immediately next door was Tite's Place, which was then relatively new offering the same services as Gilbert Cousin's, but with the addition of a lounge.

A romantic experience in water-front dining was Vera's Restaurant that specialized in soft shell crabs and boiled seafood overlooking the lake.

At the first road off the bridge was the mile-and-a-half drive to the end of Lakeview Drive. The drive along the way was pervaded by camps, both old and new, which protruded into the lake atop pilings accommodated by ribbons of piers for each fishing lodge.

I-10 bridge span on horizon

Along the opposite side, were rows of condominiums with water access bordering alongside the roadway to the end of Lakeview Drive.

At the dead end point, taking a northward turn on Harbor View Court, was George Kendrick's *Harbor View Marina* and fuel dock. In 1999, it was relatively new, complete with a bar & lounge that offered karaoke entertainment on weekends.

Retracing back to Hwy. 11 and continuing northward were a number of establishments that included Jay's Dockside Café, Frisand's Post Time, Hazel's Bar & Lounge, Pier 11 Lounge, The Landing Bar & Grill, Fisherman's Wharf Restaurant, Campy's Lounge, Eden of King Chinese Restaurant, Salvaggio's Restaurant and

Lounge, and Andi's Bayou Bar & Grill. All along the way on the canal side, were fishing camps. On the east side were condominiums, townhouses, and apartments.

In 2005, Hurricane Katrina ravished the area.

North Shore in 2015

Eden Isle from Pontchartrain Drive (Hwy 11) restaurant and bar locations are the Dock at Slidell at end of Lakeview Drive, and the Landing Bar and Grill, Tooloula's, and Michael's Restaurant and Lounge are set back from Pontchartrain Drive into Slidell.

Michael's

The Dockside

The Landing

Tooloulah's

An Aerial Photo circa 2014

Pearl River

The Pearl River was called the *Riviere Perle* by the early French explorers in 1699. Bienville had explored the mouths of the East and Middle Pearl rivers and a group of French adventurers found pearls from oysters near the banks. These pearls were sent with Iberville's first return trip to France as proof of treasures from the new colonies. The area became one of the oldest communities on the Coast following Ocean Springs and Biloxi.

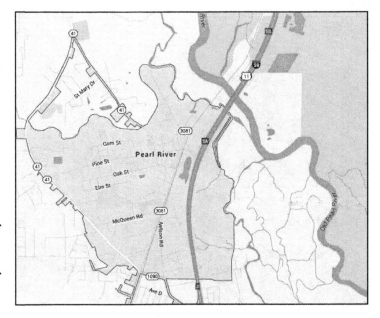

Honey Island Swamp

Honey Island Swamp, called *Marais de l'Île-de-Miel* by the early French, is a marshland located in St. Tammany Parish, deriving its name because of the honeybees. The swamp is bordered on the north by U.S. 90, on the south by Lake Borgne, on the east by the Pearl River and the west by the West Pearl River.

The Swamp covers an area that is over 20 miles long and nearly 7 miles across, with half of its 70,000 acres being a permanently protected wildlife area. The swamp is also the home of the legendary Honey Island Swamp monster.

Early Logging Town

The community of Pearl River was originally known as **Halloo**, a name reputedly garnered from loggers yelling to one another as they labored along the nearby Pearl River. Early on, Halloo was a small railroad town, located at the junction of The Northeastern (_N.O. & N.E. RR_) and Poitevent and Favre's East Louisiana Railroads. In 1886 a train station was constructed at the site, and two years later, Samuel Russ Poitevent established the first store in the village. The community's name was first changed from Halloo to Pearl, later to Pearlville, and eventually Pearl River, in 1888, after the train station was built at the town.

During the Mississippi logging years, many of these villages were similar in culture. Some of these towns have

Logger Tom McQueen leads his oxen team with Bill Favre in Honey Island Swamp   (Courtesy: Bob Moore)

Pearl River Station was built in 1888

disappeared from the maps – such as Westonia and Log Town.

Logtown was located about three miles north of Pearlington facing the east side of Pearl River and the Honey Island Swamp. It was originally called *Chalons* for Joseph Chalon, one of its early French settlers from 1805.

The name was changed to Logtown when it became a focal point for log shipments. This was the home for the large H. Weston general store, several schools and churches and the huge lumber plant covering one mile of water front on the Pearl River.

Transporting lumber and its by-products from the heart of the piney woods was the major industry of the area abounding the Pearl River. Before rail spurs were run, oxcarts dragged or hauled the cut timber to the nearest water access. Cypress and pine logs were manufactured into lumber, staves and shingles; then shipped by schooners and brigs to the markets at New Orleans or Ship Island for export.

The Community Grows over the years.

On July 13, 1898, the 200 citizens of Pearl River voted to petition the state of Louisiana for incorporation as the "Village of Pearl River", a request which was granted nearly a decade later, on May 24, 1906, naming G.W. Fuller as the first mayor.

Museum Image of Pearl River School built in 1900

During the heyday of River Sawmills, Italian fruit peddlers from New Orleans would maneuver their barges upriver to sell their wares door to door. Also, there were "floating saloons" which operated on the Louisiana side of the river because Mississippi went "Dry" in 1908. Taxi boats were pressed into service to carry the flourishing bar-trade back and forth.

The village slowly modernized over the course of the next half century, acquiring land for a courthouse in 1935 and building a town hall ten years later. Pearl River Junior High was opened in 1963. *(Later, in 2005, the building was made into a police training academy.)*

In 1964, with 1,500 citizens, the village was designated a "town."

In 1968, Pearl River High School was established on Taylor Drive with Mr. Rowley as principal.

James "Jim" Lavigne served as Mayor of Pearl River from 1992 to 2014– reserving the title of serving the most years in mayoral office.

In 2000, the population was approximately 2200 within its corporate limits. Along with its surrounding subdivisions, it is primarily a residential community counting many churches of various religious faiths.

> **1999 Town Officials**
> James Lavigne, Mayor
> David McQueen, Mayor ProTemp
> Board of Aldermen
> Patsy Ellis
> Richard Karchner
> Pat Walsh
> Theresa Zechenelly
> ***
> Ruby Gauley, Town Clerk
> Ron Guth, Town Attorney
> Elizabeth Allen, Deputy Clerk

Having served as Alderman for 28 years, in November 2014, David McQueen became Mayor. He stated, "Pearl River is a family oriented Town and my family has been part of this Town since its existence."

Mayor David McQueen

Pearl River Veterans Memorial and the Flag Plaza are located by the Museum across from the Town Hall.

A peek inside the Museum

Pearl River Schools

Milton Craddock's first campaign for the St. Tammany Parish School Board, Ward 8, included his dream for a high school in the Pearl River area. With help from Sixth Ward Board Member "Siggy" Halverson, in 1968 a one wing Pearl River High School was erected on Taylor Drive. The school began with tenth grade, and added a grade each year until the first graduating class in 1971, having 42 students.

Craddock was also successful in getting a band funded in the parish junior high schools, and the program grew to include elementary and high school bands.

Another major contribution was the School Board sponsored bus transport to Southeastern Louisiana University in Hammond, which allowed many students to continue their education after high school because of this service.

From 1968 to 1982 Ewell L. Rowley was principal of Pearl River High School. A former agriculture teacher, he was charged with opening the school and guiding it during its formative years. Disaster struck PRHS in 1981 when the entire administration building, including several classrooms, burned to the ground. Faculty, staff, and students banded together to return the school to its usual operating schedule, and within one week all classes and students were back on track using more portable buildings.

In the summer of 1982, Lawrence F. "Moose" Matulich, a former mathematics teacher and head football coach, was named the second principal. Louis Austin was appointed the third principal in 1987, followed by Ronald "Ron" Styron became Pearl River's principal in 1992.

In 1998, Scott King, former assistant principal and band director at PRHS, was appointed principal. In 2000, Ms. Karen Myles Devillier became the first female principal to lead Pearl River High. Because Ms. Devillier was also technology focused, she increased the number of computers and meaningful software.

Michael E. Winkler has been principal since 2003 and has transformed the school into a perfect learning environment.

The 2005-2006 school year began smoothly until disaster struck again in the form of Hurricane Katrina. On August 29, 2005 Pearl River, Slidell, and much of Southeast Louisiana were devastated by the storm.

During, and after Hurricane Katrina, Pearl River High served as a shelter for two Slidell nursing homes as well as numerous people from the Pearl River and Slidell areas.

Mr. Winkler remained on campus throughout that period to assist the Red Cross in its work and to oversee the repairs of the school. The result of his efforts was a safe and successful school year despite all the difficulties encountered with the storm.

Throughout the years, Pearl River's curriculum has been focused on meeting the needs of its community.

Pearl River Youth Band Won House of Blues Contest

In November 2012, a newly-formed band made up of students from Pearl River High School won top honors at a New Orleans "House of Blues" Band competition. The band won first place in the 'Bringin' Down the House' youth band competition at the House of Blues.

The band was comprised of Kelsey Parker, lead singer; Traven Handley, lead guitar; Nick Ranatza, rhythm guitar; Brennen Ouder, drums; and Bryan Spencer, bass. The four boys were members of the Pearl River High School Band.

Figure 8*2014 Pearl River High School Marching Band*

In 2014, under the direction of Stephen Abadie, the 32 member Pearl River High School marching band traveled to San Antonio to perform in competitions.

Schools in 2015

Pearl River High School (776 Students Grades: 8-12) 39110 Rebel Lane;

Creekside Junior High (511 Students Grades: 6-8) 65434 Highway 41;

Riverside Elementary School (442 Students Grades: 1-5) 38480 Sullivan Drive;

Sixth Ward Elementary School (414 Students Grades: PK, K-5) 72360 Highway 41;

Little Pearl Elementary School (159 Students: Grades: PK,K)38480 Sullivan Drive;

Children's Playground to rear of Town Hall

Police Department

The Town Hall was dedicated in 1996.

Pearl River History Museum

The children's playground and a gazebo were opened in the late 1990s.

The Pearl River and Honey Island Swamp Museum and Research Center was opened in July 2012 with many items and photographs— and more memorabilia added each year.

The Pearl River Veterans Memorial and the Flag Plaza are located by the Museum across from the Town Hall.

Poitevent Lumber Company

Pearl River as I know it

(*by **Donald Moore** -Gulf Coast attorney lives in Pass Christian, MS.*)

I grew up on the outskirts of Slidell, always just a few miles from the small town of Pearl River. In fact, I attended kindergarten in Pearl River with Ms. Ruby Gauley who would later serve for years on the Board of Alderman and become a champion of preserving the town's history.

We were regulars in Pearl River, visiting family, attending the annual Catfish Festival (it was huge!) and swimming at the train trestle (actually, more like jumping off of it).

While growing up, I used to tell everyone that I was related to more than half of the town of Pearl River with the McQueens, Friersons and Flemings and other aunts, uncles and cousins populating most of the town.

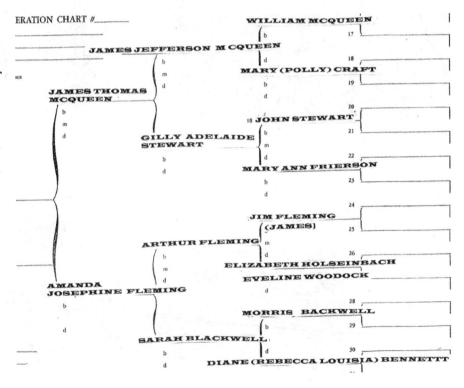

ERATION CHART #_____

WILLIAM MCQUEEN

JAMES JEFFERSON MCQUEEN

MARY (POLLY) CRAFT

JAMES THOMAS MCQUEEN

JOHN STEWART

GILLY ADELAIDE STEWART

MARY ANN FRIERSON

JIM FLEMING (JAMES)

ARTHUR FLEMING

ELIZABETH HOLSEINBACH

EVELINE WOODOCK

AMANDA JOSEPHINE FLEMING

MORRIS BACKWELL

SARAH BLACKWELL

DIANE (REBECCA LOUISIA) BENNETT

Thomas and Josephine McQueen & Family, Circa 1925
FRONT (LR) **Clarence, Harold, <u>Thomas</u> (F), Gladys, <u>Josephine</u> (M), Lena Mac and Lela**
BACK (LR) **Auther, Reva, Dan, Lula, Rand** (died 1930), **Rosa, Oather**

My grandmother was one of multiple McQueen siblings whose early ancestors had made their way to Pearl River from logging settlements and towns in the swamps of south Louisiana and Mississippi, probably lured by the railroad and the major north-south thoroughfare, Highway 11.

Pearl River was a place where a family could earn a living off the natural resources offered from the Honey Island Swamp and the Pearl River. Logging and catfish were the mainstays. Almost everyone I knew had a family member with a log truck and a fishing camp on the river.

We grew up hunting, fishing and boating in the area and my family always enjoyed the leisurely lifestyle that the small town of Pearl River offered. Even though Pearl River is only a few miles from Slidell and New Orleans, it has maintained its small town charm and remains a sleepy town nestled against the Lazy Pearl River, the last stop before heading north into Mississippi.

My family's roots are entrenched deep in Pearl River, a town where you can still stop at the local corner coffee shop and know everyone who walks through the door. Pearl River hasn't changed much over the years, and there's nothing wrong with that.

Brother loggers – Auther and Oather McQueen circa 1935

Several photos credited to Donald Moore's father, **George "Bob" Moore**

St. Joe

The St. Joe Brick Works is located at the small community of St. Joe, a few miles south of the Town of Pearl River.

Owner, Pete Schneider's great grandfather, a German brickmaker, bought the brick-works in 1895 and it's been a family run business ever since, passed down from father to son and, eventually, to a great-grandson.

1990s– St. Joe sign.

2015– St. Joe sign.

The reason this brick company is located here is this sandy clay. For more than a century, St. Joe brick has been made from either clay that's dug on site or within a couple of miles.

St. Joe is one of only a half-dozen brick makers in the country that still uses an old-fashioned wooden mold.

Schneider says, "It gives the aesthetic appeal that has been around since colonial times through where we are today."

The bricks get their color when they are baked in the massive brick kilns.

Schneider says, "The family has a love for the making of the product because it's part of their being. All of the kids have grown up in the business from 12 years old up and we've all learned how to do it."

It's a hands-on process that has put a bit of Louisiana on the fronts of buildings all over America.

It takes about three weeks for each brick to go from wet clay to a finished product. The St. Joe brickyard produces bricks at a rate of 30,000 a day.

The Robert School
St. Joe Village
A Two-Room School House

There were several 2-room school houses built around Slidell including Lacombe and Pearl River.

One of the first philanthropists was Edgar P. Robert who sold one-acre plots for school construction for only $ 1.00 in exchange. He also donated the wood for some of the schools as he realized the need and benefits of educating the folks in the rural areas.

In the schoolhouse located in St. Joe at Pearl River, the architectural design was typical to other schools built at that time. It consisted of two rooms with twelve foot ceilings, each with its own front door entering from the sheltered porch. There was a center chimney with ducts for a wood stove in each classroom.

Clothing lockers were located along each side of the extended and gabled porch gallery. In the rear back yard there were separate boys and girls "out-houses," painted green.

Two of three oak trees that remain standing today, were named Ms. May and Ms. Rosa. These trees are registered with the Live Oak Society.

During the early days, James H. Robert provided housing for the teachers, including Erma May, Miss Merritt, John Holcomb, and Emilie Kahl. Another teacher was Rosa Adelle Robert whose niece Alice, sat through grades one to six. Rosa Crawford was another of the well known teachers at the school.

Original titled owners to the Two-Room School House
Edgar P. Robert - Land owner
1914 St. Tammany School Board
1928 East Union Church
1930 Louise Alexandria Woolums
1953 Beauchamp Sharp
1954 Forrest S. Cole

The owner in 1999 was Gail Mingesz, she, as did her predecessors, maintained the heritage of the school house with but few changes. The photo below shows the original porch gallery is opened on each side and windows were installed in each of the front walls.

This is a wonderful example of preservation and pride of heritage. This same architectural design is represented in the Lacombe Museum, which was also one of the several "Two-Room Schoolhouses" of St. Tammany —
A memorial tribute to Edgar P. Robert.

According to Elizabeth Cole Malley, whose father owned the property from 1954 to 1962, in front of the former school house was a tree that was actually a dividing line. One classroom was located in Slidell, while the other was in Pearl River.

She related another story remembered while she was living there.

Sheriff deputies passed by to find out why her mother was buying so much sugar. After searching around they found her pantry filled with home-made jellies – "they actually thought she had a covered up 'still' hiding somewhere."

A story of Railroading at Pearl River
Shortest-lived Rail-Ferry services in Louisiana

Between 1887 and 1892, W.J. Poitevent and his brother-in-law, Joseph Favre constructed the main line of the East Louisiana Railroad westward from the community of Pearl River where it made connection with the NO&NE. Tracks were laid from Pearl River community to Covington, and from there, a branch line built down to Mandeville at Lake Pontchartrain.

Shortly after it began operating, the East Louisiana obtained trackage rights over the NO&NE to carry its own passengers between Pearl River and New Orleans. In New Orleans, the East Louisiana also built its own depot located at the corner of Press and Royal streets situated between the south end of the NO&NE yard and the Mississippi River.

Wanting a route of its very own

Although the NO&NE trackage rights gave the East Louisiana a quick and convenient entry into the Crescent City, the little railroad wanted a route of its very own; so, on November 15, 1895, it purchased the New Orleans, Spanish Fort & Lake RR, a 'street railroad' which ran from the intersection of Basin and Canal streets out to Spanish Fort, where Bayou St. John flows into Lake Pontchartrain.

To complete its routing, the East Louisiana also purchased a 10-year-old ferry, the Cape Charles, and began ferry service between Mandeville and Spanish Fort. This new operation allowed the railroad to offer its very own service from the heart of the New Orleans business district to Mandeville and Covington. Needless to say, the 25-mile voyage across Lake Pontchartrain took several hours, resulting in the ferry service being more expensive to operate than a train!

Thus, it would appear that the Poitevent and Favre dream of a ferry service lasted less than two years.

Area Authors

Dana Holyfield-Evans has written and produced several books and films. One of her most recognized productions available on DVD is *"The Legend of the Honey Island Swamp Monster."* Some of her published books include; "Swamp Cooking With The River People," "Cajun Sexy Cooking," "Honey Island Swamp Monster Documentations."

Holyfield has made many guest appearances on credible TV shows and speaking tours. She has also written and produced a feature film title, *"Infidelity"* that was distributed by Showcase Entertainment.

Items are available at Amazon.Com.

Elizabeth Hilby – Writer

Pearl River resident Elizabeth Hilby says she has been on a journey that began when she heard a presentation that indicated a large portion of the homeless population was widowed women.

The devotional book, "Audience of One at the Mercy Seat," is on prayer and building an intimate relationship with God, is available at Amazon and Barnes and Noble.

Bayou Liberty

Taking Highway 11 from Pontchartrain Drive, the Old Spanish Trail convenes into Bayou Liberty Road, being part of the LA Hwy 433 roadway. (Alternate route, by accessing Hwy. 190 to reach LA Hwy 433 junction.)

Before Hurricane Katrina, the picturesque drive crossed Bayou Liberty on a bridge that replaced an older one that in former days required a hand crank to open and close it. A bridge attendant would take a wrench and put it on the middle shaft and walk around a treadmill to open it to cars or boats. A new heavier bridge is now located there.

Before crossing is the Bayou Liberty Marina.

Upon crossing the steele Bayou Liberty bridge, the refurbished brick chapel fronts Bayou Liberty, replacing the old one.

The new St. Genevieve church being prominent at the end of the curve.

Pirogue
Races
are held
on the
first
Sunday
in June
on
Bayou
Liberty.

Lacombe

Lacombe is easily reached from U.S. Hwy. 190 driving eight miles west from Slidell.

The unincorporated village, once a stagecoach route, is a laid-back community known for its Creole observance of All Saints Day. Rich in traditions, "Les Toussaints les Lumieres du Morte," an All Saints Day event, the day after Halloween, when families clean and decorate their familial graves and honor their dead by candle light at dusk. Lacombe residents believe in honoring their traditions and living life to the fullest and with great meaning.

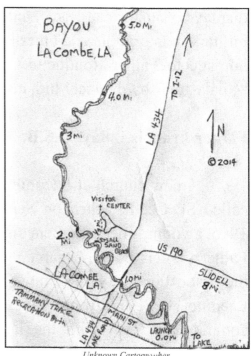

Unknown Cartographer

Lacombe
A survey map dated 1805 indicated that D. Morana resided on the west side of Bayou Liberty and to his north, was property that was first owned by a Mr. Blau, who sold to one of the Cousin family members. Other ownerships were: M. Dubuisson, Sanlarge Milan, Urban Rose, and Maria Caue, the widow of Gabriel Peyroux, – and nearby was the property of a Mr. LaChaise, who later sold to Nicholas Duere.

The ***Bayou Lacombe Museum*** which archives Choctaw Indian relics and early European pioneering artifacts.

This old schoolhouse was built in 1912 with heart-of-pine construction. Within its walls are

displays of historic artifacts, antique tools, 100-year-old furniture, clothing, dolls, military memorabilia and other interesting items. The Choctaw Indian exhibit pays homage to Father Rouquette (1813-1887), the famous missionary priest named "Chata-Ima" by the local Indians, meaning. "He who is like a Choctaw."

Father Francis Balay, O.S.B.

A new church at Lacombe was to be called St. Cecilia when on September 15, 1915, a young, energetic Benedictine monk, Father Francis Balay, became the pastor of the first official Catholic church building in Lacombe. Being from France he could communicate well with the large French speaking population, and like Pere Rouquette of the 1800s, Father Balay became supportive to all the people, many of Choctaw descent.

A week after his arrival, on September 21, 1915, a devastating hurricane hit the Northshore. The windows, statues, furnishings, and even the high altar were destroyed. Except, the life-size statue of the Sacred Heart of Jesus that was spared.

Father Balay and those who found the statue were convinced that the church's new name would be Sacred Heart of Jesus. On September 29, 1918, three years after the storm, Sacred Heart of Jesus Catholic Church was dedicated with a Maltese Cross in the front yard.

Our Lady of Lourdes Catholic Church at Lacombe as it appeared in 1925.

A new rebuilt Sacred Heart Church

Our Lady of Lourdes Shrine

To reach the remaining Choctaws who lived above Lacombe, Father Balay built a chapel at a site in Lacombe that reminded him of his homeland, Lourdes, France.

This humble chapel and shrine, located on Davis Road (also known as Fish Hatchery Road) in a wooded area north of Lacombe known as Forest Glen, was built in 1923 by Father Francis Balay, O.S.B and the people of Lacombe. Father Balay was inspired to build the shrine in that particular area since there was a ravine through which a small stream meandered and because it reminded him of the famous shrine in Lourdes, France. The chapel is a favorite place of prayer and devotion. Spring water flows into a basin in the little chapel where pilgrims leave their personal mementos in prayer. Many believed that the artesian water which gushed from the well on the hill has curative powers.

Roquette's Chapel as it was photographed in 1890.

The lives of two men, Pere Adrien Rouquette and Father Francis Balay, were consecrated to the bodies and souls of the Lacombe people. That love and devotion was returned and has been remembered. When a visitor sits on a bench outside of Sacred Heart of Jesus Catholic Church, the massive oaks' protective limbs seem to stand still.

Our Lady of Lourdes Shrine – 2015

Lacombe

Lacombe Community Cannery - 1930s

The Town of Lacombe evolved around Bayou Lacombe from its early days

The 1930s photo at right shows the Lacombe Community Cannery when it was an early industry for its marine life in the Bayou and Lake Pontchartrain.

Lacombe is proud of its small businesses, its industry, and the pending economic developments planned for the Highway 434 corridor. With renowned- area restaurants and people visiting from all around America, Lacombe also boasts corporations and other blooming business. This township is home to hospital facilities like the Louisiana Heart Hospital and other state of the art medical complexes offering innovative, cutting-edge medical therapies.

Governmental agencies, including the St. Tammany Parish Social Security Administration and the Coroner's office serve the entire parish from the heart of Lacombe's budding 434 corridor.

Frequently visited restaurants in the area are Sal & Judy's, La Provence, and Alice's.

Sal and Judy's

La Provence

Alice's

Lacombe is situated in the heart of St. Tammany Parish, having convenience to all other cities in this thriving parish. Lacombe is bountiful and serene in its setting as being a sportsman's paradise. It is a small town with Bayou Lacombe providing many outdoor activities enjoyed by its residents, and to the happy sportsmen who visit and enjoy the varieties of fishing the waters of Lake Pontchartrain.

Life in Lacombe is as much about the cultural differences of its people as it is about their hospitality and earnest welcome. New neighbors find solace in the region's majestic oaks, natural wetlands, and dense, wooded surroundings.

Lacombe Library

Bayou Lacombe Bridge – 1938

St. Tammany Trace Draw bridge at Lacombe

59th Annual Santa on the Bayou Parade in 2014

Camellia City Nature Park

Joseph Laurent built his trading post in the early 1800s. It is now called the "Salmen Lodge."

Laurent was a trader who used his schooner "Marguerite" to carry the neighboring settler's products and produce to New Orleans across the lake and bring back manufactured goods. He likely used the wide part of

Joseph Laurent home and Lodge used as local area trading store.

the bayou in front of his store as a turning basin for his schooner when making trips. Clay pit remains found on his property indicate he may have made his own bricks. His house and store was the neighborhood general store for almost a century.

In 1901 Fritz Salmen bought the "Lodge" and the surrounding land for his timber industry. Eventually he donated the property to the Boy Scouts of America which they named as Camp Salmen. Some sixty years later, after nearly 400,000 boys had stayed at Camp Salmen, the Scouts relinquished the property.

As a Boy Scout, this writer enjoyed three years of annual scouting in the pirogues and canoes at Camp Salmen jamborees.

The St. Tammany Parish Government acquired the property in the early 2000s. The old building still stands and is named the "Salmen Lodge" in Camp Salmen Nature Park.

Camp Salmen Nature Park has many large, fine old Live Oaks (*Quercus virginiana*) scattered within its 130-acre boundaries. Their greatest concentration is on the high ground by Bayou Liberty. Well before the Boy Scouts came, even before Joseph Laurent built his trading post on the bayou two

The Dock and Amphitheater on the Bayou.

hundred years ago, the people who occupied this site enjoyed the shade and beauty of the trees.

In 2011, the Boy Scouts of America turned 100 years and numerous observation ceremonies were held at their old camping grounds in Camp Salmen Nature Park.

Slidell Area Monster Legends

Onion Head

The legend of Onion Head begins many years ago in the small town of Slidell, Louisiana. There was a giant of a man with a grotesque face who roamed the woods. He lived there in a shack with his mother and seldom left his home.

He was disfigured by a childhood disease that distorted his head. The locals cruelly nickname him Onionhead. To escape their taunts, he stayed out in the woods with his mother and never ventured into town.

One day, a young girl was found murdered out in the woods. The local people decided that Onion Head must have killed her. Before the police had a chance to investigate, the townsfolk formed a mob and went out in the woods to capture Onion Head in his shack.

The mob hunted Onion Head down and found him hiding. Filled with rage, they killed him and dismembered his corpse.

The next morning, the police captured the real murderer. It was a drifter who was passing through town. The townsfolk realized that Onion Head had been innocent.

The Legend continued to reveal that every member of the mob who killed Onion Head was mysteriously slaughtered and that he makes appearances at one of the area cemeteries.

> *Proteus syndrome causes an overgrowth of skin, bones, muscles, fatty tissues, and blood and lymphatic vessels. Also called the "Elephant Man's" disease is a progressive condition wherein affected children develop skin tumors and bone growths that appear as they age.*

St Tammany Times Picayune – 1993

Somewhere amid the twisted, moss covered oaks of Haaswood lies something deeper and darker than soft marsh grasses and swampy pools that catch the moon.

In the heart of the sleepy community northeast of Slidell, a legend creeps larger than life. Ask anyone who has ventured down a gravel road at night to a secluded civil war cemetery, and they will tell you more than memories haunt these parts. The legend of Onionhead is alive.

Locals say that Onion Head is a man whose tragic life has chained him to the cemetery.

The story varies. His name is said to come from a disease that distorted his head. He is now the perpetual caretaker of a cemetery, legends says, and he waits to capture those who wander into it.

The Haaswood cemetery, which has no clear owner since it was donated by the Edmundson family decades ago as a public burial site, has become a favorite haunt in recent years for teen-agers seeking the ghoul. No one reports ever seeing him, but that doesn't stop teens from looking around Haaswood and other secluded locations where he has been reported to lurk.

The Swamp Monster

In 1974, Pearl River resident, Harlan Ford and a hunting buddy sited what has become known as the Honey Island Swamp Monster. Not only did Harlan spot the odd fellow, he also made plaster castings of the animal's foot prints. Harlan was later the subject on an interesting and very popular documentary called *"In Search Of"* which still airs recurrently on television's Discovery Channel.

Ford's granddaughter, Dana Holyfield, has kept the Swamp Monster (also known as the "Wookie") legend alive in her book *Encounters With The Honey Island Swamp Monster*. The book reveals how Ford tracked the creature over the years and also includes reports of sightings by other individuals.

Holyfield remembers how Ford once took a live goat into the back woods to use as bait. "He hid in a tree blind with a camera but the creature never appeared.

We (children) were happy to see the goat come back," says Dana, "He was kind of our pet."

Every day, visitors explore the Honey Island Swamp with the help of local guides and tour operators in the area.

The creature is described as bipedal, 7 feet tall, with gray hair and yellow or red eyes, and accompanied by a disgusting smell. Footprints supposedly left by the creature have four webbed toes.

According to the Author, "This book documents sightings of a mysterious man-like creature that roams the dense foliage of the Louisiana Honey Island Swamp, where few men have ever ventured. Evidence found (as seen on Discovery Channel's In Search Of) was studied by reputable cryptozoologists who claimed that is was not a hoax."

—And from Internet's Wikipedia. . . .
A legend tells of a train wreck in the area in the early 20th century. A traveling circus was on the train, and from it a group of chimpanzees escaped and interbred with the local alligator population.

Slidell TimeLine Significant Dates

1718 - Founding of New Orleans.

1722 - LaCombe's tarpit constructed on Bayou Lacombe.

1737 - Francois Rillieux settled on Bayou Bonfouca.

1737 - Bayou Vincent was named after his son, Vincent Rillieux.

1781 - Francois Cousin claimed 4800 arpents of land, from Bayou Paquet to Bayou Castine.

1850 - Most major parish roads were put in place.

1854 - Aug 8, the New Orleans, Jackson, Great Northern Railroad opened.

1854 - John Gusman granted lands that later composed the settlement of Slidell.

1857 - Panic of 1857 affected businesses on the north shore.

1861 - Jan. 26, Civil War began and Louisiana joined the Confederacy.

1863 - Jan 1, Emancipation Proclamation gave freedom to slaves.

1865 - Civil War ended.

1868 - George Ingram organized Mandeville and Sulphur Springs Railroad Co.

1869 - L&N RR line completed between New Orleans and Mobile.

1870 - Capt William H Hardy acquired Ingram's RR and changed its name to New Orleans and Northwestern RR Co.

1874 - Discovery that creosote lumber prevented shipworms.

1877 - Federal troops leave Louisiana resulting in free elections.

1880 - The St Tammany Farmer reported possible spanning of the lake with 22 mi. bridge.

1881 - The St Tammany Farmer reported preliminary survey to complete trestle for N.O.

1881 - Ferry put into operation at Robert's Landing on Bayou Bonfouca behind current Depot. A work camp formed around Robert's Landing, which becomes the center of activity for three years.

1881 - Aug. a telegraph line installed connecting Slidell Station, New Orleans and Meridian.

1881 - Creosote plant built near Robert's Landing.

1881 - Dec 3, work commenced on Northshore for the NO&NW RR.

1882 - Work commenced at Meridian Jan 7, for the NO&NW Railroad.

1883 - Oct 15, Completion of NO&NW RR bridge across Lake Pontchartrain.

1883 - The first train arrived in N.O. from Meridian MS.

1883 - Slidell town site surveyed and mapped. Baron Erlanger named it for John Slidell after his father-in-law.

1883 - The Wooden passenger depot was located on the west side of the tracks between Maine and Pennsylvania Streets.

1884 - East Louisiana Railroad constructruction started by W.J. Poitevent and his brother-in-law Joseph Favre.

1884 - Area now known as Olde Towne was established as Slidell Station.

1886 - Fritz Salmen started manual brickyard north of the train station on Front St.

1887 - June, the East Louisiana Railroad is completed between Pearl River and Abita Springs.

1888 - Nov 13, Slidell incorporated, with 2,320 acres within its limits.

First governing officials: Mayor Seth H. Decker; Board of Aldemen, H. Mandin, Oscar L. Ditmar, A.C. Vrovost. Fritz Salmen and Charles McManon.

1888 - Dec 19, Town counsel appointed Edgar P. Robert as town marshall.

1889 - Slidell jail and mayor's office built for $275.

1889 - Gause family built a lumberyard and Fassman family started a brickyard.

1890s - Creosote plant bought by N.O. businessmen and renamed Southern Creosote.

1890s - Local farming products developed; Sugar cane and molasses exported by schooners and rail cars. Truck farming exports corn, potatoes, vegetables and fruits such as satsumas. Tung orchards introduced, as well as rice farming.

1890 - Poitevent and Favre constructed the largest mill in the world, at Pearlington, MS.

1890 - Albert Salmen joins his brothers - started sawmill between RR tracks and Bayou Bonfouca.

1890 - June 12, the St Tammany Farmer: McCaren and Sons brickyard 2 miles south of Pearl River. A.C. Prevost builds a hotel, the Pioneer House. Slidell's population is 364.

1891 - St Joe Brick Works is started south of Pearl River and soon bought by the Schneider family - renamed it Schnieder Brick and Tile Company.

1894 The Schneider Brick and Tile Company produce 175,000 bricks and tile per day, employing two hundred workers and a special Haig Continuous Kiln, the largest in the U.S.

1894 - Bird Cage Hotel and Saloon located on corner of Fremeau and Front streets, owned by E.H. Litton – followed by a total of 13 saloons being built on Front St. Other businesses around Cary and Cousin included drygoods and medical establishments.

1895 - Salmen Bros. built shipyard on west side of Bayou Bonfouca and began building ships.

1895 - Mississippi voted itself "Dry" and Slidell escalated "jug trade".

1895 - Eunice Carroll's Hotel burns down.

1898 - Dr. Joseph Feston Polk set up practice in Slidell.

1900 - Slidell population is 1,129.

1903 - The brick Railroad Depot in Slidell was built for the New Orleans & Northeastern/New Orleans & Great Northern railroad,

1904 - N.O.&G.N. RR, "Great Northern," formed by F.H. and G.W. Goodyear.

1904 - Salmen Bros. started building RR from Slidell to Mandeville.

1905 - Salmen RR completed and eventually linked up to the N.O.G.N. line.

1907 - Slidell jail moved and permanent 2-story brick building built. Downstairs was Marshall's office and five jail cells. Upstairs was mayor's office and meeting room at cost of $3,865.40.

1909 - The N.O.G.N. RR completed.

1909 - Street name change after 1909, Salmen Avenue became Cleveland Avenue

1910 - Salmen brickworks employed 800 men; 20 clerks employed at its company store.

The Salmens had timber operations within 75 miles of Slidell supplying the lumberyard that covered 40 acres. Its sawmill had a 60,000 foot daily capacity and the planing mill could produce 50,000 feet daily. Salmen also operated a 100,000 shingle a day factory as well as producing 50 cords a day.

1910 - Slidell population 2,188.

1911 - September 5, 1911, the Slidell City Council authorized Mayor Paul Gardere to acquire a small track of land that would open up Front Street as a throughway.

1914 - World War I starts. Salmen Shipyard became Southern Shipbuilding Corporation, owned by Fritz and Albert Salmen and Andrew W. Canulette.

1915 - Pontchartrain Drive extension completed to Lake Pontchartrain

1915 - James Howze, president of the St Tammany Parish Police Jury, completed Howze Beach Road. Night time cruises to the Rigolets departed from the Howze Wharf.

1915, Sep 29 - Hurricane hit New Orleans and Gulf Coast area

1916 - Southern shipyard employed 1500 workers and specialized in steel framed, wood planked. composite construction, under government supervision.

1917 - Southern shipyard completed a 229 foot ocean going vessel. Also the Norwegian Line's Baltic I, II, III, and IV are constructed.

1917 - June 2, the St Tammany Farmer reported a highway development study between N.O. and Chicago. They considered connecting Robert Rd to the Rigolettes. These routes become Highways U.S. 11 and U.S. 90.

1918 - WW I ended; Dr. Polk returned having served as a medic and buys a Model-T Ford.

1920 - Slidell population of 2,958, reported as largest city in St Tammany parish.

1921 - Pravata family started selling gasoline at Triangle Garage, which began 24 hour-a-day service to travelers from N.O. and the Gulf Coast.

1922 - The Slidell Savings and Homestead moved from the bank building on Front St to the Carollo Building on Cousin.

1925 - Old Spanish Trail completed, between St Augustine and San Diego. Slidell became a major stopover for the cross-country highway 90.

1925 - Clyde Polk opened Cresent Drug Store at the corner of Cary and Cousin.

1926 - Oneisime Faciane opened the White Kitchen Cellar, the forerunner of a chain of three White Kitchens, each with the neon sign of an Indian cooking over a fire.

1927 - Major Flooding conditions throughout town.

1928 - The new wooden Bay Bridge eliminated the Bay St Louis ferry and the present Hwy 11 bridge was built as a private toll bridge, charging $3.50 to cross Lake Pontchartrain.

1929 - The Rigolet Bridge is completed and Slidell becomes a major crossroads.

1930, June - Rigolets Bridge opened for traffic.

1933, 4th Anniversary observance of K of C – local members with their families and friends assembled at the City Café to partake in their fourth Anniversary Banquet.

Forty-five persons celebrated while various guests offered talks enthusiastically received.

1943 - By mid-WWII, the Canulette Shipyard employed 1900 shipbuilders.

1947 - Hurricane

1950 - Haas 5 and 10 Store was opened.

1954 - 5,000 citizens reported.

1950s - Neuhauser store on Front Street burned down.

1961 – Alan Shepard was first American to fly in Space.

1962 – Haas Fabric Store opened.

1962 - Slidell became the hub for the space program when NASA built the Slidell Computer Complex to support Michoud and Stennis Space Center.

1962 – Frank Cusimano elected mayor.

1962 – Slidell Little Theatre was formed.

1962 – Slidell Art League was formed.

1964 – With 1500 citizens, Slidell was designated a Town.

1965 – West Hall was paved partly paid for by Pete Pravata.

1966 – Fire station dedicated as Pete Pravata Fire Station.

1967 – Slidell Memorial Hospital was accredited.

1968 – Gause Blvd. widened.

1969, August 17 - Hurricane Camille

1970 - Slidell population was 16,000

1970 - Father Richard Carroll appointed Pastor following death of Father Tim.

1970 - Krewe of Perseus established

1971 - Junior Auxiliary of Slidell kicked off its annual charity ball

1972 – Interstate 10 was opened.

1972 - Fort Pike place on National Register of Historic Places.

1972 - American Creosote plant burned down with remains torn down in 1973.

1972 - The Elementary school was renamed Brock Elementary after former Principal Glynn Brock

1973 - Third street was widened and in 1975, renamed Sergeant Alfred Dr. and reconfirmed in 2015.

1973 - The 3rd City Hall was constructed on the Second St site of former Our Lady of Lourdes school

1976 June - Aldersgate United Methodist church was formed.

1978 - Krewe of Bilge formed

1979, March - Mayor's Commission on Arts was formed.

1980 - Slidell population count was 26,700

1983 - Krewe of Troy was organized

1984 - Chamber of Commerce moved to its new home at 118 West Hall

1984, March - The North Shore Rotary Club was formed

1984 - Slidell Musical Arts Association was formed

1984 - Krewe of Mona Lisa and Moon Pie organized

1985 - Sam Caruso began his first term of office
1985 - Krewe of Dyonysus organized
1988 - Commission on Arts instituted the Bravo! Arts Award
1988 - The "Centennial Camellia" was named for the Slidell Centennial celebrations.
1988 - Veterans Park dedicated by Mayor Sam Caruso
1994, Dec - NASA Computer Complex donated to City of Slidell
1996, Nov - St. Tammany Trace Slidell span opened
1998, July - Heritage Festival inaugurated at Heritage Park
1999, Sept - First Edition release of "Slidell - Camellia City"
2001 - Mayor Ben Morris began his first term
2000 - Flag Plaza and John Slidell Monument dedicated
2002 - Freddy Drennan elected Chief of Police
2002, April - Volunteers headed by Gina Beck and Rene Legrand completed the Heritage Playground
2005 - August 29 – Hurricane Katrina devastated the town.
2009 - Mayor Freddy Drennan began his first term
2010, March - Dedication of Slidell City Council Administration Building with grand affair
2010, August - Hurricane Katrina Monument, donated by sculptor John Doherty, was dedicated
2011 - March – Minicapelli's 6,000-square-foot building, while operating as Club Phoenix, caught fire in Olde Town
2011, Sept - Dedication of 9/11 Memorial at Heritage Park
2012 - Five Mile Maestri Bridge closed while major repairs performed
2012, March - rebuilt Senior Center building formally opened
2012, April - City Auditorium Ribbon Cutting – "Arts, Camera, Action" gala event celebrated
2012 - Crystal Gavel Award presented to City Court Judge Jim Lamz by Ls State Bar Association
2014 - Mayor Freddy Drennan reelected to second term
2014, March - 1st phase of Fremaux Town Center opened
2014, May - East St. Tammany Chamber of Commerce new offices opened on Front Street
2015, Feb - Judge Fred Ellis tendered the Commission on Cultural Affairs' President Award.
2015 - Slidell Memorial Hospital received coveted Economic Development Pioneer Award
2015 - Southern Surgical Hospital celebrated its 10-year anniversary
2015, March - Olde Town Merchants Association held its 42nd Annual St Patrick's Parade
2015 - Krewe of Poseidon authorized to ride as a Day Parade
2015, June - Slidell Rotarians celebrated their 50th Anniversary with a gala Dinner
2015 - 10th Year Anniversary of Northshore Harbor Center celebrated

"More than $70K was raised for the Slidell Alumni Hurricane Relief Fund and distributed to fellow alums that suffered heavy Hurricane Katrina losses," reported John Doherty.

2010 stainless steel version of John Doherty's "Twisted Fleur de Lis" over water.

Dan Ellis Books available on Amazon Books
Entire Gulf Coast Area

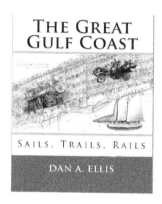  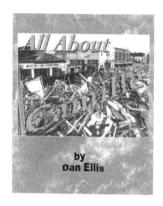

 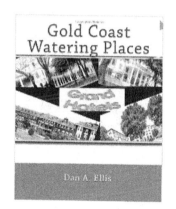 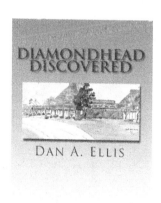

 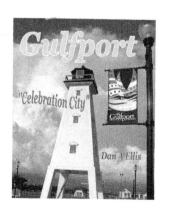 

Dan Ellis Books available on Amazon Books
Pass Christian Area

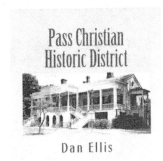

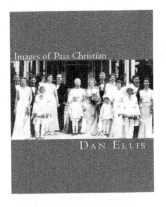

www.DanEllis.Net

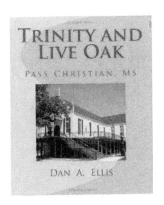

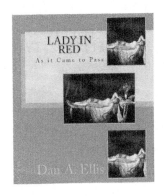

-332-

Unsolicited Commendations

Dan,

I must confess that I never knew what you were doing all those years. I was writing the history of this school, and I didn't leave here for nearly eight years.

But what you did was magnificent. The illustrations are stunning in many cases. A great many of them I have never seen - for example the Ford dealership in Biloxi that may be the first one in the state.

I wish now that I had been tuned in and involved somehow in what you were doing. In any case your collection is now the Dan Ellis Collection in the Mississippi Gulf Coast Community College Archives and it will carry your name from now on. The photographs and other materials represents the finest collection of its kind relating to the Mississippi Gulf Coast in view of the destruction of the other historical repositories by Katrina.

I will as per your instructions get copies of these files to the other historical societies that you wish them given to. Once again, thanks so much for all you did.

Charles L. Sullivan
Mississippi Gulf Coast Community College
Perkinston, MS 39573

****

Hi Dan,

I haven't written you since Katrina, I understand you suffered quite a loss in the storm. I am saddened to read that you have left the Gulf Coast. I won't tell you anything you haven't heard many times, but you are the greatest researcher of Coast history that I've ever known. Others are not even close.

Even the academics who have written books on coast history never seem to get down to the real everyday info that you do. And, the old photos are unbelievable!

Juan de Cuevas (author - writer)
****

Dan,

I want to tell you that we continue to use your Slidell book at least weekly. Someone regularly needs information on Slidell and your book is the most informal and easy to use book written to date.

Best Wishes,
Becky Taylor
Librarian – St. Tammany Parish

CPSIA information can be obtained
at www.ICGtesting.com
Printed in the USA
LVOW03s2147131115
462560LV00003B/6/P